UFOs

Over

COLORADO

A TRUE HISTORY OF
Extraterrestrial Encounters
in the Centennial State

PRESTON DENNETT

4880 Lower Valley Road • Atglen, PA 19310

D1446650

Other Schiffer Books on Related Subjects:
Ghosts of Colorado. Dennis Baker. ISBN: 978-0-7643-3052-0
Ghost Towns of the Rockies. Preethi Burkholder. ISBN: 978-0-7643-3569-3

Copyright © 2017 by Preston Dennett
Library of Congress Control Number: 2017935606

All rights reserved. No part of this work may be reproduced or used in any form or by any means—graphic, electronic, or mechanical, including photocopying or information storage and retrieval systems—without written permission from the publisher.

The scanning, uploading, and distribution of this book or any part thereof via the Internet or any other means without the permission of the publisher is illegal and punishable by law. Please purchase only authorized editions and do not participate in or encourage the electronic piracy of copyrighted materials.

"Schiffer," "Schiffer Publishing, Ltd.," and the pen and inkwell logo are registered trademarks of Schiffer Publishing, Ltd.

Designed by RoS
Cover design by Matt Goodman

Type set in FauxCRA/Chaparral Pro

ISBN: 978-0-7643-5424-3
Printed in China

Published by Schiffer Publishing, Ltd.
4880 Lower Valley Road
Atglen, PA 19310
Phone: (610) 593-1777; Fax: (610) 593-2002
E-mail: Info@schifferbooks.com
Web: www.schifferbooks.com

For our complete selection of fine books on this and related subjects, please visit our website at www.schifferbooks.com. You may also write for a free catalog.

Schiffer Publishing's titles are available at special discounts for bulk purchases for sales promotions or premiums. Special editions, including personalized covers, corporate imprints, and excerpts, can be created in large quantities for special needs. For more information, contact the publisher.

We are always looking for people to write books on new and related subjects. If you have an idea for a book, please contact us at proposals@schifferbooks.com.

A TRUE HISTORY OF

Extraterrestrial Encounters

in the Centennial State

To all UFO witnesses;

THE TRUTH WILL SURVIVE

A TRUE HISTORY O

Extraterrestrial Encounter

in the Centennial State

WE HAVE STACKS OF REPORTS ABOUT FLYING SAUCERS. WE TAKE THEM VERY SERIOUSLY WHEN YOU CONSIDER WE HAVE LOST MANY MEN AND PLANES TRYING TO INTERCEPT THEM.

—**GENERAL BENJAMIN CHIDLAW**
ENT AFB, COLORADO, 1953[1]

THE MUTILATIONS ARE ONE OF THE GREATEST OUTRAGES IN THE HISTORY OF THE WESTERN CATTLE INDUSTRY. IT IS IMPORTANT THAT WE SOLVE THIS MYSTERY AS SOON AS POSSIBLE. THE CATTLE INDUSTRY IS ALREADY HARD HIT FROM AN ECONOMIC POINT OF VIEW. FROM A HUMAN POINT OF VIEW, WE CANNOT ALLOW THESE MUTILATIONS TO CONTINUE.

—**COLORADO GOVERNOR RICHARD LAMM** [2]

I AM HOPEFUL THAT, WITH THE COOPERATION OF LOCAL LAW ENFORCEMENT OFFICIALS, THE CBI [COLORADO BUREAU OF INVESTIGATION] WILL BE ABLE TO LEARN WHO OR WHAT IS BEHIND THE MUTILATIONS AND PUT AN END TO THE FEARS OF RURAL COLORADANS.

—**COLORADO SENATOR FLOYD HASKELL**[3]

Contents

Introduction

Humans have lived in the Colorado area for at least 13,000 years. Human artifacts dated 8710 BCE found in Larimer County show evidence of Native American settlements. The area that would eventually become the state of Colorado was inhabited initially by the ancient Pueblo people. Various other tribes also occupied the area, including Apache, Arapaho, Cheyenne, Comanche, Shoshone, and Ute, some of who moved there in the 1800s to escape the growing European invasion on the eastern coast of the newly forming United States.

In 1803, some of the Colorado area was bought with the Louisiana Purchase. The remaining area was purchased from Mexico in 1848. In 1876, exactly one hundred years after the United States was formed, Colorado achieved statehood.

With just more than 104,000 square miles, Colorado is the eighth largest state. Due to the Rocky Mountains and the Colorado Plateau, it has the highest average elevation, with about seventy-five percent of the nation's land higher than 10,000 feet. Its lowest point is about 3,100 feet.

In 1860, the population was about 34,000. Thirty years later, in 1890, the population boomed to about 413,000. Population grew steadily since then, reaching more than two million by 1970, three million by 1990, and in 2016, just more than five million people. The state has a diversified economy, is rich in minerals with a large mineral belt stretching from Cortez to Boulder, and is a leader in tourism.

Colorado's UFO history stretches back more than a hundred years and involves a dazzling variety of encounters. The entire gamut of the phenomenon is represented including sightings, landings, face-to-face encounters, onboard experiences, UFO crashes and more, including mysterious animal mutilations.

The Centennial State has produced several high-profile cases that have influenced the evolution of the UFO field.

In the fall of 1949, a young college student by the name of Leo Sprinkle saw a UFO over the University of Colorado in Boulder, prompting an interest in the subject that would lead him to become one of the first academics to investigate UFOs, and the first researcher to use regressive hypnosis to investigate cases involving missing time.

In 1966, the Air Force contracted the University of Colorado to study the current UFO situation, leading to one of the biggest fiascoes and widely criticized official government investigations in UFO history.

September 8, 1967, the shocking mutilation of "Snippy" the horse at an Alamosa ranch sent shockwaves across Colorado and the world. It was the first animal mutilation to gain widespread attention and connect the mutilations to the UFO phenomenon. The case was a foreboding sign of future events that would make Colorado one of the states hit hardest by the mutilations, with a wave involving hundreds of animal deaths in the mid-1970s and continuing waves to the present day.

December 31, 1992, San Luis Valley-based researcher Christopher O'Brien launched an official investigation into the San Luis Valley UFOs, revealing the area to be the most active UFO area in the state and one of the most active in the world.

January 12, 1994, a call from NORAD to the local police regarding an unexplained heat signature on Greenie Mountain, which had been detected by satellite, revealed itself to be a complex UFO event involving multiple UFO reports, a possible crashed object, and an investigation that raised more questions than answers.

August 27, 1995, videotape footage taken by café-owner Tim Edwards of a UFO over Salida made international news and became some of the best verified UFO footage on record.

September 21, 2001, retail manager Stan Romanek was abducted from his Denver home by gray-type extraterrestrials, beginning a series of intense encounters that would result in one of the best-documented alien encounter cases on record, including multiple eyewitness testimonies, photographs of UFOs and aliens, videotape, landing traces, medical evidence (including injuries and healings), implant evidence, government harassment, and more.

These are just a few of the cases representing the tip of the iceberg of UFO activity in Colorado. Like most states, the vast majority of UFO incidents have received little or no publicity.

Collected here for the first time is a comprehensive compilation of Colorado UFO encounters, including little-known, well-known, and some published here for the first time. The cases have been organized both topically and chronologically, starting with sightings, then moving on to more extensive encounters, such as face-to-face encounters with humanoids, UFO landings, onboard UFO experiences, UFO crashes, and more.

The aliens have arrived! And the evidence is in the pages that follow.

Early Encounters

It is difficult to pinpoint the first actual extraterrestrial encounter in the state of Colorado. Some of the earliest evidence of alien activity comes from the Native American population before Colorado had achieved statehood. Native American legends speak of "the ant people" or "sky people" who traveled in "flying baskets" or "flying seed pods," moving to other star systems, or carrying people to safe caverns beneath in the Sangre de Cristo Mountains. The San Luis Valley was considered a sacred area for this reason, and warring tribes refused to fight there.

What Is it?

One of Colorado's earliest recorded encounters occurred more than a hundred years ago, on September 7, 1917. According to the *Salida Record,* throughout the first week of September, numerous upstanding residents of Salida observed strange "vehicles of the air" on a nightly basis. The objects were seen very high in the sky, repeatedly appearing and disappearing, or hovering over Tenderfoot Mountain, over Mount Shavano, and again in the northern sky.

Reverend and Mrs. Oakley used a telescope to observe the object, and saw what appeared to be a wheel with colored lights around it. Mr. and Mrs. F. C. Woody, and their family, also observed the objects, as did C. F. Bode and his family, among other residents.

The article discounted the possibility that the object might have been an "aeroplane" as the description didn't match. The article concluded: "is it then some genius who has discovered some new principle of flight, and is trying out his invention? It's your guess. What is it?"[4]

At this time, the idea of extraterrestrials had not fully entered the public consciousness. The residents of Salida apparently had no explanation for what they had seen.

A Disk-Shaped Object

Another early encounter occurred in April 1929. Hetty Pline was six years old when her father, Edward, came home and announced that something very strange had happened to him at the sawmill in Ward. Hetty's father had been there to photograph the sawmill, he explained. Says Hetty, "As he was taking the photo, he described a 'terrible thunderous bellow,' and a large round thing as big as a very large boulder moved through the air above them. You can see it in the picture. None of the sawmill workers saw the thing in the photo, but they all heard the sound and felt the ground shudder."

Hetty's father showed his family the photo, which clearly showed a strange disk-shaped object in the air. Edward died a few years later. Hetty tried to research the incident but was unable to find any of the sawmill workers.[5]

UFO activity over Colorado didn't begin in earnest until the dawn of the Modern Age of UFOs in mid-1947. At that time, a massive super-wave swept across the United States and the world. From that year on, UFO activity remained very active.

Manitou UFO

May 19, 1947, a silver-colored UFO appeared over the Colorado desert in Manitou, hovered, and performed a series of acrobatic maneuvers, including climbs and dives, reversing its course, circling the area, and then taking off against the wind over the horizon. Says Vallee, "These acrobatics are typical behavior . . ."

The witnesses watched the object for twenty minutes, during which its metallic surface repeatedly reflected the afternoon sunlight. They estimated the object was about 1,000 feet high. The witnesses were interviewed by Air Force officers who concluded that the men had seen birds![6]

One month later, June 13, 1947, Kenneth Arnold would sight twelve disks over Mount Rainier in Washington State, causing a media firestorm and ushering in the Modern Age of UFOs.

Two Huge Silver Disks

As reported in the LA Times, May 21, 1950, rancher Felix Zanon (age sixty), who owns a ranch five miles east of Montrose, told reporters that he sighted "a huge silver disk" hovering over the city during the early morning hours. Almost immediately, an identical disk joined it. The two of them flew to the east, through a cut in the Rocky Mountains at Cerro Summit, and moved out of view.[7]

Circular and Metallic

April 27, 1950, seven witnesses across the town of Rangely, located in an oil basin, reported seeing an unusual object in the sky. A. W. Jay (the Continental Oil Company superintendent) and his wife and daughter observed a glowing object "flash" across the sky.

At the same time, Ronnie Risdale and Carley Cook (both oil field workers) saw "a strange glow that seemed to hang in the sky."

A third account of the event comes from Glen Holden and his wife who sighted the object from a distance of less than seventy-five feet. They said it was circular and appeared to be covered with "phosphorescent metallic paint."[8]

A Skyhook Balloon?

June 29, 1950, a high-altitude Marine pilot became puzzled by the strange object he was seeing over the skies of Denver. He knew that sky-hook balloons were used in stratospheric research; however, that was far away, in Little Falls, Minnesota. Was it possible that one of their balloons had drifted from there all the way to Denver, a distance of more than 900 miles? The object wasn't moving and remained stationary in the sky. Furthermore, the pilot was not the only witness. Civilian control tower operators at Stapleton Air Field also observed the object. They estimated that it was at an altitude of 45,000 feet, and confirmed that it hung motionless in the sky, despite an eastward wind of sixty mph. Marine Colonel T. V. Murto believed that the object was not a balloon as it could not have drifted that far.[9]

The Arrival of Blue Book

The US military had just begun their struggle to deal with the new high levels of UFO activity. One result was Project Blue Book, one of the Air Force's early UFO study projects. The first Colorado case to be declared unexplained by Project Blue Book occurred September 20, 1950, in Kit Carson. At 10:49 a.m., a "reliable source" observed two large glowing objects that hovered in the sky for about one minute. Then three smaller objects were disgorged by one of the larger objects, at which point, all five objects sped upward and were gone. Investigators were baffled and declared it unidentified: case 807.

The second unexplained case from Blue Book occurred to Air Force pilot Major C. K. Griffin over Colorado Springs. July 9, 1952, at 12:45 p.m., Griffin observed a glowing white object shaped like an airfoil. For the next twelve minutes it moved slowly and erratically, then finally disappeared. Blue Book officers investigated and, unable to find an answer, declared it unidentified, case 1405.

Nine days later, at around 2:45 a.m. on July 18, 1952, American Airlines pilot Captain Paul L. Carpenter was approaching Denver at 17,000 feet when he noticed a yellow light to the south. Earlier Captain James Smay had radioed and reported odd lights. The airfield in Denver warned Carpenter of the lights and told him that they had captured them on radar. Captain Carpenter observed what were apparently the same lights as they began to dart across the sky, covering large distances in seconds. No sooner had he seen the first light when he saw two more anomalous lights, followed by two more.

The lights appeared to dart sharply back and forth in an arc measuring thirty degrees. Carpenter estimated that the objects were over Colorado Springs, which meant they were moving at a speed of 3,000 mph. If they were further away, Carpenter pointed out, they would have been moving even faster.

Just more than a month later, on the evening of August 29, 1952, pilot C. A. Magruder was flying over Colorado Springs when he saw three objects, each fifty feet in diameter and ten feet high, flying ahead of him. Each was moving at about 1,500 mph and emitting a red-yellow trail of exhaust. Magruder watched them for four or five seconds. Blue Book officers were unable to identify the objects and declared it unidentified—case 2013.

The 1952 wave wasn't over yet. One month later, on the afternoon of September 29, 1952, Air Force Sergeant B. R. Hughes sighted five or six bright, white objects that trailed each other, circling over the Aurora-Denver area. Blue Book officers were called in to investigate and declared it unidentified: case 2138.[10]

An Unnerving Experience

While the military was busy investigating cases involving their own personnel, civilians were dealing with their own influx of cases. In 1953, a young college student spent the entire night studying with his friend and their teacher at a home in Colorado Springs. Just before sunrise, they ended their study session and exited the house. Looking up, they saw a giant blimp-like object hovering in complete silence about forty feet directly above the house. It was so large that it blocked out a large portion of the sky. They stared in shock for several seconds until it disappeared. The college student later told his daughter about the encounter, who said, "He could not give an explanation how this huge UFO disappeared, but said it was the most unnerving experience he ever had. He later speculated that the UFO either cloaked itself or maybe shifted into another dimension as he did not see it move before it disappeared."[11]

Ranch Family Encounter

In 1953, a ranch family from Estes Park were retiring for their evening in their home when the son (age fourteen) began to scream in his bedroom for everyone to come. His family ran into his room to see "an extremely bright white light coming through his bedroom window from an aircraft floating above the tall pine trees."

The sister, age nine, remembers the event vividly. "It came from a ship, for want of a better word, that looked like the fuselage of a large airplane, but there were no wings."

The family stared at the object, which remained still and silent until suddenly darting quickly upwards. It began to glow, and then moved toward Twin Sisters Mountain and the Boulder/Denver area.

The brother remembers the incident and learned later that the object was viewed by others. Employees at the Twin Sisters fire lookout station saw it. The *Rocky Mountain News* reported that the object moved over Denver, and the Air Force sent planes after it.

The mother called the police, who told her, "Don't tell anyone what you saw."

The family later discovered that their neighbor had also seen the same object while driving her daughter home from a school dance.[12]

State Senator Sees UFO

There is a long list of highly-placed government officials who have seen UFOs. November 25, 1955, Colorado State Senator S. T. Taylor observed a dirigible-shaped object over La Veta. The object glowed blue-green and had a jelly-like appearance. He estimated it was moving about half the speed of a shooting star, and appeared to be at about 15,000 feet elevation. It dived overhead at a forty-five-degree angle, leveled off, and moved upward at a thirty-degree angle and off over Mount Mestas. Senator Taylor estimates it was in view for about five seconds. It made no sound and had no exhaust. Senator Taylor reported his case to the FBI and to Blue Book, who were unable to identify it and declared it unexplained: case 3869.[13]

Ground Observer Corps Sees UFOs

In early May 1956, members of the Pueblo Ground Observer Corps stationed at the local courthouse observed what they believe were UFOs. The objects were spherical, glowed white with flashing lights on them, and moved at very rapid speeds. The objects first appeared May 1, 1956, and continued for six successive nights. As the reports piled in, Sergeant Gilbert Nelson, a member of the intelligence squadron, was sent to Pueblo to investigate.

Nelson himself became a witness and reported his observation of six objects. "They were dull, more or less fluorescent glows, faint but bright enough to see," he said. "Most of them were triangular in shape, but one was round and brighter than the rest." Each object moved so quickly across the sky, that they remained in view for only about six seconds.

Despite Nelson's confirmation of the reports from the Ground Observer Corps (trained observers), Colonel John M. White, commanding officer of the 4602 Air Intelligence Service Squadron at Peterson AFB in Colorado Springs, issued the following statement regarding the witnesses: "They saw nothing other than ordinary celestial activity."[14]

"I Was Delighted"

June 1956, a gentleman from Denver stopped at a stop sign, looked up, and saw "a huge egg-shaped-like cloud-thing" zooming upward across the sky at about 1,000 feet elevation. The object was silent and about 500 feet wide. The witness caught the attention of the people in the car next to him, who also observed the object. In a few seconds, it had traversed the sky. A short time later, two jets appeared in apparent pursuit of the object. Says the witness: "I thought it was a UFO . . . I didn't feel threatened by it. I was delighted that I had observed this strange phenomenon."[15]

Paperboys See UFO

Early one morning in the fall of 1956, John DeHerrera (age sixteen) and his brother were delivering the *Valley Courier* newspaper to local residents along Highway 160 in Alamosa when it happened: an egg-shaped object came into view, flying below treetop level. It was moving in a straight line toward the west.

The teenagers pulled their pickup truck off the road and stopped to observe. Right when they stopped, the object changed directions, veered toward them, and moved directly overhead. "There were no windows on it, no airfoils, no nothing," said DeHerrera.

Other than the object itself, the only other detail was a flaming tail. "It was amazing," explained DeHerrera. "It was almost like an electrical flame."

The object then zipped off at an incredible speed. The witnesses were shocked and impressed. They later discovered that many residents saw the same object over Highway 160, stretching from Alamosa up to Walsenburg.

Years later, DeHerrera still felt the repercussions of his sighting. In an effort to discover what he might have seen, he joined MUFON and became a field investigator.[16]

Air Force Navigator Sighting

"I have a Bachelor of Science degree in general engineering and numerous post-grad courses. I have been an Air Force navigator, private pilot, and engineer, among other things. I would prefer that my name be kept out of this . . ."

In July 1957, "Kenneth" (not his real name) was at Lowry Air Force Base training to be an Air Force navigator. One evening, while training with a "bubble sextant" that mimics an airplane cockpit, he observed what he first thought was a star. To his shock, the "star" began to move. Says Kenneth, "I took my eye from the eyepiece and watched the 'star' moving to the right and slightly downward in relation to the other stars."

He pointed it out to other cadets, but they were busy with their own training. Says Kenneth: "I watched the 'star' continuing to move for a distance of about ten degrees across the sky—perhaps it was less—and then it stopped and just stayed in place with the other stars once more."[17]

Many other similar cases have been reported of UFOs mimicking stars.

Blue Book Returns

July 27, 1957, J. L. Siverly observed a very strange-looking object hovering over a hilltop in Longmont. The disk was "ice blue" with a thick center. The top was honeycombed with interconnecting hexagons. The middle section had a scalloped appearance, and the bottom of the craft had four kidney-shaped forms. Siverly watched the object for ten minutes as it hovered and rocked at hilltop level. Blue Book officers were called in to investigate but could not identify the object, and declared it unidentified: case 4841.

Five months later, another case caught the attention of Project Blue Book. Early in the evening of December 17, 1957, seventeen-year-old F. G. Hickman observed a round object over his home in Fruita, near Grand Junction. He watched the object for forty-five minutes as it flashed yellow, white, green, and red. It had a tail twice the size of its body. At one point, it stopped its movement, then reversed its course. Blue Book officers declared it unidentified: case 5559.

November 18, 1957, a cement worker from New Mexico was driving near Fort Carson when he saw a bright object rising from the horizon. He first thought it was the moon until it began to ascend quickly. Realizing he was seeing something unusual, the cement worker stopped his truck and stepped outside on his running board. "In about a minute," he says, "it was passing overhead, and never made a sound. But I could tell it was moving along . . . I don't know how high it was, but it was big."

The object arced overhead and descended on the other side of the horizon. It moved so quickly, the witness braced for an explosion, but none came. "Whatever this thing was," says the witness, "it made the hair stand up on the back of my neck like I never felt before or since."

Only nine cases in Colorado were designated unexplained by Project Blue Book, including the following. At 10:46 a.m., on June 14, 1958, airport weather observer and meteorologist for the US Weather Bureau Orville R. Foster was on duty at the MST Memorial Airport in Pueblo observing a weather balloon through a theodolite. A theodolite is a telescope equipped with a device to measure the angles, allowing the observer to triangulate the observed object and measure its speed.

As Foster tracked the balloon, a strange object entered the field of the lens. It was silver-white, Saturn-shaped, and tilted forward. He estimated that it was at least thirty feet in diameter moving about 500 mph. He watched it through the theodolite for five to ten minutes as it went from horizon to horizon. Foster says its shape was sharply defined and it was definitely not a balloon.[18]

So closes the 1950s. During this time, numerous cases of landings, face-to-face encounters, and onboard experiences were just beginning to occur. Again, these cases are covered in later chapters. Meanwhile, the following decades would bring new levels of activity.

CHAPTER 2

Sightings 1960-1969

While the 1950s were active, the 1960s brought an escalation to the phenomenon. Not only were there more sightings, they involved deeper levels of interaction, such as cases of UFOs being chased by military aircraft, objects hovering over sensitive installations, objects stopping traffic, disabling vehicles, or chasing people down the highway.

In 1967, UFO activity over Colorado exploded, producing more cases than ever before, including several sightings by police and government officials.

By this time, the US government was neck-deep trying to deal with UFOs, and the infamous Condon Committee was formed. The 1960s proved to be a very interesting decade.

An Extraordinary Feeling of Peace

At 3:10 p.m., August 11, 1960, Henry Hawks (an employee of a Boulder trucking company) was operating a tractor in Left Hand Canyon, near Buckingham Park, southwest of Boulder, when he heard a strange, muffled detonation sound coming from the sky above him. At that moment, his tractor engine died. Looking up, he saw disk-shaped craft drop from the sky. When it reached about 200 feet altitude, it stopped, hovered, wobbled slightly, and stabilized. At this point, it was only 650 feet away. It looked like two bowls stuck together and had a dull aluminum-looking surface with a "velvety" appearance. It was about one hundred feet in diameter and twenty feet thick.

He tried to re-start his tractor engine, but it wouldn't start. Hawks told investigators that an extraordinary feeling of peace and contentment came over him. The object, he saw, appeared to be malfunctioning. Shiny metal plates lined the perimeter of the craft. One of these plates was leaking a royal-blue smoke, and the craft was making an intermittent humming noise, like an out-of-phase motor.

Hawks was surprised to see the apparent malfunctioning metallic plate withdraw inside the saucer, leaving an empty gap, which was immediately filled with an identical plate. He heard an audible click as the new plate fell into place.

Seconds later, the hum of the saucer increased to a high pitch, and it became surrounded by a shimmering haze. The disk then rose up into the clouds and was gone.

At that point, the strange feeling of calmness left Hawks, and he felt like he was "coming to his senses." He tried again to start the tractor, which now started normally.

The case was investigated by APRO [Aerial Phenomena Research Organization] who believed it was an instance of a UFO in distress. It was their first case of a UFO being repaired. Coral and Jim Lorenzen write, "Although Hawks was the only witness, to our knowledge, of the 'repair job,' our investigator felt, after a long interview with him, that he was an intelligent observer and was telling the truth, and that therefore this particular sighting is considered to be one of the best, mainly because of the integrity of the observer and the amount of detail observed."[1]

Saucer Stops Traffic

While UFOs are generally evasive, in some cases they hover brazenly in full view, such as the following. In August 1962, three Army soldiers, their Sergeant, and his son were returning from a fishing trip in the Denver area. As they came over a hill heading west towards the setting sun, they saw a large circular craft about fifty feet wide hovering above an electrical tower. About twenty other cars had already pulled over, with the passengers standing outside to observe the object, which appeared to be rotating silently.

After twenty minutes, helicopters could be heard approaching from the direction of nearby Lowry Air Force Base. Immediately, the disk began to move leisurely east, keeping about a mile from the helicopters.

After the disk left, everyone returned to their cars and left the scene. The Sergeant telephoned Lowry Air Force Base to report the sighting. Says the son, "He was told they knew about it, and requested he keep silent about the sighting. This is the first report I've made about the sighting to anyone."[2]

Jet Chases UFO

Late one evening in June 1963, a father and son ventured outside to watch the night sky. Suddenly their attention was drawn to a "single lighted object" moving above the mountains, northwest of Colorado Springs where they lived. It moved "at right angles up and down" for a few minutes, before circling, gaining altitude, and hovering an estimated seven miles away. Says the son, "While it hung in this position, two bright orange objects came out (about a minute apart), one from the top and then one from the bottom. Once they were a short distance above or below the craft, they shot off at an incredible rate of speed in opposite directions, and disappeared immediately."

Suddenly they noticed a jet approaching on a collision course towards the UFO. As it got close, however, the UFO accelerated upward to the south at a forty-five-degree angle and was out of sight in two seconds. Says the witness, "I have never seen anything accelerate that fast in my life, except for in sci-fi movies. At no time during the sighting did this object make any noise whatsoever. I have not shared this story with many people. I recently had a massive heart attack and felt it was time to tell my story while I can."[3]

Sheriff Chased by UFO

In the early hours of June 10, 1963, the deputy sheriff and boat warden at Horsetooth Reservoir (west of Fort Collins), received complaints about an unidentified light in the water. The reservoir was seven miles long and nearly a mile wide. The deputy and the head of the Larimer County Recreation District took the police patrol boat to the north end of the lake. They approached the blinking light and discovered it was actually a buoy placed by the State Game and Fish Department to record water temperature.

Believing they solved the mystery, they were getting ready to leave when they saw "a huge bright object" hovering above the hills on the east side of the lake. Says the deputy, "I could not make out a structure. It was a very large, oblong-shaped, brilliant white light. We commented on it and couldn't imagine what it was."

The deputy gunned the boat toward the south of the lake.

"This thing is moving with us," his partner said.

Says the deputy, "I stopped the patrol boat and the object continued just a little farther south along the ridge and then it stopped. We started south again in the patrol boat; the object continued to parallel us."

The object followed them for seven miles, the entire length of the lake. At times it lit up the mountainside "as if it was almost daylight."

The deputy turned to his partner and said, "This is getting too creepy." He turned off the boat and shut off the light. Less than a minute later, the object darted away to the north over Wyoming. Says the deputy, "The acceleration of the object was absolutely phenomenal, and there was no sound whatsoever."

The deputy started up the boat and turned on the lights. The two of them stared at each other in shock, trying to figure out what had just occurred.

"Do you need the publicity?" his partner asked.

"No," said the deputy, thinking of what might happen if word got out. The last thing he wanted was to be in the uncomfortable situation of talking about his sighting without any proof.

"Let's go home."

Says the deputy, "The entire situation really shook us up a lot, and I honestly don't believe we ever talked about it to each other again."[4]

Another UFO Traffic Stop

On June 10, 1964, a father and son left their home in Montrose to go to work at the Uranium mine in Uravan. About twenty miles into the trip, the father saw a brilliant light ahead of him over the ridge. It was too bright to be a plane. He approached the source of the light, and as it came into view, he realized it was too bright to look at directly. He pulled over and alerted his son, who had already seen it.

They exited the car and stared in "total wonder and stark fear." Neither had any idea what the light could be. Before long, numerous other cars approached and pulled over on both sides of the highway.

The light was oval-shaped, intense white-blue like a welder's arc, and lit up the entire valley around. It moved at a slow pace across the valley to the east. The witnesses all spoke with each other for a few minutes, then departed for their various destinations. Both father and son reported feeling "absolute astonishment" and were glad that other witnesses shared the experience with them. Following the incident, they had to drive the same stretch of road traveling to and from work, and always felt "unnerved."[5]

The Last Unidentified

The ninth and final case (#5559) to be declared unidentified by Project Blue Book occurred on July 27, 1964. At around 8:20 p.m., A. Borsa observed a white ball of fire the size of a car move through the sky over Denver. As he watched, the object climbed slowly, and then accelerated quickly until out of view. The sighting lasted about two or three minutes.[6]

Prison Guards See UFO

On the evening of August 2, 1965, during a nationwide wave of UFO sightings, two tower guards at the Colorado State Penitentiary at Canon City saw something that they couldn't explain. One of the guards, Don Stites, noticed the object at 2:15 a.m., hovering between Colorado Springs and Pueblo. It appeared to be a glowing white object, which remained stationary, but dimmed and brightened. After thirty minutes, it suddenly winked out.[7]

Mass Sighting Over Denver

One week after the above sighting, on the evening of August 9, 1965, a particularly brazen UFO was seen by numerous witnesses putting on a fabulous display over the skies of Denver. Reports had been coming into the *Denver Post* steadily for the last week, but the night of August 9, proved to be the busiest yet.

At 5:50 p.m., Bill Lamberton (age seventeen), driving with two passengers down Mississippi Avenue saw a silver cylindrical-shaped object hover momentarily, then dart upward and to the west over the mountains. The object was in view for about six seconds.

Three hours and twenty-five minutes later, at 9:15 p.m., the UFO was back. Randy Holmes (age sixteen) saw a "bright, yellow, cigar-shaped object going along the horizon." He viewed it from his residence on Everett Street as it moved off to the northeast and vanished.

Forty minutes later, at 9:55 p.m., Don Storres (age eighty-one) observed it from Greenwood Boulevard. "It was coming from the north at a very high rate of speed and going straight north," said Storres. "It covered three-fourths of the sky in just a few seconds and disappeared in a bright, red glow." By this point, the *Denver Post* was receiving a flood of calls. The next sighting occurred at 10:05 p.m., to Mrs. Lawrence Ausdahl who said, "We picked up a UFO with our binoculars. At first it went to the right and after a while came back very fast and stood there for a few minutes. It appeared to be a dome-shaped object with red and green lights on its edge, like headlights on a car, and very luminous."

Five minutes later, at 10:10 p.m., Barbara Fisher watched multiple UFOs moving southward over Buckley Field. "There were three lights," said Fisher, "and the first two appeared to be moving faster than the third."

Fifteen minutes after that, Dan Terkins watched the object from his home on Independence Street. "It was a cone-shaped object with a dome on top of it, and lights changing from yellow to red to green."

Five minutes later, (at 10:25 p.m.) C. I. Speaks of Tennyson Street and several others became witnesses to the event. Speaks told reporters, "My wife and I and our neighbors saw a light streak by the North Star and disappear over the mountains toward Boulder."

At 11:00 p.m., Mrs. William McCall and her two daughters observed three glowing red dots that were clustered closely together in the sky. Says McCall, "Then they separated and circled over the city from southwest to southeast. There was no sound of an engine."

Ten minutes before midnight, high school math teacher Vaughan Aandahl had the last recorded sighting for that night. He was doing his evening running exercises around the school track when he saw "a very large, white, luminous flash" in the sky over south Denver. "It was considerably larger than any commercial aircraft," said Aandahl, "more like the size of the football field that I was running around."

After interviewing the witnesses, the *Denver Post* contacted The North American Air Defense Command space detection and tracking center at Colorado Springs. A duty officer told them that they had no explanation for the sightings and that: "We're not in the UFO business."

He told the *Denver Post* that witnesses might have been viewing the "Echo 2 satellite."[8]

The Condon Committee

When it comes to official governmental investigations of UFOs, one of the biggest fiascoes of all times has come to be known as the Condon Committee. It not only was a travesty of justice, it did untold damage to the UFO field.

In 1966, Project Blue was still in existence, but they were looking for a way out of the UFO business. Blue Book had become a public relations project whose purpose now appeared to be to deal with the public and downplay or debunk valid sightings while the real government UFO investigative projects took place at higher confidential levels. In 1966, the Air Force contracted the University of Colorado to study the current UFO situation. The study was headed by Edward Condon and Robert Low. Condon was a nuclear physicist and pioneer in quantum mechanics who worked on the super-secret Manhattan Project. He was chosen to head the Boulder Project because of his eminent position as a scientist and his supposed "lack of any stated position on UFOs."

The study was prompted by widespread sightings of UFOs over Dexter, Michigan, which had been explained away by the Air Force as swamp gas. The explanation was ludicrous and caused a public outcry against the Air Force. As a result, the Air Force gave the University of Colorado $313,000 dollars to fund the study. They ended up spending more than $500,000. (In 2016, this would equate to about 3.7 million dollars.)

Although it was targeted as a two-year investigation, Condon's objectivity was questioned from the start when he announced before the investigation was even complete: "My attitude right now is that there's nothing to it . . . but I'm not supposed to reach that conclusion for another year."

More problems erupted when two scientists who had been assigned to the project were fired for leaking a memo from Condon that said: "The trick would be, I think, to describe the project so that to the public, it would appear to be a totally objective study but, to the scientific community, would present the image of a group of non-believers trying their best to be objective, but having almost zero explanation of finding a saucer."

Needless to say, the UFO study was a complete disaster. Much of the staff ended up leaving, disgusted by the attitude of Low and Condon and their obvious prejudice against the UFO subject. Using only cases from Blue Book, the Condon Committee was shut down on December 17, 1969, officially concluding that "nothing has come from the study of UFOs in the past twenty-one years that has added to scientific knowledge. Careful consideration of the record as it is available to us leads us to conclude that further extensive study of UFOs probably cannot be justified . . ."

They wrote "We have no evidence of secrecy concerning UFO reports."

To put the nail in the coffin, they wrote, "A related problem to which we wish to direct public attention is the miseducation in our schools, which arises from the fact that many children are being allowed, if not actively encouraged, to devote their science study time to the reading of UFO books and magazine articles . . . Therefore, we strongly recommend that teachers refrain from giving students credit for school work based on their reading of the presently available UFO books and magazine articles."

Not surprising, the methods and conclusions of the Condon Committee came under immediate and almost universal attack, including from several members of the committee itself.

The American Institute of Astronautics and Aeronautics formed a committee to study results of the Boulder Project and after a year, rejected Condon's conclusions, stating "We find it difficult to ignore the small residue of well-documented but unexplainable cases that form the hard core of the UFO controversy."

J. Allen Hynek pointed out that thirty percent of the sightings investigated still remained unidentified.

John G. Fuller (author of the Betty and Barney Hill incident) called it a "flying saucer fiasco."

Dr. James McDonald slammed the study, writing, "In all, I believe the contents of the Condon Report fail dismally to support the strong negative recommendations that Condon has presented in his own summary analysis."

John Northrup of Northrup Aircraft and Lockheed said that the Condon Committee was "one of the most deliberate cover-ups ever perpetrated on the public."

After Look Magazine wrote a scathing article about the study, US Congressman Representative Roush said, "The story in Look raises grave doubts as to the scientific profundity of the project . . . I am recommending that we launch a Congressional investigation."

Congressman William H. Bates wrote, "I think it would be good to get another group of scientists to take a look at this matter so we can be more certain of the decisions that are being made."

Despite the protests, the damage was done. In 1969, Project Blue Book was shut down on the basis of the conclusions from the Condon Committee.[9]

Unfortunately for the Air Force, people continued to report UFOs. In fact, 1967 brought a massive wave of sightings across the state.

Meteorologist Photographs UFO

On March 22, 1967, professional meteorologist Robert Rinker snapped a photograph of the weather station where he worked as a field technician. The station was located at 11,000 feet elevation on Chalk Mountain, near Climax. Rinker saw nothing unusual when he took the photo, but upon examining the negative, he was shocked to see an enormous glowing white disk with a dark ring around the circumference. The disk appears to be hovering less than a hundred feet above the ground and covers at least a quarter of the field of view.[10]

A Daylight Disk

Following the termination of Blue Book, consultant J. Allen Hynek published *The UFO Experience*, in which he criticized Blue Book, writing that it was nothing more than a public relations exercise to rid the air force of the UFO problem. He said that valid cases were not properly investigated, and more attention was placed on cases with prosaic explanations. The policy was to debunk good cases and publicize bad ones.

Hynek's book covered encounters of all types from sightings to humanoid encounters. Among these was the category of "Daylight Disks." This next case is one of fourteen he included. At 11:30 a.m., on April 1, 1967, two people were driving through Kenosha Pass when they saw a metallic disk for about two minutes. Says one of the witnesses: "I have traveled US Highway 285 over Kenosha Pass for over twenty years, day and night. This was my first sighting of a UFO." Hynek found the case particularly convincing as he felt certain the witness was not lying and was telling objectively what he had seen.[11]

Eight Encounters

UFOs have often been reported disabling vehicles. As reported to the *Alamosa Valley Courier*, a student from Adams State College (in Alamosa) told local authorities that throughout the month of May 1967, he had seen "strange objects" on eight different occasions. The most dramatic occurred one night while driving; he saw a cigar-shaped object hovering over a field about 150 yards away. It flashed lights that changed from blue to red, to orange, and blue again. As he approached, both rear tires of his car went flat.[12]

Low Flying Triangle

Around 10:30 p.m., July 1, 1967, a group of five friends (all about ten years old) decided to go camping out in the fields near their homes in Colorado Springs. One of the children reports that they all looked up to see a large object passing about 500 feet overhead. "The object had red and white lights in the shape of a triangle," he said. "We could not see the actual shape of the object itself. It moved very slowly and quietly. Everyone in the group saw the object. None of us had ever seen anything like it before."

He was so impressed by his sighting that thirty-four years later, he reported it to NUFORC.[13]

An Invisible UFO

According to pioneering UFO researcher, Donald Keyhoe, the following case appeared in the Condon Committee's files, which surprised air force officers as they believed the case had been marked "Secret." On the evening of May 13, 1967, radar operators at Colorado Springs were startled when their scopes at two different stations showed that an aircraft was approaching the airport; however, visually, no aircraft could be seen. The radar scopes showed solid images of the UFO as it flew right over the airport at a height of about 200 feet, very much like an F-100 or F-104 jet interceptor would do if practicing a landing, but not actually touching down.

Writes Keyhoe, "According to the radar track, the UFO came to within one-and-a-half miles of the control tower, but the tower operators could not see it, even with binoculars. To the CU radar expert who investigated, this was the most baffling radar case on record. He admitted he could not find an explanation. But for the air force it was far more than puzzling. Their own radar experts had reached the same conclusion. Some unknown high-speed aircraft had maneuvered over the airport, absolutely unseen. Could the technically advanced UFO aliens have developed a means for making their spacecraft invisible? It seemed fantastic, but what other answer was there? If true, they could be in serious trouble in case of UFO attacks."[14]

Near Landing in Littleton

According to Eric (pseudonym) one summer evening, around June 1967, he and a group of others were playing in his front yard in Littleton when they saw a light swoop down from the nearby mountains and hover over the field of wheat next to them. Says Eric: "It then moved toward us at about thirty feet above the wheat tops until it was approximately 300 yards away, and stopped."

The object appeared to be forty feet wide and fifteen feet high. It had glowing white panels around the circumference but was otherwise light gray in color. Eric called for his parents, who came out and also saw the UFO.

Soon a crowd of people from the neighborhood gathered to watch the object, including several workers from the nearby Martin Plant and one police officer.

After a short while, the object retreated back to the mountains, accelerated, and then zipped upward into space.[15]

UFO Shoots Airplane(?)

Keyhoe's concern about UFO attacks might be validated by the following incident. One evening in August 1967, Scott (pseudonym) and his friend (a private pilot) were heading west toward Alamosa on Highway 160, also known as the "gun barrel" as the road is perfectly straight for a stretch of fifteen miles. Suddenly they noticed an orange light directly ahead of them. They watched it for about five minutes, then decided to pull over and get a better look. Still unable to identify it, they returned to their car and continued to drive. As they watched, the light turned randomly from orange to green and then back to orange.

They stopped the car again, and after still being unable to understand what they were seeing, continued driving. A few minutes later, a third stop produced no answers. They had observed the light for about twenty minutes as it approached the mountains west of Alamosa. It now appeared to be cigar-shaped and about 200 feet long, moving at an estimated 200 miles per hour, about 1,000 feet overhead. Says Scott, "When it was very near the mountains, we suddenly saw a blinding white light and then it was gone."

They arrived at Alamosa and checked into a hotel. They talked about officially reporting their sighting. Realizing that most people don't report their sighting, and that others might have seen the same thing they saw, they decided to call the local newspaper.

The editor was very interested in their story and drove to their hotel to interview them personally. After interviewing them he said, "Now let me tell you what other stories I have heard."

He proceeded to tell them several other local accounts, including an elderly woman who saw a "huge UFO" that hovered above her house for several minutes.

The next day, a story about their encounter appeared in the paper. Scott and his friend quickly regretted going public, as their friends, coworkers, and others who had read about the sighting teased them. They were then approached by the hotel manager who asked if they were the men from the article. By this point they were wary of sharing information, but admitted that they were.

The manager said that her eight-year-old daughter had seen a strange light on the same evening in the same location. She said that she saw a jet chasing the light. Suddenly, a beam of light shot out from the object and struck the jet, causing it to crash. The police were called, but as the story involved an eight-year-old who saw a UFO, it was not taken seriously. Scott, however, interviewed the young girl and learned that they had all seen the flash of light in the same location.[16]

300 Police See UFO

The 1967 Colorado UFO wave was now in full-swing. One evening around September 1967, Nathan (pseudonym), and several of his cousins were camping near Crestone when they saw a large fireball-like object descending from space. At around 30,000 feet altitude, it split into three balls of fire, each about the size of a house. They were trying to decide if the objects were meteors or missiles. Says Nathan, "We started to take cover behind a very large boulder when the three objects made a ninety-degree turn and came across the valley straight at us. Our thoughts later were that they were intelligent and had detected us watching and decided to buzz us."

The objects moved on a horizontal trajectory across the forty-mile-long valley in about five seconds, each of them leaving a long contrail of sparks. They roared loudly overhead and disappeared over the mountains behind them.

The next day they investigated, buying newspapers and calling the Alamosa Sheriff's office to report their sighting and ask about any others. Unfortunately, they were unable to obtain any corroboration.

The day after that, however, they found a newspaper article that told an amazing story. On the night of their sighting, the Colorado Highway Patrol and local police had seen the three lights hovering around the Colorado Prison on the east side of the Crestone Mountains. They had chased the lights for more than two hours. Fearing a prison break, the prison called in off-duty guards. According to the article, nearly 300 police saw the lights that night.

Meanwhile, the Colorado Highway Patrol contacted Petersen Air Force Base to report their ongoing sighting. Petersen was able to locate the objects on their radar-scopes and, at the request of the highway patrol, launched two F106 interceptors.

As the interceptors approached the targets, the lead pilot asked for permission to fire his weapons. Immediately the three UFOs accelerated at high speed straight up into outer space. The F106s followed them as high as they could, then gave up the chase.

Nathan and his cousins each purchased a copy of the article to keep as a memento. Unfortunately, recent attempts to locate the article have proven unsuccessful. Nathan, however, is sticking to his story. He was a college graduate at the time of his sighting, only days away from leaving for Air Force Officer's Training School and pilot training, which he successfully completed. Writes Nathan, "None of us have ever taken drugs or had enough alcohol to impact our judgment, even though we are all over fifty now . . . I have a security clearance and still work for the US Air Force. One of the cousins is now a lawyer and the other is an emergency inhalation therapist and ex-Green Beret."

It was during this month that the famous mutilation case of "Snippy the Horse" occurred, marking the beginning of a rash of animal mutilations (mostly cattle) that hit Colorado hard, and continues to plague the state today.[17]

UFO Wave Over Alamosa

September 1967, marked the beginning of a wave of sightings around the Alamosa area. At 9:30 p.m., on September 28, various board members of a Blanca Water and Sanitation meeting observed a UFO over Mount Blanca. The object pulsated red and green, and it had a white light on the bottom. The witnesses had binoculars, but were still unable to identify it.

Two of the witnesses were Mr. and Mrs. Burl Lewis, owners of "Snippy," the horse who had been mutilated three weeks earlier. As they drove home they kept an eye on the object, which hovered for a while, then moved north and hovered over Mount Blanca.

They continued driving and soon sighted another object near the Brown Hills—similar looking to the first—only this new object suddenly appeared to explode, disappearing into a cloud of smoke.

Frank Malouff, a farmer living east of Monte Vista also observed the display. He called the police, who ran a search for missing aircraft, but found none.

Two days later, September 30, 1967, a civil engineer was with his son in their backyard in Lakewood. They had a 250-power telescope and were hoping to see some satellites. Instead they saw a bright glowing object—a UFO. They watched it through the telescope, which revealed its elliptical shape. The engineer estimated it was at about 5,000 feet. Suddenly it moved, then flared up, split off two separate objects, each of which took off in opposite directions and disappeared.

The original object began to move away. At the same time, three more lights swooped down from the sky and followed the first object off to the horizon. The engineer concluded that the objects were self-illuminated and moving under their own power.

They saw another glowing object again the next evening. The engineer was outside watching the sky with his telescope when the UFO appeared. He called out to his family, and they watched it together for three minutes until it moved from sight.

Five days later, on the evening of October 5, 1967, superior court judge Charles Bennett, his wife, and mother saw three circular, red-orange objects move overhead, taking about six seconds to cross the sky. The judge reported hearing a faint but distinct "humming or whirring." His wife also heard it and described it "like the low tone of a whistle, almost like a whisper." Unknown to the Bennetts, a young schoolgirl also sighted the object, and was so impressed by the sighting that she reported it to officials.

Less than a week later, on October 11, 1967, the UFOs were back when an anonymous witness reported seeing another green and red object over Manassa, south of Alamosa.

Three days later, on October 14, the police received a call that a bright object was hovering in the east. A number of police officers were able to observe the object for more than an hour as it bobbed and swerved. Suddenly a small red object was sighted moving at treetop level. It quickly rose in the sky and joined the larger object, which now departed the area.

On the same evening, two students, Edward Boggs and Bill McFedries (both age nineteen), were camping out on Mount Blanca. They had heard about Snippy the horse and the UFO sightings, and were hoping to see something themselves. At 1:20 a.m. their patience was rewarded when they saw a brilliant white light appear. For about an hour and forty minutes, the object traveled at varying speeds, dimming and brightening as it moved over the Great Sand Dunes. At one point, it came close to their car and then swung back to where it had first arrived, and then finally disappeared. Their case was researched by APRO investigator, Don Richmond, who was impressed by the young men's sincerity and objectivity.[18]

"I Was Scared"

It was 8:00 a.m., on October 26, 1967, and Dan Kiscaden (age twelve) was running an errand for his mother. He left their home in Commerce City and was walking alone when he saw a glowing red spherical object "kind of floating around in the sky."

Suddenly the object began to move toward him. Realizing he was seeing a UFO, Kiscaden ran home, grabbed his mother's camera, and ran back down the street to take a picture. The object, however, was gone. Kiscaden was walking home when the object reappeared, dropping out of the sky and moving toward him. He quickly snapped two photos and ran home.

He didn't see the object leave. "I was scared," he said. "I just ran home after that."

When the film was developed, Kiscaden was baffled by the images. He had seen a glowing red sphere. The two pictures that he had taken showed a disk-shaped object. Jim and Coral Lorenzen of APRO reviewed the case and write, "This is one of several incidents in which the developed film did not exhibit what the eye saw."[19]

College Professor Photographs UFO

At 11:00 a.m., March 12, 1968, a college professor with a double major in astronomy and world literature, was leaving his home when he had an incredible sighting. Because he was teaching photo journalism at the time, he happened to be carrying a camera. Writes the professor, "I heard a jet aircraft flying low coming from the east. I turned to watch it. It was flying low, at about 1,000 feet. I reacted when I saw the silver mirror-like sphere following the fighter plane just below the tail and about one hundred feet behind it. I thought it was being towed by the fighter. When it was just overhead, the sphere moved in an instant to below the front of the aircraft— about fifty feet in front—then it moved instantly to behind the plane again. I shot a whole roll of film from overhead until it was out of sight."

The professor took the film to the photo lab at the college where he taught. He gave it to the grad student who ran the lab and told him to develop it. The next morning the two of them returned to the lab and entered the darkroom to view the film. Mysteriously, the negatives were gone. The student insisted that he had developed them and hung them on the clamps to dry. The clamps, however, were now empty. Somebody had stolen them.[20]

UFOs Over Delta

In the spring of 1968, a man was standing in his front yard with some of his relatives when they saw a bright red, glowing sphere rise upward. After about twenty seconds, the object split into two, with each half traveling in opposite directions. Says the witness, "They both were moving at such a great speed that they were out of vision in just a few seconds." Thirty-two years later, the witness reported his sighting to NUFORC in the hopes of finding corroboration of his account.[21]

A Mother Ship

September 10, 1968, Caleb (pseudonym) was in the backyard of his friend's house at the base of the Rocky Mountains outside Colorado Springs admiring the sunset when he noticed "four bright spheres of light" moving at high altitude toward the west.

Caleb was in the Air Force and worked at NORAD inside Cheyenne Mountain analyzing secret data about satellite launches across the world. "Though I witnessed hundreds of all types of aircraft in the skies," says Caleb, "I never saw an event like I did on that one day."

Three spheres were small and one was much larger. They appeared to be metallic as they were glinting in the setting sun. Not only did the objects look strange, they moved strangely. "These craft as a group did not form either a V or a diamond or box pattern, which is required by military law. Instead the three smaller craft seemed as if they were 'hot-dogging,' and at the rate of speed they were traveling, and as close as they were, this struck me as very dangerous."

He watched the objects for about five minutes until they disappeared over the mountain range. The incident inspired him to buy several books about UFOs. After reading the accounts of others, he concluded that he had seen a mother ship being followed by smaller craft. Thirty-five years later, he reported it to NUFORC.[22]

UFO Over Main Street

At 7:00 p.m. on June 15, 1969, fourteen-year-old Richard (pseudonym) was walking with his brother down Main Street in Grand Junction. They were on their way to the bookstore when they became distracted by a whistling sound coming from above. Says Richard, "We looked up and saw a silver saucer that had windows and lights flashing underneath. It wasn't dark yet. It stood there for at least two minutes. It was parallel with the Mountain Bell Tower on 8th and Main Street. Then it flew in a flash towards the southern sky."

Both witnesses were impressed. "But we did not report it," says Richard, "because we were afraid people would make fun of us." Forty-four years later, at age fifty-eight, he reported his sighting to NUFORC.[23]

Independence Day UFO

One of the worst days to see a UFO is the Fourth of July. With so many fireworks going off, the chances of misidentifying a UFO go way up. And yet, it does seem to happen, in this instance, on Independence Day 1969 over Lakewood. Writes the witness: "This has stayed with me my entire life. I'm fifty now; I was seven when it happened . . . it sticks because even at seven I knew what I was watching couldn't really be doing what it was doing. My brother, myself, and a friend were sleeping out in the backyard as kids do, and spotted something very high moving in the night sky. It was silent and clearly reversed directions numerous times. We watched it for about ten minutes. It was a steady light. Yes, it was the 4th of July; no, it wasn't fireworks."

The witness still remains baffled and writes that they had "no idea what we were watching. Planes don't reverse directions, and it was way too high and silent for a helicopter."

One month later, in July of 1969, five young teenagers decided to go camping on Flagstaff Mountain above Boulder. They had a perfect spot which gave them a clear view of the sky and the city lights below. Suddenly a strange object appeared in the sky and began to perform maneuvers none of them could believe. Says one of the witnesses: "This object looked like a bright star, zigzagging, abruptly stopping, and then zigzagging at a high rate of speed . . . [It] went from one end of the sky to the other."

The witnesses reported their encounter to their parents and quickly received a lesson about skepticism. Says the witness, "We were all just kids, and no one would believe us."[24]

With the end of the 1960s, the UFO situation was on the verge of a significant change. Up to this point, most of the studies of UFOs were devoted to sightings, with some landings. The contactee phenomenon of the 1950s (involving friendly contact with human-like ETs) was slowly being overtaken by a new type of UFO experience: the missing-time abduction by gray-type ETs. While the 1960s did produce a number of abduction-cases, it wasn't until the next few decades that the phenomenon increased in scope and began to draw the attention of investigators.

Meanwhile, the sightings continued.

CHAPTER 3

Sightings 1970-1979

By the time the 1970s arrived, a number of UFOs had apparently crashed on our planet, and people across the United States and the world were being regularly visited and abducted by aliens. The Modern Age of UFOs had moved to a new level involving an escalation of the phenomenon. Even simple sightings began to exhibit new features, with cases involving vehicles disabled by UFOs, people struck by beams of light, brazen UFOs hovering in full view as though putting on a publicity campaign, UFOs hovering over sensitive installations, radar cases, and more. The endless stream of cases seems specifically designed by the ETs to convince us of their presence without actually landing on the White House lawn.

UFO Stops Car

January 24, 1970, Chris (pseudonym) was driving along Interstate 70 heading from Denver to Golden to get her graduation pictures when she saw a cigar-shaped object appear in the sky on the left at a very low altitude. At that moment, her car engine died, and she coasted to a stop. Observing the object, she saw that it had two bright orange bumps on top, a blue stripe around the circumference, and a green bottom. The colors strobed brightly from top to bottom.

She watched the object for the next twenty minutes until "it just kind of faded away." She then continued her drive to Golden. More than three decades later, Chris reported her account to NUFORC, writing, "I have only told this to one other person until now."[1]

A Report from Cheyenne Mountain

The Cheyenne Mountain Complex is a well-known US military underground installation used to protect the security of the United States. In May of 1970, a nineteen-year-old employee worked the night shift monitoring the early warning radar stations. The third weekend in May, the employee writes that they began to receive reports of four objects at an altitude of 25,000 feet and moving at 2,500 mph over the Bering Sea, along the coast of Alaska and down to British Columbia. Two fighter jets were launched from Alaska but were unable to intercept the objects. Upon reaching Vancouver, the objects (each about the size of a Bomber) moved straight up and beyond the range of their radar scopes.

Although the employee was not on duty the next week, he learned that the UFOs had come back and put on a repeat performance. The first week in April, the UFOs returned again. That's when the employee learned that this sort of thing was not unusual. "I was nineteen at the time, and naïve," he explains. "All the old-timers, who were mostly radar techs and former radar system techs, let me in on the secret. This kind of thing happened all the time. But you learned to never report it in any written reports and to never question it."

The employee decided to share his account with NUFORC, writing, "I have never reported this to anyone or put this into writing before, knowing all the truth will never be out there in print."[2]

Beamed by a UFO

In the summer of 1971, ten-year-old Ricky (pseudonym) was sleeping in the backyard of his home in Westminster. Around 3:00 a.m. he woke up to see a "silent, blinding white light" directly above him. It moved south at about ten mph, illuminating the entire block. He watched as it moved over Westminster for another two blocks before suddenly winking out. This turned out to be the first in a series of sightings which he would have throughout his life.[3]

Low Level Sighting

August 6, 1973, at around 11:00 p.m., James (pseudonym) and his friends were hanging out in his 1963 Chevy Convertible on the backroads of Aurora, which they later found out was immediately adjacent to Buckley Air National Guard Base, known for testing experimental aircraft. Little did they suspect they were about to see something very unusual: a giant-sized, boomerang-shaped UFO.

"We did not notice it until it was directly above us," explains James. "This thing was very large, at least a city-block long from tip, and had dim white lights all around the edges. The color was gray-black and it blocked out the stars as it passed over us at approximately treetop level and very slowly. There was no sound, nor was there any wind . . . we watched it as it slowly made its way west and disappeared into the distance."

None of the witnesses were frightened by the encounter. Says James, "We kept asking each other, 'Did you see that?'"

Although the sighting took place next to an advanced air force base, James is convinced it was of alien manufacture. "The craft we saw as related here," he says, "in my opinion, was not made by humans. It far surpassed any of the stealth-type aircraft that I have seen currently deployed by our USAF. It is something I will never forget . . ."[4]

A Rotating Craft

On October 11, 1973, Mrs. Robbins of Boulder noticed a strange object hovering in the sky. She pointed it out to her husband, Allen. Together they watched the mass of lights approach. As it got closer, they could see it was rotating and maintaining a steady speed. A string of lights on the bottom was divided into thirds. Unknown to the witnesses until later, on the same day as their sighting, Charles Hickson and Calvin Parker were abducted at Pascagoula, Mississippi, a case which would generate national headlines.[5]

Airline Passenger Sees Disk

On the afternoon of December 23, 1973, Philip (pseudonym) sat in the window seat of a commercial airliner flying at about 30,000 feet over Colorado when he had a remarkable UFO sighting. "I was gazing out the airplane window towards the west," says Philip, "when a light from behind the plane caught my eye. I looked back and saw a saucer/disk flying parallel to the plane . . . I watched while the disk caught up to the plane, passed it, and continued on ahead of the plane until I lost sight of it."

Although the sighting was brief, it was close enough that Philip was able to get a great view of the UFO, which appeared silvery, metallic, with orange lights around the circumference, some of which were rotating. It was about forty feet across and fifteen feet high.

The disk was gone before Philip had a chance to alert any other passengers. He looked around the cabin, but nobody else seemed to have seen it. He later reported the incident to the Center for UFO Studies (CUFOS), where it was written up by J. Allen Hynek in their journal.[6]

An Ever-Changing Craft

Not all UFOs involve the classic triangle or saucer shape. Some actually seem to change shapes. On April 1, 1974, a man from Aurora had an experience he won't soon forget. "I clearly observed a silver-gray, ever-changing craft of some sort, approximately twenty-five feet above the ground . . . I believe that it was definitely from out of this world, and able to change its physical structure. It was as if it was alive."

The witness viewed the object from the second story of his home. He watched it for only a few moments before it suddenly disappeared or accelerated away at super-high speeds. He ran outside, but by then it was gone. "I have told only a few individuals this story," says the witness. "I am now fifty years old, and decided to share it. It is definitely real—no joke—and I am sure that other life forms exist."[7]

UFO Over Shopping Mall

"Look up, Mom!"

It was the day before Mother's Day in 1974, and Elizabeth (pseudonym) was picking up her children at the Sears department store in Denver where they had been shopping for gifts. "Look up, Mom!" her daughter insisted.

Elizabeth finally looked up. "I was astounded to see an enormous metallic disc-shaped object sitting a couple of hundred feet over the mall's north parking lot," says Elizabeth. "No one else in the parking lot seemed to see it, or were concerned about it."

She wondered if it might be an advertising gimmick, but it was much too large. It started to move west toward their destination, so they got in their car and followed it for several blocks until it moved off into the distance.

Elizabeth and her children were impressed by the sighting and the next day watched the local news hoping for confirmation of the sighting. There were no other reports.

"Another strange part of the experience," says Elizabeth, "was that we all seemed to have some sort of amnesia about the sighting [and] seemed to forget about it for several years."

Today, all of them have slightly varying memories of the event. As to what it was, says Elizabeth, "We will never know."[8]

Eight Round Disks

"I swear to God that what I witnessed is true and will continue to believe it until the day I die." So says Greg (pseudonym) regarding his UFO encounter. It was around noon on a warm day in June 1974, when two twelve-year-old boys were in the front yard of one of their homes in Colorado Springs. Greg's friend, Jason, turned to him and said, "Look up into the sky."

Says Greg, "I looked, but didn't see anything. Then he pointed up with his left arm and I followed his line of sight and saw eight round disks rotating in a circular motion directly above us."

The objects were a metallic silver-white. The boys were familiar with aircraft as they lived close to the Air Force Academy, and both their fathers were employed by a government subcontractor for NORAD. They were both convinced the objects were not conventional.

"What was most shocking happened next," says Greg. "The eight objects were rotating in a circular motion and then they suddenly stopped moving. The objects remained motionless, without falling from the sky, and all were perfectly separated from one another. Then they suddenly accelerated at an astonishing speed from one another in exactly opposite directions."

Greg followed one object as it disappeared over Pike's Peak, while Jason watched another. Both of them were "amazed" by the sighting and reported it officially after watching the Peter Jennings UFO Broadcast in April 2005.[9]

Rectangle and Triangle UFOs

One of the red-flags pointing toward a genuine UFO sighting is unusual movement. In the summer of 1974 (date approximate), two brothers and two of their friends witnessed a very unusual display of UFO movement over their hometown of Ovid. Says one of the brothers, "[We] watched a light zip in and stop above us in the sky. Then, in the blink of an eye, it shot straight across the sky and stopped. It then dropped straight down . . . from there it shot across the sky and stopped directly under where it first stopped. It then shot straight up to complete a perfect rectangle. From that point it shot back out into outer space so fast that you could barely see the light trail from where it left."

The witnesses were impressed by the sighting. Says the brother, "I swear to God there is nothing on Earth that can move as fast as this object did. And the fact that it formed a perfect rectangle proves to me that we are not alone. I guarantee that every one of us that saw this will be able to pass any lie detector test you want to shove at us."

Later, it turned out that there were other people who saw the same objects, including the witnesses' older brother and his friends.

A similar case of unusual UFO movement occurred on September 11, 1974, over Denver. It was in the evening when the man noticed a triangular-shaped, black object obscuring the stars above him. Without warning, the craft emitted three smaller lights from each corner. Each light moved directly to the center of the craft, then stopped. After a few minutes, the craft shot straight up "at speeds faster than I can guess," followed by the smaller lights. The witness is convinced he saw a dramatic UFO display. As he writes, "Normal heavenly bodies do not travel in geometric patterns."[10]

"It Was Real"

One afternoon in 1974, Angelica (pseudonym) stepped outside to sweep the deck of her home in Greenwood Village. Looking toward the mountains in the southwest, she was admiring the view when something very strange happened. "There was nothing but a beautiful day out there, and then suddenly, a ship just appeared, right in front of me," says Angelica. "It was out in front and a little to the right of me, maybe 500 feet, and I would estimate 150–200 feet from the ground."

The object was grey-metallic, about 300–400 feet wide and fifty–seventy-five feet in height. It was stationary in the sky. "It was real and solid appearing," she says. "It may have been there for thirty seconds or more, and then it vanished just as quickly and in the same manner as it appeared. It didn't fly off; it just disappeared."

This event caused Angelica to re-evaluate her feelings about UFOs. "After that, my opinion concerning the origins of UFOs changed to thinking that perhaps they were not from outer space, but were from another dimension, perhaps time-travelers, or that they had a cloaking device and could be hovering over us all the time without being noticed."[11]

Drive-In Movie UFO

There are a number of cases in the UFO literature involving UFOs that hover over drive-in theaters, such as the following incident. One evening, sometime in 1975 (exact date unknown), a lady was at the Mile High Drive-In theater in Denver to watch *Dr. Zhivago*. More than one hundred people were there when a large circular disk with lights around the perimeter showed up, apparently to investigate. As explained by the witness's husband: "Everyone there saw a huge flying saucer rising up behind and somewhat to the left of the screen. Everyone got out of their cars and watched as this thing slowly rose then came to a complete standstill, hovering."

The object remained for only a few moments, then tilted at a forty-five-degree angle and accelerated out of view, leaving everyone astounded.[12]

Rifle UFO

One evening in June 1975, eight-year-old Chase (pseudonym) was lying in bed when he heard a low humming noise. Looking outside, he saw a light hovering over a lake about six miles from his home in Rifle. He assumed it must be a helicopter, perhaps scooping up water to extinguish a fire, and he went to sleep.

An unknown time later, he spontaneously woke and found himself sitting up, looking outside to see that the object was now directly outside his window, about twelve feet away.

Following the sighting, several cattle were found dead under mysterious circumstances. Says Chase, "To this day I still remember this thing. I have never told anyone about this."[13]

Saucer Over Fort Carson

One afternoon in March 1976, an Army soldier driving through Fort Carson saw a saucer-like object hovering at a low altitude on the other side of the interstate. He was impressed by the object, which had several tiers, lights around the circumference, and appeared to be glowing internally. He saw it briefly before it became obscured by the road and trees. He pulled a U-turn but was unable to find it. Says the witness, "I was dumbfounded, and to this day wonder what it was. I never saw it move, never heard anything."

He wondered if it might have been an advertising balloon, but was puzzled by his inability to locate it. He thought about pulling over at a nearby restaurant and asking if anyone saw it, but was too embarrassed.[14]

Another Drive-In UFO

A particularly dramatic example of a UFO attracted to a drive-in occurred in July 1976, at a drive-in theater in Boulder. Kedrick (pseudonym) was with his girlfriend at the drive-in when she shouted out, "What's that?"

"At the same time," says Kedrick, "I noticed a lighted craft approaching from the southwest. At first it appeared to be a helicopter flying low and making slow, gradual turns back and forth. As it got closer, I could see that the lighting and motions were definitely not standard for a helicopter (or any other aircraft). The object seemed to be attracted by the movie playing on the screen and approached and hovered over the cars parked at the theater."

Kedrick estimates that the object was about 200 feet above. It was a "classic domed saucer" with red, orange, and yellow lights flashing slowly. The disk then began to descend lower; at the same time, the lights became brighter and began to flash more quickly. Suddenly the disk began to extend a "rectangular structure" from the bottom, which flashed extremely bright green, blue, and purple lights. Says Kedrick, "The intensity of the lights became almost painful to look at. The other people at the drive-in reacted by honking their horns and flashing their headlights, at which point, the object moved away."[15]

Dillon Dam Disk

In July of 1976, the town of Silverthorne had a population of fewer than a thousand people. It stands at 8,000 feet elevation below Dillon Dam, which feeds into a small lake directly below. The city itself is located in a little valley surrounded by mountains. One evening around that July time, Colby (pseudonym) and his friend were getting ready to start fishing in the lake. Looking up, they saw a metallic saucer with small windows moving across the lake toward the dam. Colby estimated that it was about 2,000 feet away and 1,500 feet high. It zipped fairly quickly across the sky below mountain-level.

Colby called out to his friend, who looked up. At that point, the object disappeared. Colby's friend glimpsed it briefly. Colby, however, got a good look at it. "It was traveling fast," he says, "but not too fast for me to observe the little portholes. The object was very bright. I followed it for probably eight seconds, and it just disappeared in front of my eyes."

The next day, Colby called a UFO hotline and learned that several other people had also called to report their sighting.

The event changed the way he felt about UFOs forever. Says Colby, "I rarely tell anyone of this event, as people generally seem to think I am a nut, or a druggie, or some other silly justification of my so-called 'delusion' . . . Everything that happened is engraved in my mind as if it happened yesterday. The memory of the UFO remains with me, as clear as when it happened . . . It is an event I shall never forget. From that day on, I not only believed in UFOs, I knew they existed."[16]

Prison UFOs

One afternoon in August 1976, a correctional officer performing tower duty at Colorado State Prison saw an oval-shaped disk about one hundred feet in diameter arrive from over the nearby mountain ridge about 200 yards away. It made a low-pitched humming sound and moved at about twenty mph. The officer marked the event down on his shift report and afterwards, reported the incident to the Canon City Police Department.

The sighting not only impressed him, it affected him physically. Says the correctional officer, "This took a while to process as it was strange to see . . . the sighting did leave me somewhat disoriented and [with] poor sleeping for about two weeks."[17]

1977 UFO Wave

The year of 1977, produced a number of high-quality reports across Colorado. One remarkable sighting of multiple objects occurred March 17, 1977, to a young couple in Denver. They had just arrived home, and the wife, Diane (pseudonym), was unpacking in the house.

Says Diane: "At approximately 7:30 p.m., my husband came running into the house yelling my name. He was very agitated and nearly speechless, and he just kept saying my name while dragging me out to the back side of the house."

Diane's husband explained that while unpacking the car, a bright light shined down on him. Looking up, he saw a silent, spherical-shaped craft hovering fewer than a hundred feet above their house. Cube-shaped lights covered the craft and blinked in a circular pattern.

They raced outside together. "By the time I came outside," says Diane, "the object was in the distance, and it looked like a very large, bright star."

She jumped up on the truck to get a better look and suddenly saw a second craft coming from behind her and moving overhead at about 150–200 feet. Like the first, it was silent and moving slowly, but this one had a different shape. "This craft was triangular," explains Diane. "[It] had three very large amber-colored lights on the bottom. It was close enough that I was able to make out some of the mechanical lines on its bottom part."

At this point, several cars stopped in front of their house to watch the strange objects.

Meanwhile the first craft had reached the mountains in the distance, where it hovered and blinked, changing shape and blinking white, gold, and red. Without warning, the craft released a red light that floated slowly to the ground. At the same time, the craft turned bright white, changed into a circular shape, and moved toward Boulder, disappearing into the distance.

Five minutes later, a convoy of military helicopters and planes swooped over and around their home, searching the area for several minutes, and then moved off. Neither Diane nor her husband reported the objects officially until years later.

The year wasn't over yet. The summer of 1977, eleven-year-old Joseph (pseudonym) was riding his bike near his home in Fort Collins when he had an experience that he would think about every day for the rest of his life.

"I sensed there was something following me," says Joseph. "I turned my head to see what was behind me and observed that there was something flying two feet above my head. The object was about three feet long, eight inches wide, and made no sound. It was a dull glowing gray in color."

His first thought was a bird, but it clearly wasn't a bird. Then he thought maybe a toy model rocket, but it wasn't that either. Says Joseph: "I checked it out for about three seconds, and the moment that I realized that I didn't know what it was, I felt startled, and the object traveled straight out in front of me and out of view in about 500 milliseconds."

Following the incident, Joseph spent the next hour looking for it or any clues as to what it might have been. Instead, he was left with a haunting mystery. "I have never told this to anybody," says Joseph, "and have thought about it every day for the last thirty years."

He wasn't the only one baffled by what he had seen. The wave of 1977 had just begun. Late in the evening of July 30, 1977, Wendy (pseudonym) was walking next to

Hinkley High School in Aurora when she realized that a gigantic, chevron-shaped craft was hovering a mere 200 feet above her head. It was so low that it barely cleared the tops of the trees and a nearby apartment building. Wendy was stunned. "I stopped dead in my tracks, rubbed my eyes, and realized it was not an illusion."

As she watched, the object darted away with a soft whooshing sound. It stopped about seventy-five feet away and hovered only to dart again. It repeated this maneuver in a zigzag pattern over Aurora towards the mountains, until disappearing out of view.

About thirty miles away and one month later, on August 9, 1977, two friends were on the corner of 18th Street and Franklin in Denver when they both "sensed" something. "We looked up at the same time," said one of the friends, "and observed a very large triangular craft moving slowly from north to south. The underside looked gray and the triangle's tips were darkly colored. It had no lights or markings and made no sounds." The craft appeared no higher than a few hundred feet, moving at a slow cruising speed, allowing them to view the craft for about fifteen seconds.

Three months later, on November 20, 1977, UFOs were back in Aurora. Eleven-year-old Darius (pseudonym) was outside his home in Aurora when he saw a low-flying circular object moving overhead. It was shaped like a hockey puck and had round, white lights around the circumference. The object was silent and moved slowly, stopped, turned sharply, and began to move toward Denver. Darius ran across the street and got his friend to come outside and observe the object. Although Darius could still see it plainly in the sky, his friend saw nothing. "I could see it," said Darius, "but my friend standing next to me could not. It was plain as day, right there."

This confused Darius, and upset him as his friend thought he was lying. He watched the object move away. Says Darius, "Then it took off at an angle into the sky like a flash, and disappeared."

Unknown to Darius, there are now several cases on record in which witnesses see a UFO while those next to them can't see it.[18]

UFOs on Radar

One of Colorado's best radar-return cases occurred on December 17, 1977. At around 3:45 a.m., radar stations in Colorado and South Dakota tracked two "unknowns" moving more than 1,000 mph. One of the objects made a head-on pass toward an aircraft. The two objects moved over a wide area for more than thirty minutes, during which "strong" radar returns showed their paths. Strangely, a third radar station was unable to function while the objects were in the area. Furthermore, one of the two operational stations was suddenly and mysteriously put out of service when the main shaft holding the radar antenna was "severely bent by an unexplained force."[19]

Sightings 1980–1989

In the 1980s, thanks to the publication of books like *Communion* by Whitley Strieber, *Light Years* by Gary Kinder, and *Intruders* by Budd Hopkins, interest in UFOs exploded into the mainstream, and people began to officially report their encounters in larger numbers. UFOs were being taken more seriously than ever before. This resulted in more people reporting their sightings, which caused further interest.

Contact at Lake Granby

It was August 5, 1980, and Austin was camping with his girlfriend at Lake Granby. Sitting around the campfire, they saw a "shining oval orb" move across the sky, stop, descend, move to the left, descend further, and stop stationary. They retrieved their binoculars and were able to discern fluorescent-looking lights of green, purple, red, and yellow flashing around the circumference.

Then two smaller objects approached and hovered below the first. Then a fourth orb arrived and moved toward the other three. They watched all four objects for nearly forty-five minutes when a fifth object arrived.

The new object was shaped like a rectangular box, and was a copper-metallic color. It moved overhead and toward the other objects.

At this point, yet another UFO arrived, a white disk. "It was by far the closest," says Austin, "and it really scared my girlfriend."

Austin had been astonished at first. Now he felt a strange feeling of being observed and pursued. The other objects began moving. They were now looking at UFOs in front of them and on both sides. This was when they heard "a very bizarre whirring sound, unlike anything I have ever heard."

When they heard the sound of pebbles being scattered on the shore of the lake about 150 feet away, the whirring sound stopped and they both felt the sense of a presence. They retreated to the floor of their camper and lay there "in abject fear."

Says Austin: "I have never been so scared in my life, and my heart was a jackrabbit trying to kick its way out. Austin began to see "strange mathematical images of almost fractal-like patterns." He began experiencing weird impressions of vegetable-computer hybrids and other bizarre information-laden thoughts.

As they lay there, they next both felt "a real euphoria, almost like an inner levitation, which overall seemed peaceful."

Austin's girlfriend was frightened by the intensity of the feeling. They both figured they'd be up for hours, but the next thing they knew, they were both asleep and it was the next morning. Says Austin: "This was one of the most intense and staggering experiences of my life, and hers too."[1]

UFO Signals Officer

On the night of October 5, 1980, the fire department in Allenspark received a call that two fishermen were missing. Ranking officer Derek (pseudonym) responded to the call and went with a fire captain to Saint Vrain Creek where the two fishermen had last been seen. As they pulled up to the spot, Derek was surprised to see "a large bright white light" hovering downstream, where there was a confluence of two creeks.

Says Derek: "As I watched it, the light moved back and forth in a U-pattern. My immediate association was to an airplane dipping its wings. After a few seconds it faded out. I had the mental impression that this light was signaling the location of the fishermen, and letting me know if they were okay."

"Did you see that light?" Derek asked the captain.

"No," he replied.

Derek explained what he had just seen, and what he thought it meant. Since it was too dark to search, Derek assigned two men to stay on the bridge and watch for the men.

The next morning, Derek led a crew down the access road toward the creek where they met the missing men. The fishermen said that they had become lost and spent the night at the confluence of the creeks.

"Did you see any unusual lights?" Derek asked.

Both men replied in the negative. Derek wasn't sure what to make of his sighting. He had seen a strange hovering light earlier in the same area, and he had talked to another local resident who had also seen strange lights. Says Derek: "I consider myself to be a curious, careful, and scientifically-oriented observer." He is convinced he saw a genuine UFO, and more than thirty years later, reported it officially to NUFORC. In the years following his sighting, Derek became the chief of a large fire protection district in the western United States, and then changed careers and became a privately practicing psychoanalyst.[2]

United Airlines UFO

In 1981, a United Airlines pilot was flying about 140 miles southwest of Dove Creek when the crew observed an unidentified object move abeam of the airliner, heading southward at an estimated speed of 5,000 mph. After it went out of view, an American Airlines airliner following forty miles behind also observed the object, watched it reverse course, turn to the northeast, and move off.[3]

Black Triangle

One morning in 1981 (date approximate), a young man was with his family driving near their home in Colorado Springs when he saw a triangular black craft hovering near the top of Pikes Peak, just above the tree line. Says the witness: "It was a sight where you instantly know this is something extraordinary and not what our brains are used to processing and seeing . . . I was instantly startled as to what this was."

It was flat black and appeared to be rotating. "Stop the car!" he shouted.

"What is it?" his father asked, pulling over.

At that instant, the object darted away at "an incredible speed." Living near the Air Force Academy and with his father in the Air Force, he was familiar with military aircraft, but was still unable to identify it. After reading about other similar triangle sightings stretching back decades, he became convinced that the craft could not be military. "I never saw it or anything like it again," says the witness. "I hope one day I can find out what it was and solve the mystery."[4]

UFO in the Forest

Around 11:00 p.m., October 30, 1981, three men in the West Elk Wilderness Area had a remarkable encounter with a UFO. Says one of the men: "A brightly lit, white, perfectly round ball an estimated fifty feet in width dropped in a straight line almost as fast as a shooting star and began to make slight serpentine motions as it slowed down. As it slowed further, the zigzagging of the craft became much more radical until it was making large sweeping switchback-turns, going from a speed of several thousand miles per hour to about one thousand miles per hour."

The object appeared to be about one mile away. It was intensely bright, and yet failed to light up the area around it. "It didn't project light as we know it," says the witness. "It looked extremely bright at its core, but the light did not emit out beyond that core. It had the ability to zigzag in and out of heavy black timber at a speed of nearly one thousand miles per hour. It didn't bump any trees or make a single sound of any kind."

The witness was with two other men, and says: "They can verify this if they are willing. They got pretty scared over the whole thing and wouldn't talk to anyone afterwards, but I've been very gabby telling everyone I know about it."[5]

An Upside-Down Pyramid

Late in the evening of February 12, 1982, Corrine (pseudonym) was driving home from work in Windsor when she saw three bright lights hovering over the local grocery store about two miles away. As she approached, she realized the lights emanated from a huge, dark, triangular-shaped object, with the apex of the triangle pointing downward. She drove right up to the object and pulled into the grocery store parking lot. Oddly, although other cars drove by, none seemed to react.

Wondering if it was a balloon or something, she drove directly underneath the craft and got out. She could now see that it was actually a large pyramid-shaped object about fifty feet high. It was upside-down and hovered just above a group of street lights. She got out of the car and listened, but the object was totally silent. Suddenly another driver in a separate car saw the object and stopped. Two young men looked up at the object. Says Corinne: "They rolled down their window and were looking at the craft with the biggest eyes I've ever seen. Their mouths were hanging open and I could see their tongues. I waved at them, and the craft began to rotate on its axis."

The driver of the car suddenly took off, racing away from the object. Wondering if she was in danger, Corrine got in her car and pulled out from under the object. She watched it from a side view as it headed at about five mph over the grocery store, lifted up slightly, and cleared the roof by about five feet.

She estimates that she saw the object for about six minutes. A few months after the incident, her co-worker described her own encounter of a pyramidal UFO. The co-worker was on Highway 34, heading toward Greeley, when she and a group of other people stopped their cars on the road when they saw a large upside-down pyramid with lights on the tips cross low over the road. Her sighting lasted about fifteen minutes as they watched it approach and leave, moving at about five mph.[6]

Longmont Disk

Because they are often outside, many children become UFO witnesses. "Early in the evening of May 9, 1982, five-year-old Mason (pseudonym) was playing with his dog in the front of his parents' home in Longmont. Looking up, he was shocked to see "a classic saucer" hovering over the corner of the yard less than 500 feet away at the same height as the telephone wires. It remained utterly still and made a weird tonal sound. Suddenly the object sent down a colorful beam of light.

Mason felt fear sweep over him as he realized that "whatever was in that object knew I was there." That was enough for him. He jumped up and ran inside with his dog right behind him. He told his mom about the UFO. She rushed outside, but it was gone. Both Mason and his dog were nervous and upset by the incident. Years later, Mason still remembers it vividly and believes that it was "something unknown."[7]

Boulder Triangle

One evening in September 1983, a man was looking up at the night sky when he saw a large boomerang-shaped object "the size of a football field" pass overhead at about 1,000 feet. It made no sound and had no lights, and was very hard to see. The witness first noticed it because it was blocking out so many stars. It passed overhead and disappeared from view. He quickly found the nearest pay phone and called the Boulder Police Department. After reporting what he saw, the dispatch department informed him that they had already received twenty calls about the same object. Later, the witness joined the navy and spent much of his time flying. "To this day," he says, "I cannot identify a possible aircraft profile that I know of that is similar to what I saw in 1983.[8]

"A Feeling of Calm"

An undated encounter (circa early- to mid-1980s) comes from near-death experience researcher, Kenneth Ring, Ph.D., who began to look into UFO encounter experiences after noticing their similarity to NDEs.

Early one morning, a forty-year-old graduate and her ex-husband were driving from Boulder to their home in Lamar when then came upon a silver-gold metallic saucer hovering 350 yards to the left of the road and about 400 feet high. It was enormous in size, at least the size of a football field. It remained perfectly silent and still in the sky. "We stopped our VW," says the female witness, "and just looked at the object. I mentally gave a 'greeting', but I don't know why . . . at no time did we feel we were in danger, but we did get a very vivid impression that whatever we were looking at was watching us in return. About thirty to thirty-five minutes passed. All of a sudden a few scattered, very white little clouds appeared. Then one large, massive, very white cloud came in from the west traveling east over the object. When the large cloud passed over the object, the object was gone as if it was never there. On the way back to Lamar, after the incident, a feeling of calm and peacefulness came over me that I have never experienced before or since."[9]

Sheriff Sees UFO

One evening in 1985, Elbert County Sheriff George Yarnell was out on patrol with his deputy when they observed a powerful and unusual display of unexplained lights. Said Yarnell, "One night we were east of Elbert on the north Fondis road on a high hill. Right north, maybe a half a mile, it was like a football field lit up. Then we looked and it went out. Then a little while later we saw it to the east, maybe three miles." Yarnell had no explanation for what might have caused the lights.[10]

Reservoir UFO

On August 20, 1985, two friends camping at Taryall Reservoir in Fairplay saw a huge white sphere descend from the sky and start moving over the lake. It was about twenty feet in diameter and about 200 feet above the water. As they watched, it moved in an erratic, bouncing zigzag motion around the coastline, traveling around the entire circumference of the reservoir in about fifteen seconds. When it reached the place it first appeared, it rose higher and higher in the sky until disappearing from view. The witness calls it "the most brilliant light he had ever seen." Strangely, however, it cast almost no light around it.

Unknown to the two men, there are other witnesses to the Tarryall lights. One year later, in May 1986, a man and wife camping a few miles from the reservoir saw a red ball of light about a half-mile away move slowly past them. They estimated it was about one hundred feet in diameter. Says the husband: "I wished it would come closer so we could see it. A little while later it came around the mountain it had disappeared behind. It was coming back toward . . . the south side of camp. This time it was only about seventy-five yards away! It was 300 feet in diameter, and it stopped directly south of us and hovered about fifty feet off the ground. The witnesses felt a strange calmness and seemed to lose track of time. Suddenly the object took off and, in about one second, it was hovering over the mountain range about thirty-five miles from their camp. Following the incident, the witness wondered if perhaps they had missing time.[11]

Fort Carson UFO

In April 1986, Gregory M. Hansford was a legal non-commission officer at Fort Carson with thirteen years of active duty. He didn't believe in UFOs. It was just before noon and he was driving on the base. As he waited at a traffic light, a "huge silverfish-gray disk" appeared from the low cloud cover and hovered. Says Hansford: "I was in disbelief! I continued to shout in my car, 'Holy Jesus!' and other things I cannot recall. I simply would not have believed anyone's stories of UFO sightings until I saw that one that day." He watched it for less than a minutes when it suddenly accelerated away. Says Hansford: "This thing took off at a speed too hard to imagine."

Hansford reported his sighting to his fellow sergeant and his captain who "thought I was losing my mind."

The sighting changed his mind about UFOs, and to this day he's not sure if he should count himself as lucky or cursed.[12]

Ranch House UFO

Around noon on July 21, 1987, a couple was driving east from Gypsum to Eagle. They had just passed the local high school and were driving by a ranch house when they saw a strange metallic oval-shaped object hovering only about twenty-five feet above the farmhouse. It made no noise and floated around as though it was totally weightless. They stared in amazement. Although the object was clearly metallic, it did not reflect light, making it difficult to see. They estimated that it was about the size of a small passenger car. Says the wife, "Suddenly, the object shot up into the sky extremely fast. Its speed was faster than anything I had ever seen before."

"What was that?" her husband asked.

Neither of them could even begin to guess. Strangely, they discounted the entire incident and didn't talk about it for years. She says, "However, without a doubt, I believe it was something not natural or normal—definitely a UFO."[13]

Almost Abducted?

It was around 10:30 p.m. on the evening of August 10, 1987, and Martin was lying in bed watching television in his home in Snowmass. Next to him, his pregnant wife and their son slept on the couch. Suddenly he was overcome by sleepiness and a "paralyzing feeling." Then the television went blank, as though there was a power outage. Looking outside, he saw that the streetlight was also out. All his hair stood on end, and he felt "strangely light." Martin fought the feeling of paralysis and finally jumped up and tried to wake up his wife and son. Strangely, however, they wouldn't wake up.

He went outside to investigate and saw "a dark rectangular object blocking out the stars. I was awestruck," he says, "there were no lights. After my eyes adjusted, I could see what appeared to be faintly illuminated portholes around the edge of the craft. I felt like I was almost weightless and my hair was standing on end."

The object was a few thousand feet high and appeared to be as big as an aircraft carrier. Martin watched it until it disappeared behind a mesa to the north. Once it was out of view, the power came back on.[14]

Army Officer Observes UFO

On the morning of April 1, 1989, an army officer walking along Redlands Express in Grand Junction saw a dark object moving overhead at about 8,000 feet altitude. After traveling across the sky, the object suddenly dropped down until it was fifty feet over some nearby rock formations. The object then transformed into a brilliant white sphere, moved about one mile, then changed to a brilliant orange. It hovered for ten minutes then shot upward about 8,000 feet, passing underneath a jet aircraft. Finally it moved north, turned white again, and made periodic flashes before moving away.

The next day, an article appeared in the *Rocky Mountain News* that the Grand Junction Radar System operated by the FAA had experience software problems that had caused glitches that made it look like there were objects flying over Grand Junction. The day after that, the witness observed a C130 military plane travel 200 feet above the ground where the object had been hovering. The Army Officer, who also worked as a police officer and has been a candidate for public office, believes he saw a genuine UFO and says, "What I saw was beyond the scope of our military and industrial machine."[15]

A Transparent Sphere

A very unusual encounter occurred one afternoon in April 1989 at Snowmass. Matt had invited his friend over. Looking out his picture window, which overlooks the Fork River, they observed a strange light rise from behind a hill and approach. They were both "aviation buffs" and took notice when the object began to zigzag over the nearby field and across the river, heading right toward them. Says Matt, "It stopped about five feet in front of the window, and we could see its reflection on the river when it passed over it. It was about five feet in diameter, and appeared to be made of glass. An amber colored light emanated from inside."

They ran to get other witnesses. When they returned, the object was speeding south along the river. It was quickly followed by two smaller spheres (one red and the other blue.) Says Matt, "We were both shaken up and in awe."[16]

Enter Christopher O'Brien

In July 1989, musician and construction worker, Christopher O'Brien moved to Crestone in the San Luis Valley. At the time, he had no idea that he would soon become a leading UFO and cattle mutilation investigator. He had long been interested in UFOs and the paranormal. Yet, he was surprised when only a few months after moving there, he had his first of what would become many UFO sightings. August 13, 1989, at 10:00 p.m., O'Brien was sitting outside watching the sky and saw "a bright point of light" heading across the valley.

He shouted for everyone to come outside. He and two others observed the light silently explode over the town, about two miles away. Writes O'Brien, "This was the first sighting of what I have dubbed as 'cheap fireworks.' Dozens more of these puzzling objects have appeared to me since moving here—some as close as twenty-five feet away! They are not meteors or identifiable celestial objects . . ."

This event sparked O'Brien's curiosity into the San Luis Valley area, which he would later identify as Colorado's most active UFO flap area, and one of the most active areas on the entire planet.[17]

"A Light from Space"

On the evening of November 21, 1989, two ladies were sitting on the front porch of their apartment building in Lakewood. Suddenly their daughters came running out the front door screaming that a UFO was hovering above the tree in the backyard. The ladies jumped up and followed their daughters to see a craft about the size of two football fields flashing an array of multicolored lights. It was totally silent, very low, and says one of the witness, "[It] was huge!" The object instantly darted away to the north end of Denver and began to drift back toward them.

One of the ladies was particularly impressed because only a year earlier, her daughter's friend had come running into the apartment hysterical. She said that she had been walking her dog when "a light from space" came down and "was trying to suck her up." Everyone had been skeptical, until this incident occurred during which they saw a UFO for themselves.[18]

So closes the 1980s. As can be seen, the sightings in one decade alone should be enough to convince skeptics that UFOs are real. The 1990s would bring an even more impressive parade of encounters.

Sightings 1990-1999

Each year brings hundreds of UFO sightings over Colorado. Most of these involve unexplained lights at night or brief sightings of an ambiguous nature. Others turn out to have prosaic explanations. But each year brings a smaller number of encounters that are very difficult to explain. The decade of the 1990s brought an increasing number of these types of cases.

The Colorado Hum?

Starting in May 1991, residents in Taos, New Mexico, began to report a mysterious humming noise with no discernible source. Before long, people in other areas were reporting the same (or similar) mysterious hum, including in Colorado.

Terri of Calhan says she began hearing the hum in 1990, one year before the Taos story broke. She has seen "strange lights" on multiple occasions, but starting in 1990, she began to hear a constant sound like a distant jet engine. The sound seemed to come from everywhere at once. When the hum continued for four days at once, Terri contacted the Air Force who told her that they would look into it. They called her back four days later, telling her what she already knew: that she was not in any flight paths.

When Terri questioned her neighbors, she learned that they had also heard the strange noise. Finally, after four days it stopped briefly, only to start up again a week later. It went on and off all summer long, then stopped.

Two years later, it returned for half a day. Terri wondered if it could be some type of psychological warfare device. Thankfully it stopped. Terri reported her account to the Colorado UFO Institute who published an account of her experiences in the hopes that other "hearers" would come forward.[1]

A Second Sighting

In January 1991, a year and a half following his first sighting, Christopher O'Brien saw his second UFO. He had just finished a musical gig in Salida and was driving home to Crestone when he heard "a loud crackling sound." Looking up, he saw "a huge, brilliant, green glittering ball of light! Behind it streamed a tail as it remained at a constant altitude parallel to the mountaintops." More sightings would soon follow.[2]

Buzzed by a UFO

On the evening of April 13, 1991, an uncle and his nephew were driving between Durango and Pagosa Springs just before midnight. They were traveling at about forty-five mph along a remote stretch of the highway where the mountains were close-up on either side. The nephew (a twenty-three-year-old aeronautical engineer) was in the driver's seat when they both noticed a huge disk of light about fifty feet across, hovering directly above their car and moving along with it at the same speed. They both saw that the light was actually attached to a much larger object composed of gray metal. Only then could they see that the object was gigantic and extended far ahead of them on the highway. The uncle (the president of an international trade association) counted seven lights on the object, all spaced evenly along its bottom. Says the uncle, "I had just finished counting the lights when the object disappeared in a beautiful curving motion. I then looked up in the clear dark sky and saw the object, which in a split second went from something that seemed 400-500 yards long to a tiny two-inch object way up in the sky, where all we could see were the row of lights. Then it disappeared."

They compared notes about what they had seen and agreed on everything, except one thing. The uncle thought the object was one hundred feet above their car, while the nephew believed it was closer to about seventy-five feet. The next day they reported their sighting to the local sheriff's office and learned that the airport manager at Pagosa Springs had seen a similar object hover over his home.[3]

A UFO Mimic

The evening of July 18, 1992, Brendan O'Brien (Christopher O'Brien's younger brother) and mutilation investigator Bill McIntyre were in the Great Sand Dunes area when they saw a very bright light four miles away toward Pioneer Canyon. They pulled their vehicle over and turned off the headlights but left their orange parking lights on. Instantly, the light changed to orange. O'Brien turned the headlights back on, and the mysterious light turned white and started to revolve. He turned the headlights off, and again the object turned to orange. Intrigued, he decided to approach closer. As he drove toward the light, the light began to rush directly toward them, again mirroring their actions.

It lit up the trees below as it raced toward them. O'Brien pulled a U-turn and raced away from the light, which now turned "ruby red." The object then stopped, grew brighter and smaller in size, moved to the south, then shot up at a forty-five-degree angle, turned white, and mimicked a star.[4]

November and December Sightings

Around 3:00 a.m. November 1, 1992, John Browning woke up to see a strange light outside his tent. He was about twenty miles north of Saguache on a hunting trip with his son and two friends. Crawling out of his sleeping bag, he ventured outside and saw a gigantic triangular-shaped object moving overhead. It was silent and covered with sixteen lights. "I'm telling you this thing was huge," said Browning. "It must have been at least a quarter mile long! . . . Whatever that thing was, it wasn't from this world." He rushed to wake up the others, but the object moved away before they could see it.

Three weeks later on the evening of November 25, 1992, Michael and Andrea Nisbit were in their home in the Baca Grants when the entire house became illuminated by a powerful beam of light coming from above. They ran to a window and saw an orange-white light surrounded by pulsating lights.

At 8:15 p.m., December 9, 1992, astronomer Michael Robertson and a friend went outside Denver to watch the lunar eclipse when they saw something even more interesting: an unexplained orange object approaching from the northeast at about 30,000 feet. At the same time, an identical object approached from the northwest. The two objects crossed paths over Denver and headed south. Robertson reported his case to MUFON investigators, telling them, "In thirty years of watching the skies, I have never observed anything like those objects." It appeared that they were high enough to reflect the setting sun.

One hour later, a woman down in Crestone was also outside to see the eclipse when she observed two golden-white orbs race overhead at "fantastic speed."

Two other witnesses also observed the lights. Luna Bontempe and Lucas Price were outside their home in the Baca Grants waiting for the eclipse when they saw unusual lights "bouncing around, creating geometric shapes." While watching the lights form squares and triangles, they saw two other bright orbs flying at treetop level overhead. The lights emitted bright beams of light that lit up the ground like daylight. The lights returned for the next two nights, and were seen by Bontempe, Price, and others.[5]

A Full-Time Investigation

The recent sightings were causing a buzz of gossip in the San Luis Valley area. Since moving to Crestone, Christopher O'Brien found himself regaled with stories of local UFO encounters. He had already had two sightings himself. For three years his interest mounted. But it wasn't until December 31, 1992, at a New Year's Eve party at his home that his investigation officially began. During the party, he heard one of his friends talking about a UFO she had recently seen. Intrigued, O'Brien asked for more details. She described her sighting and referred him to her boyfriend and several other people at the party who had also seen UFOs recently. He learned that there had been local sightings on November 25, 1992, and sightings that occurred over a three-day period from December 9, to December 12, only two weeks prior. Another guest mentioned that there had been a cattle mutilation on a local ranch at the same time the December lights had been seen. O'Brien was amazed:

> UNBEKNOWNST TO ME, I WAS GRABBING FIRMLY HOLD OF A TAR BABY! MY FULL-TIME INVESTIGATION LITERALLY BEGAN THAT NIGHT, AND I CAN'T HELP BUT LOOK BACK AT THAT PIVOTAL EVENING AND VIEW MY NAÏVE EXCITEMENT WITH A SMILE. IF I HAD KNOWN WHAT I WAS GETTING INTO, MY EXCITEMENT WOULD HAVE UNDOUBTEDLY BEEN TEMPERED WITH THE REALIZATION THAT YEARS OF FRUSTRATING AND UNREWARDING HARD WORK LAY AHEAD WITH NO PROMISE OF ANY FIRM ANSWERS. I NEVER ACTUALLY DREAMED I WOULD SOLVE THESE RIDDLES. BUT I FELT COMPELLED TO INVESTIGATE THE EXTANT OF THESE ELUSIVE RIDDLES.[6]

The 1993 Wave

As researched by MUFON field investigator and State Section Director David B. Clemens, the San Luis Valley produced a number of high-quality sightings throughout 1993.

In February 1993, witnesses saw unexplained lights moving below the ridge of the Sangre de Cristo Mountains, then streaking along the ridge-tops. Also in February, a man was in his car at Crestone Campgrounds when his car was struck by a beam of light from above that tried to "get him out of [his] car." Finally, two women were driving south along Highway 17 near Mosca when a "bell-shaped object" passed over their car.

In March 1993, two objects were viewed moving down the entire western length of the vast San Luis Valley. A few minutes later, military jets were seen tracing the path of the UFOs.

One month later, in April 1993, four witnesses at Monte Vista described an object as "school-bus sized."

In May 1993, two witnesses observed a thirty- to forty-foot boomerang-shaped object descending from the sky in a figure-eight pattern.

In November 1993, twelve witnesses observed a blue-white object fly at low altitude over the La Garita area. The next night, another anomalous light showed up, and so did a group of military helicopters that surrounded the object and began dropping flares.

Researcher Christopher O'Brien also received multiple reports of day and night sightings involving "a silent, large silver sphere with blinking red and blue lights sequencing around the bottom, pairs of orange orbs flying through the sky, a large triangular craft hundreds of feet long, and even seven alleged Bigfoot encounters."[7]

It Wasn't a Meteor

Jack Cookerly (a trained naval aviation navigator) thought at first it was a meteor. Early in the evening on November 30, 1993, Cookerly was getting out of his car in Crestone when something overhead caught his eye. "It was bright white as it streaked over my head," he said, "and I instantly thought it was a meteor. But as it approached the horizon, it flared up about twenty times its original size, turned into an oval shape, and stopped. It was huge!"

The object moved at right angles, changed its size, shape, and color, and began to descend.

Meanwhile, seven miles to the west, Al Koon (a former military officer) was at his home in Moffat when he, his wife, and daughter all viewed the object, which had the apparent size of the full moon. None of them believed it was a meteor. Says Koon, "I've never seen anything like it in my life."

While Koons watched the object "blink out," Cookerly believes the object came down in the valley. He was expecting it to hit the earth and explode.

In the days that followed, the area was stricken with black helicopter activity, strange explosions, mystery fires, anomalous lights, at least one cattle mutilation, and more UFOs.

On December 13, 1993, a Crestone resident observed a "glowing white object" fall to the ground. " . . . [W]hen it disappeared, it was like it went underground on this side of Highway 17," said the witness.[8]

A UFO Swarm

January 7, 1994, a resident of the San Luis Valley reported to Christopher O'Brien that he observed about twelve to fifteen unexplained lights at about 1,000 feet. The lights moved like a swarm of bees toward the western sky. "He called me to report this as soon as he got to the phone in Hooper," says O'Brien. The man had been skeptical of UFOs until his sighting. Afterward, he immediately phoned O'Brien, who had recently begun his investigations into sightings in the area.

While O'Brien had only just begun his official investigation, in the space of less than two years he would soon find himself a leading investigator. His 1996 book, *The Mysterious Valley*, recounts hundreds of sightings in the San Luis Valley area, documenting the activity there in fantastic detail, not to mention the cattle mutilations. The book, and its sequel, *Enter the Valley*, are required reading for anybody interested in UFOs and the San Luis Valley hotspot.[9]

A Memorial Sighting

On the evening of Memorial Day 1994, Chandra Chandler and her husband were sitting in their yard in Colorado Springs when she caught movement from the corner of her eye. "I had my binoculars," said Chandler, "and when I looked through them I saw four objects. They flew directly over our house. They were oval-shaped, dark if not black, and each one of them had a pale halo or energy field around it. Three of them were flying in a triangle shape going north. The fourth one came over and joined the other three, and then all four of them shot off in different directions."

She was so impressed by the sighting, she joined a UFO group called the UFO Institute of Colorado Springs.[10]

Spelling UFOs

On August 21, 1994, twenty witnesses in Del Norte observed a group of twelve objects that flew in a leisurely manner. At one point, the objects began to perform strange maneuvers, making shapes and letters. They first formed the letter "G," then a triangle, and finally a circle. The display lasted an hour until one object departed from the group, dropped down through the clouds, and approached the witnesses close enough so that they could now see red and blue lights flashing beneath the object. At this point, the objects moved southward and disappeared.[11]

Triangles and Disks

June 27, 1994, at around 11:00 p.m., six witnesses in Moffat saw something blocking out the stars. As it moved from west to east, they saw that it was "a triangular ship with no lights . . . ." The object appeared to be at an altitude of 1,000 feet. After it passed, another smaller craft followed.

Just more than three months later, on October 9, 1994, June Martin and one other witness observed a "large disk-shaped craft" over La Veta. The object was shining a spotlight on the ground. After it left, helicopters were seen searching the area.

Five days later, on November 2, Martin saw a "wedge-shaped craft" over La Veta, moving silently from east to west.[12]

A Car-Lift Case

Dozens of UFO car-lift cases have been reported across the United States and the world, including this unusual example from Rio Grande County, just north of the New Mexico border. Christopher O'Brien spoke with the witness, Alan, who told him that he and his family had been seeing "every kind of ship you could imagine" flying over the desert area surrounding their home. They saw large ships, small ones, triangular-shaped craft, disk-shaped craft. Says Alan, "My mother found out that they could come closer if you called to them in your mind."

Intrigued by the possibility of communicating with the occupants of the craft, Alan and a friend went out one night in 1994 to watch the UFOs. They sat in the friend's pick-up truck and waited to see if anything would show up. Early in the evening, "a strange bank of fog" rolled in and surrounded them. A light appeared in the fog and they saw a craft about 600 feet away. "I started to call it closer," said Alan, "and it approached and just sat there about fifty feet away. Well, my friend kind of freaked out, grabbed his rifle from the rack, and popped off a couple of shots at it. It went above us and somehow it lifted up the truck and put it in the bar ditch!"[13]

UFO-Car Encounter

For some unknown reason, UFOs seem to have a penchant for harassing drivers. Around 11:00 on the evening of May 5, 1995, three people from Conifer were driving home from a movie when they experienced an unusual encounter. Instead of taking the main road, they took a side-route called Turkey Creek Canyon Road. They were traveling about thirty mph, approaching the only street light on the road, and noticed a strange glowing light hovering above the street light. Suddenly it swooped down towards their windshield and began to pace their car. Thinking they were about to collide with the UFO, the driver slammed on the brakes and swerved. The object then flew off to the left, lighting up the trees, and moved over a ridge and out of sight.

All the passengers were stunned. They each agreed that they had seen an object about the size of an SUV. It appeared translucent and had a propeller-like device on one end.

Two of the witnesses exited the car to search the area, while one remained in the car, crying and scared. By then, however, all evidence of the UFO was gone, and they soon continued their journey home.[14]

The Salida Sightings

"Daddy, there's something up there in the sky." Brandy Edwards (age six) stood next to her father, Tim Edwards, a café owner from the town of Salida. It was early in the morning, August 27, 1995.

Edwards ignored his daughter and continued working. But as she continued to insist, he finally looked up. His mouth dropped. Hovering high above them was a gigantic, silver-colored, cigar-shaped spacecraft.

Edwards stared in shock. "They put some feelings in me I've never had before," he explains. "When I was looking at the main craft, I got like an electrical impulse through my body. It was very important for the world to know the truth. Now I'm convinced we're not alone."

Edwards grabbed his video camera and recorded almost ten minutes of videotape while his wife and daughter watched the object through binoculars. To Edwards, it appeared to be a very large cylindrical-shaped object, glowing with a pulsating light, which is what the footage shows. However, through the binoculars, the other witnesses could see a disk shape and colored lights.

"I felt deeply at the time that I was witnessing something of great scientific and historic importance for the world," said Edwards. "I believe that the August 27th craft was sending a message to the world and wanted to be photographed, that its appearance was somehow just the beginning of more to come, and that I was really fortunate to be a part of it."

Edwards released his footage to the media. The result was an explosion of publicity and attention. The media converged on the small town of Salida, and Edwards' sighting garnered national and international headlines. Before long, the leading UFO television programs, *Sightings* and *Encounters* became involved and aired segments containing Edwards footage.

"The first three weeks I was an emotional wreck," says Edwards. "Everything seemed so trivial . . . My family couldn't understand my obsession with it."

Thankfully, he soon got confirmation that his footage showed something very unusual. Bruce Maccabee, a photo analyst specializing in UFO photos called it "some of the best UFO imagery ever recorded in history." Jim Dilettoso (also a UFO photo analyst) of Village Labs in Tempe, Arizona studied the footage and declared it genuine. "It is definitely a very large, solid, and three-dimensional, possibly cylindrical object at high altitude," he concluded. "We don't know how large it is as yet, but the object clearly is emitting brilliant white and colored lights, is demonstrating unusually rapid, darting movements in the sky, and we have confirmed on the tape the presence of smaller objects coming from it, which confirms the witnesses' visual accounts."

Further analysis revealed that the object was hovering at 60,000 feet and traveling at 10,000 mph.

More support of the incident soon arrived. At least twenty-one witnesses in thirteen different locations reported seeing the same or similar object during that time.

"I feel a lot better about the whole situation," Edwards told the *Herald Democrat*. "There's a certain amount of relief involved. I put our lives and reputations on the line when I came out with this, and it's nice for someone to tell me I'm right."

In another interview he said, "I never gave much thought to UFOs before this happened. When something this unusual happens, your life is completely changed in a moment. It's been a very emotional and stressful time, but I've never felt better about life. I'm totally honored to be a part of what's transpiring."

One of the witnesses to activity on the same day was a disk jockey at a Grand Junction radio station, who had a very unusual sighting. The man was hiking in Colorado National Monument when he saw a sphere of white light across the valley. Without warning, the ball of light emitted a stream of smaller orbs, which then proceeded to strike the mountainside.

Following Edwards' sighting, more reports began to pour in from a wide number of Colorado locations. Julie Perez, office manager of Fiske Planetarium at the University of Colorado in Boulder received seven calls in the first week of September. One call came from Longmont, another from Flagstaff Mountain near Boulder. She discussed the reports with her colleagues and none of them were able to match the descriptions to any known astronomical objects. Instead, their descriptions seemed to match what Edwards saw. "It appears these people were looking at the same thing in different areas," explained Perez.

On August 8, 1995, two woman saw a "huge cigar-shaped" object over Poncha Pass and reported their sighting to Christopher O'Brien. On the same day, Sheriff Al King of Saguache County received a call from a motorist who saw a "giant cigarette-shaped object" over Highway 285. The object first hovered and then darted away at "fantastic speed."

September 12, 1995, witnesses in Leadville, Glenwood Springs, and Colorado Springs, observed unexplained objects in the sky. A man driving over Lizard Head Pass said he was followed through the pass by "silver disks."

Around 3:30 a.m., September 12, 1995, a man camping in Idaho Springs with friends woke up to relieve himself and saw what he first thought was a shooting star. Instead of burning out, however, it headed right toward him. "As it grew nearer," says the man, "it grew larger and larger. The brightest and whitest light

I had ever seen . . . it stopped right in front of me and right over my head. It was huge and I was frozen stiff." After a few moments, three jet fighters approached and chased the object away. His friends ridiculed him when he told them about the sighting, until the next day when the *Denver Post* had a front page story about the local sightings.

The sightings continued. September 22, 1995, Jeannie Shaw, her sister, and two adult children heard a "humming sound" over their home in Huerfano. They ran outside and saw a rectangular-shaped object about 300 feet wide passing over their house at about eighty feet. "My legs buckled," said Shaw. "I couldn't believe it. There were yellow and white lights oscillating around the front, which was rounded."

Her sister, Loni Smith, says, "It was monstrous. It was the mother ship . . . Our mouths were open to our navels. I felt like I was looking up at the bottom of a barge."

They watched the object for ten minutes as it moved leisurely away. "As it moved away from us, we could see red lights on the rear," said Shaw. "They looked just like giant Cadillac taillights."

After the object moved over a ridge and disappeared, a bright light rose up, flared, and went out. Then ten blinking lights appeared, flying in crisscross patterns.

She called the police who said that they had heard the object, and that it was a helicopter. A call to the *Huerfano World* newspaper yielded the same answer.

Shaw wasn't convinced, as she had already contacted several neighbors who either heard and/or saw exactly what she and her family witnessed. One of them was Jean Newland who said, "It was huge. I saw it going over the trees. It was a shock to see something that big."

Edwards' sighting changed his life. He not only became a sought-after guest at UFO conferences and media outlets, he began to take a closer look at the skies. It wasn't long before he had another sighting.

At 9:30 a.m., September 25, 1995, Edwards' mother, Jean, noticed a tiny silver object near the sun. Tim went outside and saw it, too. He immediately called the Chaffee County Sheriff's Department and the local KVRH radio station. Then he went outside and began to record the activity. He soon saw additional objects darting around the sky, some of which left contrails.

Edwards discovered something strange. The UFOs seemed to hide in the intense light of the sun, making it very difficult to see them. To view them clearly, he found that if he stood in the shadow of the eaves of his home, he was able to see them more clearly. It appeared that the UFOs were hiding by remaining at high altitude in the direction of the sun, and/or that the intense light levels in the coronal direction made the objects visible.

Meanwhile, officer Chester Price at the Chaffee County Sheriff's Station soon arrived and watched the objects with Edwards and a group of ten other people.

Officer Price said he saw "bright and shiny silver objects traveling from north to south around the sun." He counted at least ten.

Back at the KVRH radio station, Mark Roman was trying to deal with a mysterious problem with their FM signal tower, which went out around 9:00 a.m. that morning and remained non-functional for forty-five minutes. Then Edwards called to report a UFO over Salida. His call was followed by four others from different residents who also saw the object. Several employees of the radio station ventured outside and also saw the object.

The Salida *Mountain Mail* newspaper learned about the sighting and later discovered that the Cellular One tower near the radio tower also malfunctioned and was down from 1:00 p.m. to 4:45 p.m. They also received calls from additional residents who had seen the object.

The next few days, the skies were filled with military planes who appeared to be investigating the area. "It is obvious to me that something very special is happening," Edwards said.

The buzz slowly died down. By 1996, Edwards stopped searching the skies for UFOs or attempting to film them. Instead he eased back into his normal routine. Though it was clear to him, things would never be the same.[15]

A Train-like UFO

One evening in 1995 (exact date unknown), a man and his girlfriend were driving home along Airport Road in Longmont. Another car followed not far behind them. Suddenly he noticed a strange-looking vehicle passing the other direction in the opposite lane of traffic. He looked in shock. It was a long object, glowing orange, and floating just above the road. It was completely silent and looked "like a floating train," only not as tall. It took several seconds to pass, after which the car behind them began flashing its headlights and honking its horn.

By this point, the UFO was gone. The man was confused and frightened by what he had just seen, so instead of stopping, he floored the accelerator and drove off, something he would later regret.

Not long after, he married his girlfriend, and while both remember the incident, she prefers not to discuss it. Says the witness, "My wife usually denies this ever happened in front of other people [and] only confesses to me sometimes about what we saw."[16]

Caught on Video

James Armijo of Center says that he has grown up with UFOs. He estimates that he has seen them eight or nine times.

In mid-January 1996, he saw a strange object near Alamosa. "It looked sort of like a boomerang. It was near the big blue water tower in Alamosa. It was just sitting there. It didn't move. Then it disappeared."

His wife also saw the object. "I don't want to believe," she said, "but I have to. I've seen them."

When more strange objects appeared a week later, Armijo was ready. January 25, 1996, just after sunset Armijo observed silvery disk-shaped objects moving up and down, and back and forth, over Greenie Mountain. "These things were moving all over the sky," he said. He grabbed his video tape. "I saw one right over Greenie. It was sitting right on top of the mountain. When I zoomed in on it, I couldn't find it, but I saw another one."

Armijo showed his family and friends the footage, and when they were impressed, he contacted Christopher O'Brien. "This is very credible footage," O'Brien said.

The footage later appeared on the television program *Sightings*, and remains some of the best footage of UFOs over Colorado since Tim Edwards filmed an object over Salida.[17]

CSETI Sighting

June 16, 1996, Steven Greer, MD., was leading a group of individuals (including the author of this book) in an attempt to make contact with UFOs. Greer, the founder of the Center for the Study of Extraterrestrial Intelligence (CSETI), was on a mission to establish peaceful diplomatic relations with ordinary citizens and extraterrestrials. The group CSETI became widely influential, mainly because its methods worked, and many people had dramatic encounters. On the evening in question, the main group had just gone to bed while around ten people remained. It was 2:05 a.m. when Greer, his assistant Sheri Adamiak, and eight others saw an orange-red, elliptical object. Says Adamiak, "Greer signaled to it with the high-powered light three times, whereupon the craft pulsed back three times. We sent thoughts of welcome, peace, and friendship to the craft. Immediately the craft increased its illumination and pulsed brightly."

The light then winked out. However, about a half-hour later, another glowing yellow-white light appeared, followed by a smaller red light. Through binoculars, Greer observed a triangular shape to the yellow light. They watched the UFOs for a few moments, until a military jet headed toward the objects, which moved behind the Sangre de Cristos Mountains."[18]

Black Triangle

In the early morning hours of June 19, 1996, multiple independent witnesses in the Fort Collins area observed a massive silent black triangle move at low elevations over the city. Just before 2:00 a.m., one witness was on the campus of Colorado State University when he noticed a portion of the sky where the stars were being occulted. He observed the phenomenon carefully and was shocked by what he saw. "After a while," he says, "I could make out a huge triangular craft, much blacker than the rest of the sky, moving northward over Interstate 25 about seven miles east of campus. It was very large—from my perspective, about 600 yards long by 200 yards wide at the rear."

As it moved closer overhead, he was able to view its bottom side, which was dimly illuminated by the lights of Loveland and Longmont. The witness estimates that he viewed it for about two minutes, and says that there was "no way anything that size would have escaped the attention of NORAD."

Meanwhile, only a few miles away, a man in Masonville woke around 3:00 a.m. to make some coffee. Walking out onto his porch, which faces Fort Collins, he looked up and saw a large black triangle about 3,500 feet high and 5,000 feet away. "I was in awe," says the man. "I didn't hear any noise from the object. It was black, and as it moved in front of me, I could tell it was triangular. It was non-reflective . . . much blacker than the night sky." He estimated that the object was about one hundred feet long and 125 feet wide. He watched it for about ten minutes as it moved over the mountains to the north. The witness was in the Marines for six years prior to the sighting and says, "I'm pretty level headed, never did drugs, and don't drink alcohol."[19]

A Red and Green UFO

While conventional planes use red and green navigation lights, UFOs sometimes appear to use the same colored lights and mimic the appearance of planes. March 7, 1997, Nancy Brown of Aldasoro Ranches, near Lone Cone, woke up at 1:30 a.m. and, looking outside, saw something spectacular: five UFOs hovering high in the sky outside her home. They hovered as a group off to the southwest, above Lone Cone. "They all looked the same," said Brown, "except for the one that went over the house, which I saw the bottom of. That one had two circles, where one was red and the other light green, and they were circulating and pulsating. It was really bright. The others that looked the same were really bright, also with red and green lights pulsating."

They clearly weren't planes, but what were they? She woke up her husband and asked him what he thought; could they be planes? "No," he told her. "It's too bright."

She retrieved her binoculars, and then knew that they weren't planes. "It was way too obvious that they couldn't be planes," she said.

One of the objects was larger than the others and appeared to be the mother ship. "There were other UFOs spinning around it," says Brown. "It was oval shaped, like the [apparent size] of a planet, with a red station pulsating in there . . . It felt really organized and technical. Especially that one station that was at one place."

Brown felt no fear during the sighting, and watched the objects for more than an hour. But having to work the next day, she finally stopped looking and went to bed. In the morning, the objects were gone.[20]

March Lights

March 1996, proved to be particularly active. March 14, Undersheriff Brian Norton of the Rio Grande County Sheriff's Office received a report of UFOs over Greenie Mountain. Says Norton, "There were four objects reported, and eyewitnesses claimed that two of them appeared to be shooting tracers at each other."

On March 22, the UFOs returned. Mary and Ed Johnson, Kris Kroll, and other residents of Creede (west of the San Luis Valley) saw a bright red explosion over Snowshoe Mountain. The Johnsons had exited their home to walk their dog in the early morning hours when Mary saw what she first thought was an exploding plane. "Then it seemed to stop, and had a bunch of little fizzly tails coming off it," said Johnson. Unable to identify it, they got their neighbor, Kris Kroll, to take a look. He was also mystified, as was Kenny Wyley, another Creede resident. He tried to take photos of the object, but the pictures didn't come out.

The last week of March brought more reports. Sergeant Harry Alejo of the Alamosa County Sheriff's office received a call from Helen Willhite of Blanca who told him that a light was hovering over Mountain Blanca. She had seen it for four nights in a row. Alejo found the woman's testimony credible. However, after contacting various Colorado Air Bases, he was unable to obtain any verification of her sighting.[21]

A Very Close Sighting

While distant sightings of anomalous lights in the night sky are relatively common, much rarer are close-up sightings. Extremely close sightings, within a few feet are the rarest of all. These cases provide a unique opportunity to observe the phenomenon so closely that it virtually removes any chance of misperception.

On November 12, 1997, two brothers and their cousin had spent the day fishing at Rampart Lake just outside of Divide. The sun had set, and a thick fog settled over the lake as the men waited for their wives to come pick them up.

Suddenly one of the brothers noticed a "white ball of light" hovering about 900 feet away over the lake. The sphere was so brilliant that it pierced through the fog. The men watched it move in a ninety-degree arc over the lake. They thought at first it might be a boat.

Says one of the brothers, "The object then moved directly at us doing about five miles an hour or so. It got so close at this point—I would say no more than twelve feet. The light was about the size of a basketball. At this point we started to get a little concerned about our visitor."

They had been watching the light for about fifteen minutes and had been talking about it the entire time. The object now edged even closer to them until it was about twelve feet above them and seven feet to the side. "This was a little too close," said the brother. "So I picked up a rock [and] threw it right at the object. I did this several times and came very close, if not hitting the light. The action had no effect on the ball of light."

The cousin wanted to shoot at it, but the others believed that it might be "a bad mistake." Shortly later, the mysterious sphere of light retreated and moved away in the same direction it had arrived, and left.

The witnesses returned the next day to investigate. They concluded that the light was not ball lightning, nor any type of reflection.[22]

Prison Sighting

On the afternoon of January 10, 1998, a correctional officer at Canon City prison was taking his crew of inmates back to the shop to turn in the tools and return them to the prison population. He and a prison inmate looked up to see "a very large sphere, chrome in color with three brown spots on the side." It hovered an estimated 60,000 feet high and appeared to be gigantic, big enough to fit ten full-sized airliners. Says the correctional officer, "The inmate and I just looked at each other and said, 'What in the hell is that?' To this day I have no idea what it was."[23]

UFO Fleet

On the evening of April 3, 1998, six people traveled in three vehicles southward down Interstate 25 above the southern border of Colorado just north of Walsenburg.

"As we came to the crest of the hill," says one of the witnesses, "we were presented with a scene that brought us to a stop in the middle of the road. It was like a scene from a movie. The valley was filled with lights and ships."

Two large ships glowed orange and hovered still in the sky while several other smaller yellowish objects maneuvered "almost as if playing." The ships were about 600 feet high. At least eight other vehicles had also stopped on the highway, and a small crowd of people stood outside their cars to watch the display. Two jets and helicopters appeared, but stayed on the perimeter of the activity. Meanwhile, the smaller objects maneuvered around in the larger objects.

Says the witness, "The objects were moving south at a slow rate, and seemed totally unconcerned with the helicopters or the jets. The smaller objects did maneuvers unlike anything we had ever imagined and seemed to glow and blink at each other as if interacting . . . we were all so stunned; we realized we were holding hands and just asking each other if this was some kind of beginning, or maybe an end."[24]

UFO Affects Car Radio

Around 11:30 p.m., March 21, 1998, a small group of friends were driving home after visiting a coffee shop in Broomfield when they heard a police siren. They pulled over, but strangely there was no emergency vehicle. Suddenly the passenger in the back seat shouted, "Look!"

Outside the car, three teardrop-shaped objects hovered in a triangular formation. At that exact moment, the radio station went out and became static for the next two minutes. "Then the objects just disappeared," says one of the witnesses. "The radio came back on."[25]

Pueblo Triangle

According to Peter Strescino of the *Pueblo Chieftain,* just after 9:00 p.m. on the evening of April 10, 1998, two seventeen-year-old boys observed a triangular object in the southwestern skies over Pueblo. The object was zigzagging the area and sending down a spotlight as if searching for something. At this point, a passenger jet approached from the north, heading south. The triangular object began to circle around the jet; at the same time it changed color and shape. "It looked like cells dividing," explained one of the witnesses.

The jet raced away and the object departed, leaving the witnesses impressed enough to report their encounter to authorities.[26]

Four Low Level Sightings

On the evening of June 6, 1998, just off Interstate 265 between Bailey and Fairplay, two college students and friends were sitting on the hood of a car, talking. Suddenly, one of them yelled, "Look at that!"

Together the two friends observed a bright circle of light about sixty feet in diameter, with a red halo and a deep-blue tail. It was silent and appeared to be about

500 feet high, flying slowly. Both witnesses felt "completely at peace," and both had an "out-of-body experience." They saw the light for about five minutes until it reached the trees behind the house, at which point, it promptly disappeared.

They rushed inside the house to get other witnesses and went back outside with two other people, but the objects were gone. Strangely, two planes flew overhead, which was unusual as there was no flight path nearby. Only after returning to the house did they learn that twenty minutes had passed, and not the five that they had thought. Says one of the witnesses: "The whole experience felt very peaceful, but afterward both my friend and I were terrified of seeing it alone."

Just more than a month later, on July 18, 1998, a Longmont family was driving their car when they saw a triangular-craft. Around all three edges of the craft were yellow-white lights like neon tubes. The object appeared to be about fifty feet high as it passed over the road, hovered, and moved on.

On September 3, 1998, a man from Cherry Hills Village reports that, at 10:20 a.m., he saw a silver, dome-shaped craft with a spike on top. It hovered about 200 feet above the ground. Says the witness: "It left so quickly, just sped up until I could not see it anymore. I couldn't believe it." Colorado State MUFON Director Michael Curta says that there were other sightings in the same area around the same time.

One month later, on the evening of October 8, 1998, Robert Kelly-Gross observed "an intense red light sitting in the sky." As he watched the light, it suddenly "bolted across the sky at an incredible speed." The light stopped over Battle Mountain (located near Vail), about eight miles from Kelly-Gross's home.

A jet appeared and followed the light. After about thirty seconds, the light disappeared.[27]

As can be seen, the 1990s proved to be very active. The above sightings are a cross-section of the more extensive and dramatic sightings. For each case listed here, there are dozens of others. And these are only the *reported* cases. Most people don't officially report their sightings, so the actual number of cases is substantially larger.

As humanity moved into the new century, UFO activity continued at a steady rate. The UFOs, it appeared, were not going to go away anytime soon.

Sightings 2000-2009

By the time the new millennium arrived, UFO activity had occurred for more than fifty years, including sightings, landings, abductions, and UFO crashes. Like it or not, Earth was being invaded by aliens—and had been for decades. The 2000s were largely a repeat performance of the previous decades. One difference was that more people seemed to be more aware of the phenomenon. UFO reporting centers like MUFON and NUFORC now received hundreds of cases each year. The disclosure movement continued to make strides. While the subject still isn't being taught in schools or officially and publicly recognized by the US government, it appears that things are trending that way.

A Confrontational UFO

As investigated by Colorado MUFON state section director, Davina Ryszka, on the evening of March 7, 2000, a woman was driving with her baby along a back road to her home in the small town of Olathe (population 1,300.) Suddenly the mother saw a very bright light in front of her. Seeing a red and green light on either side, she assumed it was a low-flying plane. But as the object came toward her, the object seemed "confrontational," heading directly toward her car.

She slammed on the brakes to avoid a collision. At this point, the craft stopped directly in front of her car. She moved the car, and the object moved with her. She pulled a U-turn and the object hopped around and moved right in front of the car.

The witness became "really frightened," for both herself and her baby. She turned around again and though the UFO tried to block her, she managed to get in front of it and began the drive home. For several moments, it appeared that she had escaped the attention of the strange visitor until suddenly, a bright light came on above her, illuminating her car and the area around it. The witness then drove home, shaken but unharmed.[1]

The UFO Watchtower

Judy Messoline was frustrated. Once again, she had found people camping on the front yard of her property, located about two miles north of Hooper in the San Luis Valley. She knew what they were looking for—the same thing the other campers were always looking for: UFOs. Her home, she knew, was smack in the middle of Colorado's biggest UFO hotspot. She could hardly blame people for being curious.

Then, in 1999, she had an idea. If you can't beat them, join them. Why not build a UFO watchtower and invite people to come look for UFOs? She sent design plans for her idea to the Saguache County commissioners. She soon received approval to build a ten-foot watchtower, with a fifty person capacity.

The watchtower and adjoining gift shop and garden, opened in May 2000, and quickly became a popular local tourist attraction. It continues to be popular, and according to Messoline, it actually works! Many people, she said, have seen UFOs from the watchtower.

On Memorial Day, May 29, at 10:45 p.m., a "watcher" visiting the tower saw two star-like objects racing across the sky when one stopped for a moment, allowed the second one to catch up, and then both darted into a cloud. The next week, more watchers saw five star-like objects when one of them instantly began moving in the opposite direction.

Hooper resident (and store owner), Candace Knolan had seen UFOs before. In early June, she was with a group of researchers on the tower when a circular object with red, white, and teal lights appeared. One of the researchers flashed twice at it with a 250,000 candlepower flashlight. "The object blinked back twice," says Knolan. "The guy with the flashlight went blink-blink again, and the thing moved across the sky and went blink-blink, too."

The light exchange happened a third time before the UFO disappeared. "It blew me away," said Knolan.

Messoline had seen UFOs in the area before. On Father's Day, June 19, 2000, she saw them again: a string of silver objects. She thought they were Mylar balloons until they stopped and began to maneuver into different shapes. She ran to get her binoculars, but when she returned they were gone.

In late June, around 11:00 p.m., Messoline was in the tower with several others when she saw a bronze-colored, cigar-shaped light zip quickly across the sky. She was hesitant to mention it until other people in the tower shouted out that they had also seen it. Says Messoline, "It scared one gal so much she left."

The UFO Watchtower appears to be a huge success and has attracted upwards of one hundred visitors a day.[2]

UFOs over Boulder Jail

In March of 2000, Elliot (pseudonym) was pulled over by the police and arrested for driving without a license. As a result, he was ordered to serve eight days in Boulder County Jail. To pass the time, he would stare out the window that faced east overlooking the train yards and baseball fields on the east side of town.

For the first three days he noticed nothing unusual. But on the fourth day of his incarceration, about 1,000 feet from his window, he observed a "dark green craft with a white glow around it" rise straight up from behind a hill, then dart around, up and down, back and forth, then finally fly in a straight pattern to the north looking strangely like a plane. "Trust me," says Elliot, "it was no airplane . . . I could see the detail of the craft. It was diamond shaped, with strange small details."

As it moved off and disappeared, another object appeared, rising straight up, and like the first, began performing "weird maneuvers" and then straightened out and moved north. Four more objects followed.

At this point, Elliott had to go eat dinner. When he returned, it was now dark. Before long, he saw more objects. He was freaked out because they looked very much like planes. "Yet I saw them in the day, fairly closely," he says. "Close enough to know they were definitely not planes."

He asked his cellmate to look at the objects. He refused. He saw a few more objects, then the activity stopped. The next morning, around sunrise, he saw one more. After that, no more appeared. He estimates the entire event lasted about fourteen hours.[3]

Vail UFO

At 10:00 p.m., July 22, 2000, a man from east Vail was outside his home walking his dog when he saw a round-shaped craft with four lights underneath it and blinking lights on the top. It flew only a few hundred feet overhead. While the witness could hear plane engines and car engines from further away, the craft, which was much closer, made no noise whatsoever. As he watched, it gained in altitude and flew east over Vail Pass.[4]

Jets Chase UFO

As investigated by researcher, Bob Fiske of Vail (a former police officer,) on November 4, 2000, a couple driving along interstate 70 in Wolcott observed an unidentified craft flying about 300 feet overhead. They flashed their headlights at the object, which promptly jumped to a higher altitude and began to move west. The object appeared to be teardrop-shaped with a dome on top. It glowed green-white, but had a red light at the rear end and multi-colored lights around the perimeter. The object made no noise as it moved westward. Suddenly, the couple saw two USAF A-10 jets coming toward the object, which now accelerated quickly and disappeared into the distance. An Eagle County police officer admitted to seeing the jets, but didn't see the UFO.

A few months later, on February 3, 2001, another married couple in Wolcott was driving along Highway 131 when they saw a bright green light swoop downward in an apparent controlled descent, disappearing behind a hill north of 4-Eagle Ranch.[5]

Moffat Cigar

As investigated by Christopher O'Brien, on March 2, 2001, a family of three driving through Moffat saw what they first thought was a small plane. The craft flew in front of their car about a quarter mile away and a hundred feet high. Only then did they see that the object had no tail and only "stubby little wings." It was moving too slowly to be a plane. Otherwise, it appeared "dull silver" and had a cigar-shaped fuselage. The witnesses viewed the object for about ten seconds, when it suddenly disappeared. "We couldn't believe our eyes," said the father. "It just vanished."[6]

UFO Surveillance

May 23, 2001, two men camping south of Kremmling saw three glowing UFOs maneuver silently for about an hour. One object appeared to be a bright white light. The second was amber/orange, and the third had multi-colored lights. The three objects moved in different directions as if conducting some sort of search or surveillance of the area. One of the lights approached to within a quarter-mile of the witnesses. Two of the objects moved away, but the third remained hovering. The campers observed it through binoculars and saw lights rotating around the perimeter of the object. They said it looked like something directly from the movie *Close Encounters of the Third Kind*.[7]

More UFO Watchtower Sightings

As reported to Judy Messoline at the UFO Watchtower in Hooper, on the afternoon of July 1, 2001, Cary observed a silver object, which traveled along the north side of Mount Blanca and disappeared into the Great Sand Dunes.

In September 2001, visitors to the UFO Watchtower saw a strange light directly above them. It flashed and moved erratically up and down, and side-to-side. It remained in view for about twenty minutes, then disappeared.

The next day around 10:00 p.m., more than a dozen people on the tower saw an unexplained light over Mount Blanca. Later, campers visited the tower and told Messoline that they had seen the same lights.

One month later, on November 24, 2001, seven people visiting the UFO Watchtower watched three lights hovering above the Great Sand Dunes. Two hovered stationary a few miles apart and flashed yellow, red, blue, and green lights. A third object appeared about nine miles away and was making "erratic movements." The objects were observed for one hour until they disappeared.

One week later, witnesses saw a UFO move at very low altitude over the Great Sand Dunes.[8]

Dinosaur Extinction UFO

"I'm currently writing a book about an important scientific discovery located within the Rocky Mountains of the United States, known as the Western Interior Seaway Impact Project (WIS). This unique discovery has allowed me to be the first person to locate and study the first major physical evidence of the dinosaur extinction, which occurred 65.2 million years ago," writes, Quentin, a WIS scientist.

The evidence is in the form of fossil dinosaur bones that show "signature" impacts from iron asteroids. On the fifth day after the site had been discovered, Quentin, who worked with his father on the project, observed a bright white light dart across the sky, then stop and hover directly over the discovery site. It remained in place for ninety seconds, then shot off "at an incredibly high rate of speed."

Five minutes later, two Air Force jets appeared, following the course of the strange object.[9]

V-Shaped UFO

At 11:00 p.m., on December 13, 2002, a witness in Denver saw a "fairly large" V-shaped object studded with more than a dozen lights fly about 600 feet overhead, just above the treeline about one-eighth mile away. It moved at an estimated speed of 2,000 mph. Says the witness: "It didn't make any noise, and it completely disappeared."[10]

More UFO Watchtower Reports

While visitors to Messoline's now famous UFO Watchtower continued to produce UFO reports, she also found that she became something of a local clearing house for UFO reports.

JANUARY 5, 2002, SHE RECEIVED SEVERAL CALLS FROM LOCAL RESIDENTS REPORTING A BRIGHT SPINNING STAR-LIKE LIGHT FLASHING DIFFERENT COLORS.

FEBRUARY 23, 2002, AT AROUND 6:20 P.M., SHE RECEIVED MORE CALLS ABOUT A BRIGHT LIGHT WITH AN AMBER BOTTOM MOVING OVER KIT CARSON PEAK. THAT NIGHT, AT 9:20 P.M., SEVEN WITNESSES ON THE UFO WATCHTOWER REPORTED SEEING A BRIGHT LIGHT OVER THE GREAT SAND DUNES.

MAY 13, 2002, CAMPERS REPORTED SEEING A STRANGE LIGHT OVER CRESTONE. IT BLINKED WHITE AND RED IN VARYING PATTERNS. THE PARENTS REPORTED THAT THEIR YOUNG BOYS STARTED ACTING STRANGE AFTERWARDS AND THAT THEIR ENTIRE DEMEANOR CHANGED.

JUNE 10, 2002, THREE LIGHTS WERE SEEN MOVING ACROSS THE SKY. TWO DAYS LATER, A LIGHT WAS SEEN MOVING UP AND DOWN, THEN IN CIRCLES, THEN MOVING BACKWARDS, CIRCLING AGAIN, MOVING TO THE RIGHT, AND FINALLY DISAPPEARING.

JULY 21, 2002, MESSOLINE'S GRANDDAUGHTER SAW A "BRIGHT LIGHT" HOVER OVER THE UFO WATCHTOWER JUST BEFORE MIDNIGHT. ONE WEEK LATER, ON JULY 27, MESSOLINE AND HER FAMILY (AND OTHER WITNESSES) SAW TWO WHITE LIGHTS MOVING IN STRANGE MANEUVERS FOR ABOUT THIRTY MINUTES.

ON CHRISTMAS WEEK, 2003, MESSOLINE RECEIVED REPORTS FROM THE RESIDENTS OF LA GARITA WHO REPORTED A BRIGHT LIGHT WHICH HOVERED OVER THE AREA, ILLUMINATING A LARGE AREA. "WHAT'S STRANGE," SAYS MESSOLINE, "IS THAT ALL THE YARD LIGHTS IN THE AREA WENT OUT."

JANUARY 25, 2003, A GUEST CAMPING AT MESSOLINE'S HOME SAW A LIGHT HOVER OVER THE ROAD AND MOVE TO THE TOWER. IT LIT UP HER ENTIRE BEDROOM, SCARING HER SO THAT SHE HID UNDER HER BLANKETS RATHER THAN INVESTIGATE.

The UFO Watchtower continued to produce reports, many of which are listed on the website. For a nominal fee of two dollars, anybody can visit the tower and perhaps see a UFO for themselves.[11]

Alien Voices

Stella (pseudonym) first began having unusual experiences around age five when she began to hear "voices" in her mind. She soon became aware that nobody else was hearing them and so kept quiet. By the time she began to attend school, the voices ceased.

Then in November 1996, when she was twenty-seven years old, the voices returned. They began spontaneously without any apparent trigger. The voices were both male and female and were human-like. They discussed a wide variety of subjects with her. Stella assumed at first she was hearing "spirits," but also wondered if it might be aliens.

She went to a catholic priest, who told her she was possessed by "demons," and that she should seek a Christian psychiatrist. She followed his advice and was told by doctors that she was "schizoaffective," and that the voices originated from her own mind.

Strangely, however, Stella had no other symptoms. She never experienced hallucinations, irrational thoughts, bizarre behaviors or beliefs, or other symptoms typical of schizophrenia. Still, she couldn't help but wonder if she was mentally ill or actually in contact with another intelligence. She tried medication, but it had no effect on the voices.

One day she had a vivid dream during which she saw "a short, gray, humanoid alien standing right in front of me, raising its hand to me." Her voices explained that the alien was greeting her. She later had another dream involving a "large, humanoid praying mantis."

Meanwhile, the voices continued to share information which she felt was too "complex" and "intelligent" to be coming from her own mind. They told her that "nature is our only friend." They said that human language is a poor method of communication and shared many other things with her.

Following these dreams, Stella began to wonder if the voices were, in fact, alien. The voices told her that yes, they were extraterrestrial. Disbelieving, Stella asked them for proof.

At first, no proof was forthcoming. Then one morning, in June 2003, she was talking with her "alien voices" while walking around the campus of the University of Colorado at Boulder, where she was attending graduate school. The voices told her to look up. "When I did," says Stella, "directly over my head flew a solid black triangular, tri-lighted spacecraft. It was larger than an airplane, but not huge. It flew at an extremely low altitude, and very, very slowly, almost stationary. It made no noise at all."

Stella was overjoyed to finally get the proof she longed for and felt as though she had reached a "turning point in my life."

Soon further sightings followed, including one in downtown Denver and other locations. Each time she was told to look up, at which point she saw the craft. She now believes she is in contact with ETs, and that they have the ability to control things "in very bizarre and profound ways."

Most recently, the voices have slowed down. Stella rarely shares her experiences as people usually assume she is crazy. Stella remains convinced, however, that her "alien voices" are not the result of mental illness and that she was in contact with actual extraterrestrials.[12]

Silverton Boomerang

In September 2003, a mini-wave of sightings swept through the small town of Silverton. At around 7:00 p.m. on September 15, 2003, Anita Steck and Tammy Rhoads reported their observation of a boomerang-shaped object in the skies over Silverton. When they first saw the object, it was stationary in the sky, then it turned and darted away at high speed leaving a smoky contrail. Four hours later, at 11:00 p.m., Steck observed the object again. She was so impressed by the sighting that she called the *Silverton Standard* to report it.

Unknown to her, another resident, Chris Tousimis, also saw the object later that night. Tousimis told the *Silverton Standard* that he watched a boomerang-shaped object as it moved over Sultan Mountain. It appeared to glow and send down two rays of lights.

The sightings weren't over yet. On the afternoon of September 28, sound engineer Tim Butler saw the same (or similar) object as it cruised over Fort Lewis College. The object was silver in color and about fifty feet long. It had no markings, no portholes or rivets, no sign of any engine or stabilizing equipment. "It wasn't thermalling and didn't make a sound," said Butler. "There was no heat distortion behind the end . . . I'm a scientist at heart," said Butler, "so I'm a pretty skeptical person. I've been going to air shows in Oshkosh since I was a kid. It wasn't like any military technology I've seen."

Butler observed the object with his friend. After ruling out birds, gilders, or conventional craft, Butler wondered if he had seen a UFO. Later, after investigating and discovering that there were additional witnesses, he became convinced he saw something unusual. He still remains uncertain whether this was advanced terrestrial technology, or perhaps non-terrestrial.

Don Brockus, financial director of the Durango-La Plata County Airport was contacted regarding the sighting and said that they received no unusual reports, and that the description of the object didn't match any aircraft that they had in the air. Then he added, "But anything other than airliners doesn't have to check in with us. UFOs never let us know."[13]

Colorado Springs Triangle

It was the evening of July 1, 2004, and Nolan (pseudonym) was walking his dog in the field behind his home in Colorado Springs. Suddenly he noticed a strange silence. He couldn't hear any traffic noises; even the crickets were quiet. He looked up, and hovering twenty-five feet overhead was a dark triangle about twenty feet long with soft white lights at each corner. It drifted for a few seconds, then angled up at a ninety-degree angle and accelerated silently upward.

Nolan knew that President Bush was due to arrive in Colorado Springs the next day to address the Air Force Academy graduation, and he wondered if perhaps he had seen a stealth bomber, or other advanced military aircraft. He finally rejected the idea. "It was too small," he explained, "too close to the ground, and I have never seen anything angle up and accelerate that quickly and silently before." He believes it must have been hovering there for a while, and left because he had spotted it. Nolan's dog, who was about a hundred feet away, showed no reaction to the object.[14]

A Daylight Sighting

At 1:40 p.m., on July 7, 2004, an Englewood resident was surprised to see a star-like light high in the sky directly above him. "I ran inside to grab my binoculars," he said, "and scanned the sky to see if it had moved to another location. I located it substantially to the east of the original location, but again appearing stationary."

He wondered if it might be a balloon, but was puzzled by the fact that it had moved so far from its original spot, and was now perfectly still. It appeared to be "a single, round, whitish object."

He had watched it for about two minutes. "Then suddenly," says the witness, "it took off, heading to the south very quickly, erasing any suspicion I had that it may be a balloon."

He reported his sighting to NUFORC. About five hours later, another witness in the area also reported a similar "star-like" object.[15]

A Huge Object

Around sunset on September 19, 2004, a man hunting in the wilderness near Grand Junction saw an enormous disk-shaped object flying above two airliners. He grabbed his pair of binoculars and saw that the object was flat except for a large dome in the center. It was much larger than the planes. "I was trying to understand what I was seeing," said the witness, "when three jet fighters banked over Grand Junction . . . one of the jet fighters got on a straight course toward the huge object and hit his afterburners."

As the jet approached, the mysterious disk-like object faded away. After the fighter jet moved on, another smaller star-like object reappeared in the same spot.

The witness thought it might actually be a star until another fighter jet flew over Grand Junction, heading directly for the object, which promptly disappeared. The entire encounter lasted about fifteen minutes.[16]

A Massive Craft

On the evening of April 9, 2005, a man from Orange observed a massive flying craft studded with colored lights flying at an extremely low altitude. Says the witness: "The object flew directly over our house and my parents' house down the road at treeline level, making a huge rumbling noise. It was a massive craft, oblong and oval in shape, bigger than a blimp . . . The lights were amazing, a white and green dot on top with a long streak of lights along what looked to be the bottom or side. The long streak had to be close to one hundred yards in length, and the streaks changed color periodically from white to red and to blue."

The witness managed to video tape the object but, as he says, "the video does not do it justice."

Perhaps the strangest aspect of the sighting was the bizarre electromagnetic effects. "As the craft moved overhead," the witness explains, "every sensor light we have around our house went off and continued to for about a half-hour afterward."[17]

Pilot Encounter

"I have 17,000+ hours of flying time over forty years. I'm a captain at a major airline and a retired USAF Lt. Col. fighter pilot. This event was unlike anything I've ever seen," says the witness to a UFO event over Denver on the evening of October 1, 2006. The witness observed a large object flying at an estimated 45,000 feet. It was being followed by four or five smaller objects moving at the same speed and altitude. The witness phoned Denver Air Traffic Control and asked if they had any traffic. They replied negative. The witness suggested the possibility that it was space junk, but another airliner was also viewing the event and said that it couldn't be meteoritic as they were moving horizontally and there was no trail.

"I agreed," says the fighter pilot. "The lights went out as they moved off to the north and east. I've seen many meteors while flying, and this was not a meteor. It was not a conventional aircraft, as it had no position strobe, or anti-collision lights."[18]

"I Just Saw a UFO"

Early in the evening of October 19, 2006, a man and woman were sitting in a hot tub with their son when he pointed up and said, "What's that?"

His parents looked up, but didn't see anything. "I just saw a UFO!" their child said. Frightened by what he saw, he jumped out of the hot tub and fled inside.

His parents told him, "Come back in. It was probably just a shooting star."

As their child came back in, he pointed to the sky. "There it is!"

The parents looked up and saw a huge V-shaped triangle made up of reddish, dull, illuminated sections. It was flying low and silent and fast, about 1,000 feet up.

The boy's parents were amazed and shocked. They all returned inside in amazement. The child explained that when he first saw the UFO, it appeared to be rounded in the front, had more lights on it, and was flying lower.[19]

The Missing Stump

Some cases defy explanation. On the morning of November 1, 2006, Mr. and Mrs. Walker (pseudonym) left their home outside Durango to conduct some business in town. When they returned to their home, they found a puzzling mystery.

Earlier they had cut a large burl from their Boxelder Maple tree. It was green wood and still growing sprouts, four feet across, and weighed an estimated 500 pounds. They had just moved it with their tractor, and when they left it that morning, the burl was still wrapped with a four-inch-wide towing strap.

When they returned home, something very strange had happened to the burl. Says Mr. Walker, "The entire burl disappeared, leaving a circular ash footprint."

The ash was a half-inch deep. The towing strap was also burned except for a four-foot section that lay outside the circle. The burl had been lying in an area surrounded by dry grass, and yet the grass outside the circle was unaffected. There was no odor of smoke or fire.

For the next several years, the burned circle remained sterile. The Walkers have no explanation for what happened to their burl, and wonder if perhaps UFOs might be involved.

Unknown to the Walkers, three days following the incident, on the evening of November 4, two people driving in Durango observed a "bright white light in a stationary position" right outside of town. Planes rarely flew over this area, especially at night. They came to a red stoplight and were able to watch the object for about twenty more seconds when "it just disappeared."[20]

A Dark Shape

May 26, 2007, a family of four from Denver was walking their dog when the eleven-year-old child pointed to the sky and said, "What's that?"

All four members of the family looked up and saw "a dark triangular or boomerang shape moving slowly across the background of light and clouds that were part of a storm front. The dark shape was clearly moving independently of the cloud movement."

The object was very hard to see. It didn't reflect light and appeared, at times, almost as a shadow. They watched the object for more than three minutes as it moved to the southeast, stopped, and reversed direction, then faded away and disappeared.[21]

"I Saw It Clearly"

On May 31, 2007, Elise Eagle of Fountain Creek was at the local nature center near her home practicing yoga when she saw a strange swirling energy in the sky above her. She had never seen anything like it before. Says Eagle, "Then a small white cloud suddenly appeared about the size of a football. An even smaller piece of this small white cloud separated from the main cloud. The main cloud quickly disappeared . . . leaving this peculiar little white triangular cloud in the middle of the blue sky . . . And behind it I saw a cylindrical-shaped, matte metal object . . . rounded on both ends. Its cloud cover completely disappeared leaving a non-shiny silver grey object . . . "[22]

Eagle watched the object for about fifteen seconds. "I saw it clearly," she says.

A Shiny Silver Egg

It was 7:00 a.m. on the morning of June 22, 2007, and Justin (pseudonym) was walking with his fellow classmates to the cafeteria at the Emily Griffith Center for troubled children in Colorado Springs. Says Justin, "I decided to look up at the misty sky and saw a shiny silver, egg-shaped thing about one hundred to 200 feet above us. It was floating completely still and made no noise at all. I stood there mystified and wondered what it could be. I watched this thing for a good five to seven minutes when it suddenly zipped away into the sky, like a bullet."

Justin started to tell his peers about the object, but it zipped away before he could. "Seeing this thing totally shocked and excited me," said Justin. "I couldn't stop talking about it all through breakfast. I had a gut feeling that this thing was a UFO."

The story wasn't over yet. Says Justin, "About two hours later, during our field activity, I was even more weirded out when black helicopters circled over our campus for a good thirty to forty-five minutes. I was skeptical about those sort of things until this happened, but not anymore."[23]

Greeley Unexplained Lights

Throughout the first half of 2008, Greeley was the location of multiple reports of unexplained lights. Clifford Clift, field investigator and the Greeley representative for MUFON says, "In the past six months there has been a lot of activity reported over Fort Collins . . . it's almost as if they, whatever they might be, want to be seen."

In late April 2008, the Weld County Sheriff's office received a call from a person reporting four lights in a boomerang shape over the skies of Loveland. The witness explained that the lights appeared suddenly, and then moved away very quickly.[24]

Near Collision with a UFO

There are many accounts of near-collisions between airplanes and UFOs. The following case provides an unusual example. At 4:15 p.m. on June 12, 2008, a man was driving east on Highway 7 and was passing the Denver International Airport when he saw a large plane taking off. Suddenly a large object appeared directly in the plane's flight path. The object was huge, saucer-shaped, bronze-colored, and had a large dome on top. There were no visible lights or portholes. Says the witness, "[It] appeared as if out of nowhere. One minute it wasn't there, and the next it was. It happened quickly, but in that time I was witness to a near air collision with the plane . . . I screamed and pulled my car over. Luckily the pilot missed the saucer by descending fast and hard in a downward direction. The saucer immediately swerved and changed direction upward in a southwest direction and was gone in seconds. The airplane ascended and proceeded in a northwest direction."

The man did not see any other witnesses. After arriving home, he called the airport and reported his sighting, asking for further information, but none was forthcoming. Says the witness, "This event has stayed with me and is as clear as if I just witnessed it."

Incidentally, the Internet is buzzing about multiple UFO sightings, not to mention several conspiracies revolving around Denver International Airport. Theories range from the existence of a vast underground city beneath the airport reserved for the power elite during a time of crisis, underground bunkers to hold prisoners, and statues, memorials and murals throughout the airport that hint at secret societies such as the Free Masons, and the possibility of an upcoming New World Order.[25]

Phone Call from an Alien?

On the evening of October 24, 2008, two friends went out UFO hunting near Mack. They didn't see anything, and when the driver received a phone call from his place of employment, they began the drive home.

A short time later, the passenger pointed to a large yellow orb." The passenger used a flashlight to blink at the orb. The orb stayed stationary in the sky, but began to release a series of seven smaller orbs, which blinked red, as if imitating standard aviation lights.

The friends pulled over, parked the truck, and observed the seven smaller lights as they began to perform a series of dazzling maneuvers. One of the objects darted at least ten miles across the sky in one second. "I was in shock and utter awe of what was unfolding in front of me," said the driver.

After watching the display for several minutes, the driver knew he had to get back to work, so he continued the drive home. To their surprise, one of the orbs began to follow. As they drove down the highway, it matched their speed and when they stopped moving, it also stopped.

During this time, the driver's cell phone rang. By the time he answered, the caller had hung up. When he reviewed the call, he got a shock. The caller ID showed that the number of the person who called him was 777-7777. Says the driver, "The correlation to seven numbers and since all the digits were 7s, it seemed to be more than coincidence."[26]

Denver Extraterrestrial Affairs Commission

In November 2008, Jeff Peckman introduced a referendum to the city of Denver to create a seven-member commission to handle extraterrestrial affairs. Initiative 300 would aim for a budget of $75,000 dollars, would depend entirely on grants and donations, and would take no city money. Its purpose was to help legitimize the UFO subject and create transparency and cooperation between citizens and government.

Peckman needed 3,974 signatures to qualify. When he was able to exceed that number, he was allowed to submit the initiative.

On November 2, 2010, citizens voted on Initiative 300. The results were decidedly one-sided. The number of those voting yes was: 31,108. The number of those voting no was: 145,022. More than eighty-percent of Colorado voters were not persuaded that UFOs deserved their own commission, and the measure was soundly defeated.[27]

Silver Sphere over Las Animas

In mid-December 2008, Mark Lucero's girlfriend told him that she had seen and photographed a strange object while driving out of Las Animas. She even managed to capture a picture of it on her cell phone. Lucero wasn't sure what to think until a few weeks later when he saw a UFO himself.

One evening during Christmas week, Lucero and his friend (who prefers to remain anonymous) were standing outside a Las Animas convenience store chatting. Suddenly something in Lucero's peripheral vision caught his eye. He turned to look at it and was shocked at what he saw. "It looked like a silver basketball, but a lot bigger," he said. "It was above the tree right here. Then it took off west and was gone."

The object was gray, perfectly round, and seemed to have three small holes along the edge. It also appeared to be glowing. It had been motionless until he looked at it and appeared to be hiding behind the tree branches. Around the object he saw a heat-wave-like distortion, "like a mirage in the desert."

As soon as they both looked at it, the object moved back, down, and shot off to the left, taking only a few seconds to disappear. "It took off pretty damn fast," said Lucero.

Lucero's friend confirmed the details and also saw it in his periphery, turned to look at it, at which point it darted quickly away. The witnesses have no idea what they saw, other than a UFO. They later learned that a couple saw something similar east of Las Animas around the same time.[28]

Underwater Lights

On the evening of May 8, 2009, two brothers (age twenty-seven and thirty-two), went fishing near their home in Hartsel. About a half-hour after sunset, they noticed a few strange lights in the middle of the lake. No boats were allowed on the lake after sunset, so they wondered what it could be. As they watched, it began to pulsate. Meanwhile, one hundred yards to the south, a "pulsating electric blue light" appeared. It sank beneath the surface of the lake but still remained visible. The brothers drove around the lake to get a different perspective. They soon observed a third light next to the others flashing blue, white, and green. They watched the lights for about a half-hour, but unable to identify the lights, decided to leave.[29]

"I Lost Interest"

It was 5:20 a.m. on September 1, 2009, when a married couple were driving two separate cars west on Dillon Road through Broomfield. The husband was first and his wife followed.

Looking up, the husband saw something incredible: a saucer-shaped craft heading toward him about 150 feet above the road. "This craft made no sound at all," said the husband. "I slowed down to take a look and rolled my window down. By this time, it was about two or three blocks ahead of me, coming directly toward us."

He stopped his car and stared in wonder. Then something strange happened. "All of a sudden I lost interest," said the husband." I continued to work and did not know about any UFO, or having seen one."

He drove several blocks before he looked in his rearview mirror to check on his wife. He saw that she had stopped her car and was looking up at an object that was passing over her car.

Unfazed, he kept driving. It wasn't until his wife called him thirty minutes later and began discussing the incident that his memory returned. He became very excited. Not only was he puzzled that he had forgotten the incident, he lamented the fact that he had a camera sitting on the passenger seat next to him. During the sighting, the thought of taking a picture never entered his mind. He later reported the event to MUFON.[30]

University UFO

One afternoon in April 2009, college student Will Chambers drove along University Boulevard heading toward his parents' home in Littleton when he saw something very strange. "I spotted a bright white object in the sky," he said. "It looked like it was either cigar-shaped or disk-shaped from the side."

He slowed down to take a better look when it disappeared into the trees. "I kept looking for it," said Chambers. "I almost gave up on it, but as I looked more westward, it had moved to a new position. It seemed like it came closer to me, almost overhead."

At this point, the object did something Chambers didn't expect. "As it came out from under the cloud, it turned blue to match the sky. It was like camouflage. It definitely looked like a solid object. I definitely felt like it was an intelligent design."[31]

So closes the sightings for the first decade of the new millennium. Many more sightings could be listed, but would only be repetitive. Enough cases have been presented to provide an accurate overview of UFO sightings. Now it's time to move on to the more extensive types of cases, including landings, face-to-face encounters, and more.

Landings and Humanoids

There are several hundred thousand cases of simple fly-by and hovering UFO sightings on record. Since its formation in 1974, the UFO hotline center, NUFORC, has catalogued more than 100,000 cases, the vast majority involving simple sightings. The same is true for MUFON.

Much rarer are cases in which UFOs come close and actually land on the ground. Unlike sightings that are often brief and ambiguous events, UFO landings are not as open to multiple interpretations. In these types of cases the chances of misidentification drop considerably. While the witnesses still do not necessarily recognize what they are seeing, they know the object is not a helicopter, plane, blimp, fireball, or other conventional object.

By far, most witnesses believe they are looking at an extraterrestrial craft, up close and on the ground. Bolstering this belief are the many cases in which people encounter humanoids of various types exiting and entering the craft, walking around it, or even peering at them through the portholes of the craft.

What follows are more than fifty cases of Colorado UFO landings and/or face-to-face encounters with strange humanoids. Again, these cases are only the tip of the iceberg. While they provide a good overview, many other cases go unreported or unpublicized. Likely, there are thousands of such cases in Colorado alone.

Holyoke Humanoid

A rare and interesting early humanoid account comes from a ranch about eight miles southwest of Holyoke. Says the witness, "In the winter of 1931, I saw a flying machine as I was riding on a horse in a draw of a pasture. I was seventeen, and I was checking on cattle after a snowstorm. I went over a small hill and down to a draw that was about twenty-five to thirty feet deep . . . I looked up to the west and saw an elongated oval-shaped flying machine in the air. It was an aluminum color, and a door that was transparent like a glass opened . . . a man appeared that looked human but was not as tall. He looked down at me, and he had a uniform on that was darker than he was."

At this point, the man's horse stumbled, and he looked away. When he looked back up, the UFO was gone. In 2004, more than seventy years later, the witness reported his account to NUFORC. Writes Peter Davenport from NUFORC, "We spoke with the witness at length, and he seemed to us to be exceptionally reliable and credible."[1]

Sightings of humanoids and landings prior to the Modern Age of UFOs in 1947 are almost unheard of, and only a small scattering of cases exist. It wasn't until the 1950s that UFOs really began to land in large numbers and humanoids began to be seen.

Landing in Boulder

April 18, 1951, two friends driving near the Rocky Flats Power Plant in Boulder City came upon something unexpected. Opposite the plant was a large field. As they drove by the plant they saw "these rotating lights in the field by the side of the road. I immediately thought that it was a flying saucer . . . We just sat there in silence watching this craft. It had a silver exterior and all the lights that were rotating around it were all white."

One of the friends wanted to get closer to the craft, but the other didn't want to. "After about twenty minutes of just sitting there watching it," says one of the friends, "it just zoomed straight up in the air and flew away vertically out of sight. We didn't get out of the car and check the field or anything, and we didn't see any little green men; we just drove away and didn't say anything to each other for a long time."[2]

The Old Wise Ones

Michael (pseudonym) grew up on a 3,000-acre ranch about fifty miles west of Colorado Springs. For as long as he could remember, there was something very strange about the ranch. Writes Michael, "There was an area on the ranch that you could not go to. Horses would refuse to go into this area, and if I forced the issue they would go crazy and start bucking. I never could walk into that range of small mountains. If I did, a very strange overpowering fear would sweep over me until I turned around and crossed that invisible boundary and instantly it would go away."

Using the horses, Michael soon learned exactly where the border of this area was, and it never changed. He was baffled by this mystery, but soon learned what the area was hiding. On Christmas Eve, 1960, when Michael was sixteen years old, he woke at 2:30 a.m. to see a strange dark object descending toward the meadow behind his house. It was lighting up the entire valley where their ranch was located, casting crisp shadows on the ground. Even though it was twenty degrees below zero with three feet of snow outside, Michael had to take a closer look.

"I stepped outside on the porch in my longjohns and gazed up. What I saw, I'll never forget: A massive black, rectangular-shaped object just floating over our meadow. I ran back into the house, jumped into my coats and snow-boots, and took off running across the meadow toward the craft."

In a few moments, Michael stood under the craft. It hovered about 300 feet high. He estimates that it was about 1,500 feet long, 500 feet wide, and 300 feet thick. "What was very strange about this," explains Michael, "was that the entire time I was looking at it, I 'felt' safe and somehow knew that 'they' were mining for minerals."

He stood under the object for as long as he could. But the object remained still, and feeling the cold seep into his clothes, Michael retreated inside.

He now wondered if the ETs were somehow connected to the area of the ranch were none of the horses or cows would go. "It was common knowledge about that location," writes Michael. "It was a family joke that we always knew where the cattle and the horses weren't. When I was a kid I would take friends to the borderline, and we would run into the area in an attempt to try and tease the aliens. I found out in short order that they weren't amused. I began having terrible nightmares. I knew it was them, so I went back to the boundary line and shouted to them that I was sorry, and I wouldn't bother them again. That night the nightmares ended, and so did my trips to the area."

It wasn't long before Michael had face-to-face encounters. "You might say I've grown up with aliens," he says. "I've seen them. Some look like us. Others—the old wise ones—are on average seven feet tall with elongated skulls and blue translucent bodies. They are trillions of years older than we are, and are very gentle and loving. I have had two of them appear before me from time to time to check in on me. They watched me grow up as the only child on our huge, very isolated ranch. I could always feel them protecting me when I was alone in the forest. They love us and consider us their children. They have come back now to help us through what is coming. They will soon introduce themselves to the world."

As in other cases, Michael has been given warnings of upcoming disasters. "They have showed me what is coming," he writes. "A global nuclear war that will destroy nearly all of America, Europe, Russia, and China." Michael says that another alien faction is controlling the New World Order. In 1989, he traveled to

Venezuela where he had another encounter with the Blue Beings. They told him that there is an underground city beneath the jungles of Venezuela inhabited by a confederation of aliens who are preparing to help humans survive the upcoming disasters. They told him that the city will be a center of growth and knowledge, and that it is safeguarded by a protective energetic dome which will keep it safe during the wars. Writes Michael, "Tesla, Marconi, and Fulcanelli were involved. I have met personally two high-ranking Venezuelan officers who interface with 'the City.' The New World Order knows full well about this city, but they are powerless to do anything about it."

Michael says that because of this city, Venezuela will be the target of growing aggression from the New World Order. "If you want a good timeline," he says, "watch very carefully what happens between Venezuela and the New World Order."[3]

Talking with UFOs

June 18, 1964, Caroline (pseudonym) had invited her friend to spend the night at her parents' home in Denver. Around dusk, Caroline and her friend were in the backyard when they saw three lights in a triangular pattern hovering in the western sky.

Says Caroline, "We were just playing, as girls will do, and started talking to the light . . . we told the light our names and talked to it quite a long time."

Caroline and her friend soon discovered that the object appeared to be communicating. Whenever they finished talking or asking it a question, the object flashed a beam of light.

After spending several minutes talking with the UFO, Caroline's mother called the girls inside. "We told the lights we had to go in and we said goodbye," says Caroline. "They acknowledged with a beam of light. We told the lights to meet us outside my bedroom window at midnight. They acknowledged with a beam of light. We waved goodbye as we were going in. They said goodbye with a beam of light. The last we saw the lights, they were still in the sky where we first saw them."

Caroline and her friend assumed the encounter was over. However, that night around midnight, she woke up to hear two men's voices say, "Where's Caroline and Tina?"

"I knew my friend was sound asleep in the bed beside me because she was breathing deeply," says Caroline. "I was so scared because we were just playing with the lights, right? They did not really understand what we said, right? But now, outside my bedroom window were two men's voices saying where's Caroline and Tina! I put the covers over my head. The next thing I knew, it was morning!"

Thankfully that was the end of the encounter, but since then, Caroline has often wondered if she was abducted that night. Years later her friend confirmed the sighting, but had no memory of the voices.[4]

Just Like You and Me

As uncovered by researcher Christopher O'Brien in the mid-1960s, Lynn Bogle, (who would later become a county deputy in Saguache) told O'Brien that he and his parents used to take summer trips to the Platoro Reservoir. During one trip, they met an old hermit by the name of Carter who lived in Summerville year-round and would take tourists on informal tours of the area. Carter told Bogle and his parents that several times during late fall and winter, he was visited by human-like aliens, who would land their craft right outside his home. He talked with them on multiple occasions and told the Bogles that "they were just like you and me."

The visitations occurred on several occasions, but stopped after a military helicopter landed on his property, and a military officer told him never to talk to the aliens again.[5]

Landing in Littleton

Around 11:00 p.m. on the evening of April 7, 1966, a group of teenagers tumbled into the Littleton Police Station in Denver to report that they had just seen a UFO. Police Chief John C. MacIvor of Littleton was skeptical at first, but admitted that the teenagers appeared to be "cold sober, sincere, and a little shaken by their experience."

An investigation soon proved that something very unusual happened. Earlier that evening, the six teenagers, all in one car, drove to Daniels Park in their 1954 Ford. They gathered at a small stone shelter against the hillside where they built a campfire. Around 9:30 p.m., they heard noises above them.

Alan Scrivner, a junior at East Denver High School, said, "It sounded like a man walking on top of the shelter."

They checked with flashlights, but saw nothing on the roof. Don Otis, also a junior at Denver High School, was worried about the car. He and Scrivner went to check on it. When they reached it, they heard "a real weird buzzing noise that seemed to be all around us." In the field across from their car they saw two red lights floating about two feet from the ground. The red lights appeared to be about a foot in diameter. Thinking it must be another car, Scrivner and Otis returned to their friends.

The four teenagers who had stayed behind reported that they heard the footsteps again. Patty Retherford and Kaye Hurley saw "a tall figure, like a man who might have been wearing a raincoat." The figure moved swiftly along the edge of the shelter and disappeared.

At this point, the six teenagers decided to leave. As they hiked back to the car, Otis looked back at the shelter and saw a bright red light behind the shelter. The light was bright enough to illuminate the entire area.

When they reached their car, the buzzing began again. "It didn't come from any particular direction," said Scrivner. Another witness said, "It was unlike anything I have ever heard before."

The teenagers now turned around and watched two pulsating blue lights that hovered in the sky about a half-mile away. Before long, two more lights showed up. They were also blue, but glowed red in the center. Finally, the teenagers saw a dark shape between the lights and realized that they were seeing a massive craft of some kind. "It appeared to be shaped like a black football," said Scrivner, "the blue lights on each end, and the reddish-orange on top. The red lights were on the bottom."

Shaken by what they were seeing, the teenagers piled into the car and attempted to flee. They took off for a short distance when their engine suddenly died. "You may think we are nuts," Scrivner told Police Chief MacIvor, "but my car did not work right. It would run up to about thirty miles per hour and then the engine would cut out. It was like someone turned the ignition off. Then the engine would catch again."

While they had trouble with the engine, the car radio also began to play nothing but static.

As they fled Daniels Park, the UFO followed. Mary Zolar got a good look at the object, which she described as a large oval circle of light, wide enough to cover the entire road. "It was huge and glowing," she said, "and came right up to the back of the car. Then it went out after about three seconds."

The object left, and immediately the car engine and radio began to function normally. The teenagers went directly to the Littleton Police Station in Denver. "I don't know what they saw," says Chief MacIvor," but I am convinced they saw something . . . I was skeptical at first, but each of the kids called their parents to tell them where they were. One thing about their story that was impressive was that all six did not claim to have seen the same shaped thing at the same time."

Confirming the teenagers account, it turned out that there were other UFO sightings that same night. Two students from the University of Denver reported seeing seven flying saucers which they described as "about the size of garbage-can lids."

Even more impressive, Police Chief D.C. Morgan and Patrolman Earnest Markley watched a very bright, glowing, green light, which hovered in the sky for two hours before rising straight up into the air and disappearing.[6]

Six Silver Saucers

On March 23, 1966, six disk-shaped, silver objects were seen hovering in the afternoon sky over Trinidad. Calls flooded the office of Arch Gibson, editor of the *Trinidad Chronicle News*. Witnesses included a few adults and several children.

One witness was John Mantera, who observed the objects around 5:00 p.m. Says Mantera, "I was walking down the street bouncing my Superball when something started flashing in my eyes. I looked over toward the ridge and saw three objects. Two were stationary, and one was on the ground. Later we found burned weeds there."

Other witnesses included brothers Raymond and Dean Hoch (aged fourteen and ten) and their mother. Says their mother, Eula May Hoch, "They were very quiet, moved very slow, and flew fairly low."[7]

Landing Traces

During an intense wave of sightings over the area, on March 18, 1967, possible UFO landing traces were discovered by Mrs. Ted Willden on Moraine Road (a gravel road) west of Montrose. There were two markings. One was a six-foot circle impressed into the ground. The second was nine feet and three inches. In the center of the larger circle was a six-inch circle of "lightly polished stones and gravel."

About six months later, the case of Snippy the Horse, the first publicized animal mutilation would occur not far from the area.[8]

MIB Encounter

Men in Black are mysterious figures that sometimes show up after UFO encounters involving physical evidence. Often they threaten witnesses not to talk about their encounter.

In September 1967, the same month that Snippy the Horse was mutilated, a resident of Alamosa, Mrs. B., sighted an unusual crescent-shaped object over the Great Sand Dunes. Mrs. B. was an artist, and being impressed by her sighting, she decided to paint it and preserve the memory of the event.

She had no plans to sell it, so she was surprised when some weeks later, a strange man visited her home, inquiring about the painting.

The man, said Mrs. B., appeared to be about thirty-five years old and in ill health. He behaved very oddly and began to make very strange statements. He told Mrs. B. that he came from a different universe. He told her: "I cannot read, but mention any book in any library and I will be able to tell you its contents."

Mrs. B. was more interested in the fact that he knew about her painting. When she asked him, the man repeated that he was unable to read, and said that humans are wasting time and energy eating food when "it could all be so easily taken from the atmosphere."

He again asked about acquiring her painting. Mrs. B. had no intention of selling, but when he insisted, she gave him a very high price. The man told her that he had no money.

At this point the stranger left. Mrs. B. marked down the license plates, which were from Arizona. She contacted authorities, but they were unable to trace the vehicle. She then told her story to reporter, Pearl M. Nicholas who published it in *The Valley Courier.*[9]

Landing in Naturita

On October 28, 1967, two brothers-in-law, David Barnard (age thirty) and Jack Kerns (age forty-one) were on a deer hunting trip in the wilderness outside of Naturita. They brought their sons along including Terry Kerns (age fifteen), and Robert and Larry Barnard (ages ten and eight.)

The hunt was successful. They had killed a deer, and around 7:30 p.m., began the drive down the mountain road back to town. As they drove, somebody noticed an object floating over Lone Cone Mountain. "When we first saw it," Kerns said, "it looked like a ball of orange fire, sort of moving along the tops of a stand of cedars."

They kept their eyes on the object and continued the drive down the mountain. When the object changed position and began to come down the ridge toward them, they stopped their jeep to watch. As they watched, the object appeared to land only 300 yards away.

Kerns and Barnard watched through their rifle scopes. Kerns, whose scope was more powerful, said that the object was round with a dome on top, and what looked like an antenna. He saw square windows, colored lights on the bottom, and blue lights flickering or revolving around the base.

Unable to identify the object, they became consumed by fear. "I never had anything scare me so much in my life," said Barnard. "If I would have had to run, I just couldn't have."

They raced away from the scene. The object then seemed to follow their car, remaining in view all the way down the mountain. When they reached Colorado Route 80, the object disappeared.

They reported their encounter to the *Denver Post*. Only one week earlier, Kerns' other son, Jack (age eighteen), had been hunting in the same area when he saw unexplained blue lights.

All the witnesses were deeply impressed by their encounter. Mrs. Barnard told reporters that her husband never believed in UFOs before the incident, but that "he most certainly does now."[10]

Lizard-looking Aliens

Amy (pseudonym) was only five years old when she had an encounter at her home in Uravan, but more than forty years later she still remembers it vividly. July

20, 1968, Amy woke to hear the family dog, Tippi, barking outside her bedroom window. The dog normally only barked when strangers visited the property. The dog kept barking and nobody else was waking up, so finally Amy pulled herself out of sleep and looked out the window into the yard. "When I did," said Amy, "I couldn't believe what I saw."

A small disk-shaped craft had landed in her yard. She saw landing gear and a hatch with stairs that folded down to the ground. "Next to the ship," says Amy, "were green lizard-looking aliens. Their eyes were bright yellow . . . they didn't have fingers, but kind of web hands . . . Their body was thin and scaly . . . their feet had V-shaped toes."

The ETs had some sort of tanks strapped to their backs. Amy had the impression that the ETs were searching for something. Suddenly another alien much larger than the others exited the ship and appeared to be giving orders to the others.

"Tippi again began her barking," says Amy, "and the alien closest to our house seemed to be upset with her barking. I could see it looking over at Tippi."

When the alien began to walk over to Tippi, Amy jumped from her bed and ran to get her mother. "I couldn't get her to wake up," says Amy. She was finally able to drag her mother to her bedroom and make her look out the window, but it was as though her mother could not see.

Her mother told her to go to bed and returned to her bedroom. Amy did as she was told. The last thing she remembered, Tippi had stopped barking and two dark figures were trying to look in her bedroom window.

Amy now "firmly believes" that the ETs did something to make her family sleep. But as she says, "It didn't work on me."

In the morning, the first thing she did was run outside in her pajamas to check on Tippi. "Sure enough," says Amy, "she was lying in the front yard waiting for kids to come play with her. She acted like nothing happened the night before."[11]

Alien Tour Bus

At 3:00 p.m. on June 1, 1969, twelve-year-old Trevor (pseudonym) walked out into his front yard in Colorado Springs and saw a UFO. "Across the street," says Trevor, "thirty feet above the neighbor's house was a UFO . . . it was close enough to hit with a rock."

The object was silent, disk-shaped, larger than a school bus, black in color, and had a dome with big windows all around it. It drifted at one or two mph. Trevor felt a strange calmness emanating from the craft. He stared up at it and looked into the windows. "There were lights on inside, and I could see dark, shadowy, human-like figures looking out at me."

Events seemed to move in slow motion. Trevor looked over and saw his neighbor, an elderly German lady who spoke no English, also looking at the object. "She also seemed to move very slow," says Trevor.

When he looked back up at the object, it was gone, and the strange slowness instantly stopped. He looked around and saw the object moving down the street about six houses down. "I have only told this story to about seven people, mostly family," says Trevor. "My impression of this whole ordeal was that of a tour bus, except that it was a tour bus for aliens."[12]

Denver UFO Landing

Around midnight on July 15, 1969, Dennis (pseudonym) and three friends were driving out of Denver when they saw a meteor blaze through the sky heading down to the ground. At least they thought it was a meteor. They found a narrow road leading in the direction of the meteor, but as they followed it toward a hill, they saw that meteor was actually a UFO, and it was landing.

One of the men jumped out of the car, whipped out his gun and attempted to shoot the craft. The gun misfired, causing him to run off alone into the darkness.

The car then stalled and two of the friends exited the vehicle and walked toward the UFO to get a better look. "It was a disk," says Dennis, "with a dome and two revolving plates going in different directions."

The disk was black and silver, with red, orange, and yellow glowing lights. As they watched, two figures, both about ten feet tall with long arms that reached to their knees, exited the UFO. "One entity," says Dennis, "picked up a rock half the size of a VW bug and carried it into the UFO. The other entity pulled a giant bush out of the ground and into the UFO."

After taking the rock and the bush, the craft glowed bright orange and yellow, lifted off the ground, and went straight up.

At this point, the three friends began to search for their missing friend who had tried to shoot at the UFO. Unable to find him, they drove back down the road. Meanwhile, the UFO followed them.

Suddenly they came on a roadblock with five men dressed in the strangest uniforms they had ever seen. They wore black shiny helmets that extended down to their shoulders, one-piece uniforms that appeared to be "braided," and boots with toes.

The uniformed men stopped the three friends. The next thing they remember, says Dennis, they were back in Denver in their building with their car parked in the lot. They had "no memory of how [we] got home."

Two and a half days later, the missing friend showed up in Denver with no memory of his return. "All four subjects had the same story," says Dennis. "It was thought it should be reported at the time, but they didn't know to who. One of the men is reporting it now in case it correlates to other events at that time."[13]

"It Was a Grey"

In the early a.m. hours of June 15, 1974, Chuck (pseudonym) was on his way to work when he saw "a strange object" hovering fifty feet above the Animas River. He slowed his car down and looked directly at the front of the craft. "I just stared at it," says Chuck, "and noticed a being through the front window, in silhouette, staring straight ahead down the river, or maybe looking at the controls. I had been reading about UFOs since 1969, and knew what I was looking at. The being inside was not human . . . He had a big head and scrawny neck, skinny body as seen from the side."

Chuck continued to drive very slowly down Main Street, still observing the craft, which began to move south down the river. Suddenly it accelerated, ascended upward, and burst out of sight to the south. "I was in awe at what I was looking at," says Chuck. "I knew what it was, but I couldn't believe it."

It wasn't until years later that Chuck saw images of Greys in the media. "At the time I did not know it was a Grey," he said. "I just realized that recently."[14]

Bedroom Visitation?

Sometimes, what at first appears to be a simple sighting turns out to be something more. The evening of August 10, 1980, two girlfriends (around age nine) were in the tiny town of Hasty playing pinball about two blocks from their home. Afterward, they bought soda pops and were returning home when suddenly they saw a large disk-shaped object hovering about twenty feet overhead. The center was dark while the perimeter had oscillating red, blue, and green lights. It was completely silent and appeared to be following them.

They quickly ran to one of the girls' homes and called out for her mother. All three watched it glide across the empty field and over the nearby homes.

That evening, when they went to sleep, one of the girlfriends panicked and said that she kept seeing "huge black eyes all around." She was too frightened to remain at her friend's house and called her own mother to pick her up.[15]

Followed

On the evening of September 13, 1972, the Ludwig family was driving to their home south of Burlington when they saw a fiery object swoop alongside their car and begin to follow them. "It stayed with us for two miles, for about three or four minutes," explained Mrs. Ludwig. "Then it veered over us going southwest into the field. We could see it was the size of a house. It got so bright it was almost like the field was on fire. Then it shot straight up into the sky and appeared as big as the moon. Then it came down again, this time landing in a field about a half-mile southwest of our house."

The object lit up the entire field, remaining only moments before shooting up into the sky so fast, the witnesses couldn't actually see it move. It was on the ground, and then the next instant, it was in the air and gone.[16]

"It Was Human-like"

"What we saw was real and the truth," writes Patricia (pseudonym) of an encounter she and her family had in Fort Collins. Sometime in 1972 (exact date not given), Patricia and two other members of her family were on the second story of their one-hundred-year-old farmhouse watching television when one of them noticed red and blue lights flashing through the window. "What's that?" he asked, alerting everyone to the object.

They first thought it might be a helicopter; it was black and similarly-shaped; however, it was also totally silent. It hovered in place, giving the three witnesses a perfect view of what looked like a pilot operating the craft. The figure wore a full helmet so they couldn't see its face. All the witnesses agreed it was human-like in form. They watched the figure for "what seemed like a short period of time," at which point the object moved upward and left.

Following the encounter, none of the witnesses talked about it. Instead, they continued to watch TV has if nothing strange had happened. Patricia now wonders if there was perhaps more to the incident than she and her family can remember. "All these years have gone by," she says, "and yet we all remember this in detail, and still can't believe we all just went back to watching TV. Did we lose time?"

It wasn't until years later that Patricia and the others discussed their experience with each other. Only then did they learn that another family member had an even more dramatic encounter at the farmhouse.

It occurred before their own encounter. She was sleeping in a room downstairs when she saw a craft covered with lights descend from the sky and land in the field next to the house. Next, three humanoid figures exited the craft. They were each about four feet tall and dressed in full suits and helmets. They came directly to the window where the witness was watching them. Patricia was unable to convince the family member to reveal what happened next. "To this day," says Patricia, "she refuses to detail her experience as it has deeply affected her. She was so shocked and scared, she ended upstairs sleeping on the floor in her aunt's bedroom . . . let's just say, after her encounter she was never the same."[17]

Christmas Eve Humanoids

On Christmas Eve 1972, Sherry (pseudonym) and her husband were driving from Denver to Colorado Springs. They had just arrived and were in a rural area when they saw what appeared to be a shooting star. Sherry made a wish: "Money! Money! Money!"

Then to her shock, the shooting star dropped down right in front of them about 1,000 feet away, and revealed itself to be a disk-shaped craft. "The top half became transparent," says Sherry, "And I could see people walking around and looking out the windows."

Sherry's husband continued driving, so the object was in view for only a few minutes, but it was long enough for Sherry to recall it and report it to NUFORC nearly forty years later.[18]

Three-Toed Humanoid

In April 1973, four men were camping at the foot of Mount Blanca in the San Luis Valley. The group included Floyd Murray (a UFO/Fortean researcher), a deputy sheriff from Colorado, and two men from Texas. All of them were there to investigate the unusual phenomenon in this area. They had retired to the mountain cabin for the evening when everyone was awakened by a loud screeching sound, like metal being shredded. Next there were heavy crashing and thumping sounds, seemingly from a very large creature.

Although armed with rifles, the men decided to stay inside. The next morning, they searched the area around the cabin and found a set of "three-toed footprints," each about ten-and-a-half inches long and six inches wide. While the sheriff replied that he had never seen anything like these prints, the others claimed that they had seen similar prints before.

They followed the tracks for about a half-mile leading away from the cabin and then lost the trail when the ground became too wet.[19]

"They Weren't Children"

In the fall of 1981, Rayna lived in a home outside of Denver. One evening, at 10:00 p.m., she was heating up some food when she "felt compelled" to look out the window. Her dog followed her. Says Rayna, "As we stood looking out together, I noticed what at first glance seemed to be four or five children standing at the edge of the lawn under a street light. I was surprised to see them there at that hour, because, judging by their size, they couldn't be much more than seven or eight years old. As I watched them, I realized that something was terribly 'off' about the scene. Their heads were oversized and bald, their arms and bodies were long and spindly-looking. Their movements were jerky, irregular, and fast, almost insect-like. Their coloring was a semi-dark shade of brown. I began to feel very frightened. They weren't children."

At this point, her dog lowered her head, began to whimper, ran from the room, and hid under the bed. This was out of character as normally the dog was aggressive and barked whenever somebody was in the yard.

Rayna says that when her husband came home, he told her that she looked like she had seen a ghost. "I didn't tell him what I had seen," says Rayna. "I actually forgot about it until a few years later, when something in a book triggered a memory."[20]

Seduced by an ET

Rick is a forest ranger stationed in a remote, unnamed area of the Rocky Mountains. In February of 1982, he received a radio call from a helicopter flying in the area that they had seen flashing lights up along a little-used mountain road and that it might be a truck that had skidded off the road. No distress calls had been received from any truckers.

There was a heavy carpet of snow, so Rick took a snowmobile to the area where the lights had been seen. He reached the location and spent an hour crisscrossing the area, and finally came upon some strange footprints. One pair of prints showed what appeared to be bare feet, while the other showed much shorter shoed tracks.

Puzzled, he stopped, got off his snowmobile, and began to follow the tracks. Looking up, he saw a man step out from the trees with his palms raised in a peaceful gesture. The man looked strange. He was five feet tall, had an enormous head, huge large eyes, a blank expressionless face, and was wearing a tight-fitting greenish jumpsuit.

Confused about the appearance of the short man, Rick now saw another figure, a blond woman, with blue eyes, wearing a thin translucent gown and no shoes.

Rick wondered if these were the passengers from the truck which had skidded of the road, although they appeared to be a couple of weirdos from a traveling carnival.

Suddenly there was a loud sound of crackling electricity, and Rick saw that the smaller man had disappeared. Concerned about the safety of the strange man and woman, Rick questioned the woman. She didn't answer, but merely smiled.

Then, says Rick, he felt compelled to save the woman. Her eyes compelled him. He found himself taking her to his cabin on his snowmobile.

He made her a cup of coffee, but she showed little interest in it. She pointed toward the bed and aggressively seduced him. Rick says that he made love with the woman three times. When he woke up the next morning, she was gone.

Rick discovered that two days had passed. There was no sign of the strange woman. It was seemingly impossible that she had left his cabin, which was located in the remote wilderness of the Rockies.

A year and a half later, Rick was washing dishes in the kitchen when he looked outside and saw the strange woman in his yard. She was dressed in the same diaphanous gown, only this time, she held a young blond-haired baby. She pointed to him, at the baby, then at her abdomen, smiling widely the whole time. He felt as though she were saying, this was his baby. Rick felt almost paralyzed as the woman turned and walked into the forest.

His paralysis broke and he rushed outside to find her. There was no evidence that she had ever been there. Writes Brad Steiger, who corresponded with the witness, "He remains uneasy with the conviction that he has fathered an alien baby. Every time he looks up at the night sky, he wonders if his child is living on some other world. Or if the child might be growing up on some alien base, one day to return to claim its Earth heritage."[21]

Thunderbirds and UFOs

Native American, Pat, revealed to Christopher O'Brien that he has witnessed an enormous thunderbird on multiple occasions near his home north of Blanca. He usually saw it near Flat Top Mountain, near an ancient stone altar. "I'd seen the bird up there before on a number of occasions," said Pat. "It's hard to believe, but the darn thing had to have been thirty to forty feet tall."

Then one summer day in 1986, a young couple from Alamosa was visiting Pat's trailer when they all saw the shadow of the bird up on Flat Top Mountain. On this occasion, it was perched on the mountain, unmoving. Pat and the young couple drove closer to get a better look. They drove to the bottom of the hill and began to climb up. "Well," says Pat, "this thing took off, and I'll tell you, Chris, this thing is huge. It would've dwarfed a 747! It was that big. It looked like a shadow. It didn't look tangible, but you could make out details. You could see split feathers on its wings and on its tail. You could see a predatory beak, but you couldn't see any eyes. It took off and flew out over the valley, headed to the east."

They watched it for a few minutes as it flew in several large circles and then disappeared. The young couple was "pretty spooked," and departed for their home in Alamosa.

That night, a thick fogbank settled down directly over Pat's property. The next morning, one of his neighbors asked, "What were all those bright lights around your place last night? It looked like a football stadium all lit up."

Pat had no answer. He had no such lights. But he was even more mystified when his other neighbors reported that they had found three of their cows mutilated and dropped from above, lodged thirty feet above the ground in the tops of a group of Cottonwood trees. Pat wasn't overly surprised. Around this time, a few ranches in the area had been hard hit by the mutilations. "One sheep rancher lost well over one hundred sheep," said Pat. "He never even bothered to call the sheriff to report them." The Colorado animal mutilation mystery is covered in a later chapter.[22]

Summoning a UFO

Gary Young, a Vietnam veteran from Colorado Springs who now teaches workshops on spiritual development, says that, in 1988, he met a man at a Denny's restaurant who told him that it was possible to contact alien spacecraft, and actually instructed him how to do it.

Young learned to telepathically communicate with the apparent ETs. Years later, he and his nephew traveled to Carson Mountain in the Sangre de Cristo Mountains, where they successfully summoned a UFO. "I tried to get onboard," said Young, "but they wouldn't take me." They told him intuitively that further contact was not appropriate for him at that time. "I'm interested in sharing what has been shared with me," he says. "I'm happy, healthy, and living in a state of peace."[23]

Saguache County Landing

Seventy miles north of Blanca in Saguache County are the Mineral Hot Springs, and a small cluster of homes, one of them occupied by Sally Sloban. July 20, 1992, Sloban woke up to hear her dogs barking at an eerie orange glow coming through her bedroom window. The glow was emanating from behind a group of small hills where the hot spring was located. Suddenly there was a bright flash, and the light went out.

Vowing to check it out the next morning, Sloban went to sleep. Hours later, she went to the hot spring with a couple of friends. They quickly discovered something very strange: a thirty-foot circle had been mysteriously impressed into the ground. All the bushes and grass were crushed and whirled. In the center of the circle was a three-foot-deep hole eighteen inches wide. It appeared to have been "caused by intense heat from a powerful, concentrated, downward blast."[24]

Huerfano Humanoids

September 28, 1995, Huerfano rancher Larry Chacon discovered a mutilated horse on his ranch (see Chapter Ten: "Cattle Mutilations.") He had been renting the ranch from an old man who lived like "a hermit." When he told the man about the mutilation event, the man told him that his ranch had been the location of many strange events.

Researcher David Perkins, who investigated the mutilation event, spoke with the man, who told him that he has had numerous UFO sightings over the ranch. On one occasion, around 1993 (date approximate), one of the objects landed. The man told Perkins that two human-looking beings came out of the craft and walked toward his cabin. They carried a flashlight, which cast a brilliant spotlight on his cabin. The light was so powerful that the light went through the walls, illuminated the whole interior of his cabin, and caused him to become temporarily paralyzed and blinded by the light.[25]

Camper Harassed by ETs?

Bill (pseudonym) has spent many hours camping, hiking, and backpacking. On the night of June 26, 1993, while backpacking alone in the Holy Cross Wilderness Area, he had one of the most frightening experiences of his life. He had just set up his tent and retired for the evening when he was woken up by what sounded like small animals scurrying around his tent. He didn't think much of it and went back to sleep. Sometime later, he woke up unable to move or hear. He struggled and managed to open his eyes. His hearing returned slowly, as though emerging from underwater. He was still unable to move as suddenly the scurrying sounds began again. This time, however, they moved from the ground to the sides of the tent.

Bill wondered if he was having some sort of weird waking nightmare. The scratching went on for fifteen minutes, then suddenly stopped. "As though somebody had blown out a candle," explained Bill. "Everything stopped and there was complete stillness."

Bill still couldn't move and was trying to figure out what was happening. Says Bill, "Then the whole tent and surroundings became brighter than daylight. A complete and encompassing white light entered the tent. It was absolutely blinding. I was still unable to move."

The light remained for a few moments, pulsating in intensity, then suddenly winked out. Bill found himself now able to move. "Needless to say, I was upset," he says. He immediately packed up camp and left the area. When he returned to the closest town to get supplies, he asked around to see if there were any other reports of strange lights.

Nobody else had reported anything strange. "I did not see a craft or see any little green men," says Bill, "but I cannot explain what happened to me that night. All I know is that it scared the crap out of me, and I am not one to get scared in the woods."[26]

The Color of Water

It was August 19, 1993, and Leslie (pseudonym) was concerned about her five-year-old son. Her husband, a famous author, had passed away, and over the past year, her son kept waking up and telling her that he saw the earth shaking. Leslie began to take notes and was surprised to find that her son's dreams or visions were coming true, and that he appeared to be predicting earthquakes. Every time he had one of his dreams, she'd read about an earthquake somewhere in the world. She began to wonder if her child had special abilities.

Then on August 19, 1993, she and her son were visited by a group of about a dozen aliens. On that night, her son was sleeping next to her, and she lay in bed feeling restless. She had just turned out the bedroom light when she heard noise in the house. She wondered if maybe a bear had broken into the house. She got up, looked around, and found nothing.

She returned to bed. Right after she lay down, ten or twelve three-foot-tall figures glided through the wall in a tight group. "When they were coming in, I could see right through them," said Leslie. "They looked like the color of water. As they got into the room, they became solid and I couldn't see through them . . . At first I wasn't afraid . . . They were cold. They seemed completely indifferent, well maybe a little curious. It was hard to tell . . . They were small and slight and they had huge almond eyes."

Leslie reported her experience to Christopher O'Brien, who was shocked. On the same evening, he had a similar impression that someone or something had entered his own home.[27]

I Spoke to an Alien

It was the fall of 1993, and Randolph, a single dad, worked two jobs to support himself and his son. During the day, he was a Colorado State police officer. At night, he managed an upscale restaurant and nightclub. One evening, he pulled out of his home in Colorado Springs and headed to work when he saw what looked like airplane landing lights coming in for a crash-landing onto the golf course across the street from his home. The lights approached to about sixty feet above the ground and stopped, hovering above a group of oak trees. Randolph exited his car and looked more closely. He watched it for a few minutes when it moved diagonally toward him, revealing a cigar shape, with a red light at the tip, white lights in the middle, and a blue light at the rear. The edges of the aircraft blurred as it began to move down the road. Randolph hopped in his car and followed the object as it moved over a section of homes, stopped, then vanished. Says Randolph, "Being raised an Air Force brat and having lived on more air bases than I want to remember, I can tell you now this was no ordinary aircraft. It made no sound whatsoever."

Mystified, Randolph continued driving to work. He arrived and began attending to management issues when he noticed a normal-looking man sitting on a bar stool, leaning against the bar and staring intently at him. As Randolph worked, the man continued to stare. Says Randolph, "At first I thought he was going to cause some sort of trouble, so I kept a close eye on him as well."

A few minutes later, the man approached Randolph and asked if they could speak outside. "I agreed," explains Randolph, "and followed him outside, half expecting to be in a fist fight or something. We stood in the middle of the sidewalk in front of the club."

"Did you see something funny on the way to work tonight?" he asked.

Randolph was shocked. "How would you know about anything funny I may or may not have seen?" he replied.

The man's response chilled Randolph. "This guy told me that they were checking up on me because I was one of the 'special ones.' To this day I don't know what he meant by that. For the next twenty minutes, he stood there and told me of my entire life from the time I was born to the present moment, reminding me of things I had long forgotten about or just kept secret from anyone else."

"Do you remember the night," he asked, "when you were a young boy playing on the floor of your parents' house, that a red light-beam came through the window of the living room, across the wall and floor, and then disappeared?"

"I have no recollection of any such event."

The man pulled out a business card and handed it to Randolph. Randolph glanced down to look at the card, then immediately looked up. The man was gone.

Says Randolph, "For years I kept this information from anyone in fear of being labeled some sort of crackpot, and I didn't want to lose my police position with the state."

Nine years later, Randolph's father died and he moved to California to live near his mother. On Thanksgiving evening, they were all telling stories when Randolph decided to tell them about the night he saw a UFO and spoke to a possible alien. "There were about twenty family members there," says Randolph, and they were all chuckling as I told the story of my strange event. When I got to the part about the red light coming through the window and across the wall and floor, my mother dropped her fork on the plate. Everyone stopped talking. It was absolutely silent when she said that she remembered that like it was yesterday. She said that this red beam of light came through the picture window of the living room, ran across the wall, down to the floor, and across the floor to the opposite wall. She also said that Dad got up out of his chair and went out on the front porch to see where the light was coming from, but there wasn't anything out front. When mom got done telling her tale of the red light, the laughter was gone. It continued to be silent for several minutes."

Randolph later tried to find the business card, but believes he lost it during the move to California.[28]

Prairie Dragons

In October 1993, Christopher O'Brien was contacted by a couple from the Baca area regarding a strange phenomenon in and around their house. On more than a dozen occasions, they told him, they saw a two- or three-foot-tall translucent glowing creature darting around their yard. Their dog also saw and reacted to the creature. They weren't overly concerned until one evening the creature came into the house, moving through the wall, across the living room within inches of the witnesses, then through the dining room, and out through the opposite wall. This event prompted them to call O'Brien. It wasn't long before the creature entered the house again.

In August 1994, O'Brien was doing construction work in the home of the witnesses when he saw the strange creature himself. "It reminded me of a two-to-three-foot-tall lizard," he said. He later learned from a local Native American that the creatures were well-known by the Native Americans who called them "prairie dragons."[29]

UFO at Musical Performance

When the leader of the rock band, Random Art Festival, learned that they were going to perform at Breckenridge at an abandoned copper mine in the mountains on September 14, 1994, he had a feeling something strange would happen. "We had a professional lighting setup with us," he explains, "and because the gig was outside at night and so high up in the mountains, I predicted for two weeks before the gig that UFOs would show up."

Sure enough he was right. "That night at around 3:00–4:00 a.m.," he said, "multiple UFOs were seen flying just overhead of the gig location. At least a hundred audience members and my six band members all witnessed the event. After finishing a song [and] playing for a few hours, all who were in attendance started to point at the sky at a very, very large double-pyramidal UFO followed closely by a large, spherical UFO, with much smaller spherical UFOs that encircled both. Six to ten of the small spherical UFOs appeared to land on the hillsides above the location where we were, and across the valley. Tall alien figures like apparitions seemed to appear near where we were."[30]

Alien Soldiers

An uninvestigated case comes from researcher David Perkins, who heard the story from a local artist, who spoke with the witness firsthand. The witness, Mark Hays, was a police officer, who, in September 1994, decided to go hunting with his friend in Huerfano County. When the men didn't return, they were declared missing. After a week, one of the hunters returned in a frightened state and left the area without saying what had happened.

Meanwhile, Hays also returned and told the local artist an incredible story. He said that on September 2, 1994, he had rented a cabin on Greenhorn Mountain, above the town of Libre where the artist lived. While at his campsite, a group of "aliens dressed in camo" appeared. They attacked Hays, knocking him unconscious with some kind of gas. When he woke, he found that he had been tied up. The aliens were human-looking and appeared to be conducting some sort of maneuvers. They paid Hays no attention, and never fed him. Hays said his only nourishment was a few grasshoppers which he managed to eat. At one point, the human-looking aliens boarded a small ship. To his surprise, the object expanded in size to fit the entire group. The ship took off, morphed into the image of a bear, then a wolf with three heads, and finally a cloud.

The artist told Perkins that Hays seemed "remarkably calm" and "did not seem traumatized." The artist did notice that Hays had a four-day growth of hair on his face.

Law enforcement officials went to investigate Hays' campsite and found that his vehicle had been trashed. The passenger-side door was still open, and his "half-burnt clothes" were scattered around. What exactly happened remains a mystery.[31]

Landing in Sanford

As investigated by Christopher O'Brien, on October 19, 1995, two men were driving west of Sanford when they saw a group of bright, white lights that appeared to be landed on the hillside. They drove toward the lights, approaching to within a quarter-mile. The lights blinked in sequential patterns. Said one of the witness: "The largest one looked like a big football field all lit up." He was eager to approach the object closer, throw a rock at it, and find out if it was metallic. The other witness refused and wanted to "get the hell out of there."

As they left, they saw about ten other vehicles also observing the strange lights. "The whole town must have seen them," they told O'Brien.[32]

Pterodactyl!

"No one believes us, but we don't care. We know what we saw that night." So says a man who—on the evening of September 30, 1994,—was fishing with his buddy at

Two Ponds, a group of small lakes in Golden, not far from their homes.

It was a foggy night and the two men were fishing for carp and catfish. "We both saw what appeared as a pterodactyl flying off like we scared it. It went over the car dealership where we could really see it because of the bright lights . . . it was big, real big, way bigger than any owls around here. It was like a small plane, but I couldn't hear anything when it flew by us. It had a long body and long wings."

While reports of pterodactyls may sound like science fiction, an increasing number of reports (including at least a few in Colorado) are beginning to raise questions.[33]

Creature in Horsetooth Reservoir?

The Horsetooth Reservoir (a 1,900-acre artificial lake created in 1949) has been the location of UFO activity. According to some sources, it is also the location of a mysterious water monster. Researcher, Mr. Morris, was able to interview the Macias family who claimed to have filmed what appears to be a large unidentified aquatic animal living in the lake. Their footage was impressive enough to interest producers at *Unsolved Mysteries*, who aired their footage in 1995.

The Macias family aren't the only witnesses. Morris spoke with another witness who was boating on the reservoir when her sonar depth finder recorded the presence of a large object moving underneath her boat at a depth of 120 feet. Writes Morris, "The image moved around the screen, sometimes going out of view completely, only to reappear again."

Morris interviewed her and learned that she was concerned for the safety of her two daughters who often swam in the lake. Writes Morris, "She was anxious for some sort of official inquiry into the allegations that large aquatic creatures are inhabiting the reservoir, and I am happy to report that the Colorado Division of Wildlife has set up an appointment to view the videotapes recorded by the Macias family."

Morris published a series of articles about the creature in the Brighton newspaper, *Standard-Blade*. Unfortunately, the identity of the creature remains a mystery.[34]

Landing in Colorado Springs

It was still dark outside at 5:30 a.m., March 7, 1997, as Kenneth (pseudonym) drove to his place of employment in Colorado Springs. He was following another vehicle, approaching the Big Thompson Reservoir when a tall, cylindrical-shaped object with tiers of lights around it began to descend in the field on the west side of the highway, next to the lake. The object was totally silent.

"The lights attracted my attention," says Kenneth. "I pulled over on the side of the road, as did the other vehicle." Realizing it was about to land, Kenneth became frightened, as did the driver of the other vehicle. Both of them quickly left the area, and Kenneth continued to work. He never forgot the sighting, however, and six years later, reported it to NUFORC.[35]

Landing in Greenwood Village

Around 3:00 p.m. on February 14, 2001, two ladies were at the dockyard of Cherry Creek Reservoir when they noticed a black triangle flying low in the sky. It darted at right angles and moved directly overhead, totally silent, then descended to the ground at a forty-five-degree angle and landed several miles away behind some trees. The witnesses were "amazed" and saw no visible cockpit, wings, windows, or markings. Unfortunately, they did not investigate any further.[36]

Men In Black

In March 2004, two friends went to the local elementary school playground in Fountain to film themselves performing stunts on the jungle gym. Suddenly, a metallic object appeared overhead, and then proceeded to land behind some trees in a nearby field. They filmed it as it moved overhead and disappeared behind the trees, then ran toward it. When they arrived, the object had already landed. Says one of the friends, "The object looked like a giant flat CD with a slightly domed top." It was shiny, metallic, and had no visible portholes, lights, or markings of any kind. They recorded it for about thirty seconds when "it lifted off the ground and sped off toward the mountains at lightning speed."

A few minutes later, six army helicopters showed up and raced toward the direction of the craft. The witnesses made three copies of the videotape. The next day, they drove to Fort Carson. They weren't allowed on the base, but the gate guard agreed to take down their information and a copy of the tape. "They took us very seriously," says one of the witnesses.

They never heard back from the base. However, it wasn't long after that they were hanging out at one of their homes when the doorbell rang. Two strange, identical-looking men, bald with very pale skin and wearing black suits asked their names. After answering, the men shoved their way into the house and, speaking in monotone, began to interrogate them, asking them about what they saw and if they had shared the tape with anyone. They became belligerent and told them that if anybody asked about the videotape, they were to say, "It was a hoax." They then threatened the witnesses and said that if they told anyone about the sighting, they would "lock up all our families and make sure nobody remembered us."

They proceeded to conduct a thorough search of the house, took all copies of the tape, and left. Later, one of the witnesses' girlfriends said two men showed up with a search warrant and proceeded to search the other friend's house. One of the friends reported the incident to MUFON, writing, "We now have no evidence of what we saw."[37]

MUFON Investigator Sees UFO Land

On June 8, 2005, MUFON National Director for Brisbane, Australia, Glynnys Mackay, was visiting friends in Blue Mountain, which overlooks Golden.

It was around 7:15 p.m., when he saw what he first thought was "a very large bird." He turned to his friend, John Tracey, and said, "What a huge bird."

At that point, it passed a grove of Ponderosa Pines and turned toward them. Mackay saw then that it wasn't a bird. "This object was flashing a blue light, and on turning toward us was silver and round, and appeared to be landing on a clear grass area between the trees across the valley. It then climbed up to eye level and started to fly toward us."

The two men called out to the rest of the people in the house, and the group of five people watched the object as it followed the contour of the hills, then turned, flew for a short distance, and took off at high speed toward Denver. The witnesses snapped two pictures of the UFO before it disappeared. Says Mackay, "This really made our trip to the USA a pretty exciting one, as our host and hostess had never seen a UFO or believed up until this time.[38]

Kissed by an ET?

One evening in August 2005, Augustine decided to go to a bar called *The Triangle* in downtown Denver. She ordered a drink and wandered onto the outside deck, which was shaped like a triangle.

"Soon enough," says Augustine, "an older gent came outside to join me, and probe me with questions to get an idea who I was."

Augustine entertained him, told him that she liked the stars, and looking at the skyscrapers around them, she said that "that building is her favorite and someday I will get to the top of it."

It was at that moment that they both noticed the stars beginning to disappear. They soon saw the cause: a "large black triangle" moving overhead. "We watched in shock as it passed over the city," says Augustine. "No lights and definitely no sound." She reports that the object was very large, at least the size of three football fields or larger. It moved overhead and disappeared from view.

Augustine was shocked and wondering if they had just seen a huge UFO. "Right then," she says, "the man grabbed me and we kissed. It must have been the moment. Still, today I wonder if that man was an ET, sharing and analyzing my reaction to something unbelievable and not easy at all to share with non-believers. Or else it's our government already advanced enough to play Star Wars," she adds.[39]

Three Aliens?

Looking out of her home in Colorado Springs, an anonymous woman reports seeing something very unusual. It was 11:00 p.m. on May 7, 2006, when the lady saw a "landed starship" outside her bedroom window. The craft was silvery green, with a dome on top and white lights around the edges. A hatch opened, dropping a series of steps to the ground.

Using a pair of opera glasses, the witness watched the lights of the craft fade to a dark blue. Three entities stood next to the craft. She watched as they walked across the street and stood by a street lamp and talked to each other. She did not see them actually exit the craft, but their appearance was so startling that she believed they were aliens. One figure, an apparent male, was five-feet-seven inches tall and had dark hair. He wore a black cape with a pointed collar and a red sash across the front, and black thigh-high boots. The second figure, a female, wore shorter boots and a pink sequined-like jumpsuit. The third figure was dressed in tan clothes with tan thigh-high booths and a chocolate-brown vest with pens clipped to it. He wore an eye patch and appeared to have burns or a rash on his face, and "worry lines" on his forehead.

The witness became so frightened that she closed the curtains and refused to look further. She admits that there may have been as many as five figures.[40]

An Alien in Deer Trail

In July 25, 2006, Marcia Burke was driving toward her home in Deer Trail when she noticed somebody following her car. They appeared to have their bright headlights on. "I thought somebody was following directly behind me too closely. I had really bright headlights in my rearview mirror. So I pulled over to let me them pass me, and I shut off my car, and I shut off the lights, and no one came. So I thought that was really weird."

Burke had started driving again when it happened again. She pulled over and still, nobody was there. That's when she arrived at her house and saw a group of objects hovering over her horse farm. She immediately thought of her camera inside the house. "As I'm driving up my driveway to get home to get my camera, my car actually starts bogging down and gives me some kind of electrical engine troubles. That was a little weird."

She ran inside, got her camera, and started recording the lights. She walked around the front yard when she saw what she first thought was a demon. It was in a red light. "It looked very scary, and I didn't know what it was. Then I started running and my battery goes. And I go inside my house and I charge my battery. The alien was actually in my front yard. It was right in front of me, ten feet in front of me. It seemed like it could have been about three feet tall . . . I felt like I got some telepathy where he was telling me not to be scared. It was too much for me handle. I went inside my house and locked the door."

She laughed at herself. If aliens could travel through space, they could probably get inside the house. But too frightened to venture outside, Burke continued filming from the balcony of her upstairs bedroom.

Burke later appeared on the *Montel Williams* show where she talked about what she had seen and played her footage, one segment of which appears to show the actual alien.[41]

Denver Landing

Around 2:00 a.m., October 7, 2006, Bradley (pseudonym) was driving with his friends near Hampton in Denver when they saw what they first thought were two planes flying at a very low altitude. It appeared as if the planes were connected by a beam of light. As they got closer to it, they realized the planes were actually one large triangular-shaped object. They watched as it began to dart around in rapid sporadic movements, making no noise at all. When it suddenly darted away and disappeared, Bradley and his friends were convinced they had seen a genuine UFO. Bradley was shocked, excited, and amazed.

They continued driving. About six minutes later, they saw the object again. This time it was much closer and moved directly over their car about 150 feet up in the air. It flew around for about a minute, then suddenly stopped a short distance away directly over a group of homes. They could now observe it better and saw what appeared to be dark windows.

Several other cars also stopped to observe the strange craft. Without warning, the craft lowered and appeared to land. Bradley and his friends drove up to where they had seen it land, but couldn't find it. They searched the area extensively for about a half-hour with no success. They wondered if perhaps it had turned invisible or cloaked itself somehow. As they searched, three helicopters showed up and also began to actively search the area. The helicopters remained for the entire night crisscrossing the area.

Unable to find the craft, Bradley and his friends returned home. Says Bradley, "Throughout the entire sighting I never felt afraid. I just felt amazed beyond belief and lucky to have seen this object."[42]

A Little Gray Man

On the evening of October 1, 2007, Erika (pseudonym) of the small town of Aguilar, was having trouble with her three-year-old daughter. "She did not want to go to bed because she was scared," explains Erika. "I asked her what she was scared of, and she described an event she said happened the night before. She said she woke up in the night and saw a little person standing next to her bed. She said it was looking at her toys. She then said it turned and looked right at her."

At that point, her daughter fled her bedroom to go find her mother. After some more questions, Erika learned that the figure was short, had gray skin, small sharp teeth, and strange segmented black and yellow eyes. It never touched her daughter or spoke to her, and her daughter wasn't frightened until the being looked at her. She even had her daughter draw the figure.

Erika asked her daughter if she might have been dreaming, but the daughter insisted that she wasn't dreaming and that it was real.

Around that time, the daughter had another strange experience. Says Erika, "My husband and I are at a loss. She also oddly enough told me of a vision she had that felt very real, where an asteroid smashed into us, killing everyone. She was really scared and I had to reassure her for a couple of days."

Erika is not sure what to make of the experience. About five years later, she sought out MUFON and made a formal report. "My daughter claims a little gray man was in her bedroom looking at her toys, then her," she says. "It was pretty frightening for her and me."[43]

A Humanoid Form

Tina (pseudonym) of Fort Collins worked the late shift at her job. Around midnight on April 29, 2008, she was walking home with her nineteen-year-old son as they usually did when she got off work late. It was a four-mile walk. They were nearing the end when they saw something about sixty feet ahead of them and to the right. There was a small "sonic boom" and suddenly they saw an oval-shaped craft about thirteen feet long and four feet tall, hovering about four feet from the ground. It was moving about ten miles an hour and had a seven-foot-long contrail following it.

The object had a translucent mirror-like appearance that Tina found mesmerizing. Her son, however, reported that he could see "a humanoid form" inside it. The object suddenly accelerated, then shot up into the sky.

Says Tina, "I was in a state of shock, as was my son . . . we went home very quickly, and for the first time, I was actually scared, even though I have seen UFOs close-up several times in my life . . . for some strange reason, this incident has really been bothering me. We no longer go on walks late at night in the summer, since that night."[44]

The Generator Alien

Pamela (pseudonym) is a generator manager who, on May 15, 2008, experienced a dramatic encounter while on her jobsite at a large generator between Sedgwick and Ovid along Interstate 76. The generator had been brought in as part of a highway construction project.

On the evening in question, Pamela arrived at the jobsite around 8:00 p.m. and sat in her truck filling out paperwork. It was her last night on this site. However, over the past two-and-a-half weeks, she had noticed amber lights, which she did not examine closely and assumed were conventional city lights. However, tonight the lights had moved much closer and appeared to be hovering over a nearby field. Puzzled, she examined them more closely and realized that the lights were not only hovering; they appeared to be attached to one large craft. The lights were multicolored, including blue, green, red, white, and yellow. Meanwhile, dozens of intense white orbs were orbiting around the stationary object. The lights covered an area nearly four miles wide. As she watched, the whole mass of lights moved, stopped and hovered, moved again, then stopped and hovered, and continued this strange behavior several times. She heard no noise.

Realizing she was seeing something very unusual, she grabbed her camera (which had full battery power) and attempted to take a picture. She tried three times to take a photograph; however, on each occasion, the camera powered off and wouldn't function. At the same time, Pamela reported an "overwhelming and extreme calmness" that came over her. Despite the strangeness of the sight before her, she felt no fear.

She grabbed her binoculars and observed the mass of lights, but couldn't see any detail. She was most impressed by the strange patterns of the lights. At this point, she felt a strong impulse to record and write down the pattern she was observing. The urge was so strong, she felt as though she was being told to write the pattern down, that there was meaning to them.

As she watched the object, she saw two semi-trucks pull over and also observe the lights for a short while. They did not exit their vehicles and both soon departed.

Without warning, the craft seemed to shrink to the size of a football field. She tried repeatedly to take photos, but the camera remained non-functional.

She had to leave the area to service another generator, but returned to see that the lights were still present.

Around this time, the witness became confused about the sequence of events. The camera, she recalls, began working, and she was able to take a series of photos. She remembers getting in and out of her truck several times, but was confused as to why she did this, or when.

She recalls the object approaching her very closely, about twenty feet away. She watched the object change to the size of a house, and then down to the size of a coffee can. At this point, the object was hovering directly over the generator she was in charge of operating.

She was able to walk up to the generator, where she took more photos. She felt like she was "allowed" to take these photos. After taking them, the camera went dead again. The object remained over the generator for another fifteen minutes.

By this point, morning was beginning to arrive and the sky was brightening. The lights promptly increased in size, spread out, and moved back over the field. The sun rose and the lights disappeared.

Pamela approached the generator and shut it off. When her coworkers arrived to take over the worksite, she told them about the strange lights.

Following the incident, she returned home and downloaded her photos to show her brother. She was shocked to see a "creature" standing near the generator looking back at her. The creature appeared to be partially transparent, and was about three-and-a-half feet tall.

A few days after the incident, she received a call from one of her coworkers who told her that they had found three dead cattle in the field where she had seen the lights. They were freaked out and left the area.

Pamela felt spiritually transformed by the experience and feels that she now has a more "carefree" view of life. She contacted MUFON investigators who conducted a full investigation. Pamela has refused all publicity and has released the photos to investigators for research purposes only.[45]

An Alien in a Suit

On the evening of February 2, 2009, Carson (pseudonym) of Colorado Springs decided to go to sleep early as he was feeling unusually tired. His girlfriend joined him and they went to bed. Sometime later, he found himself having what he assumed was a strange dream. In the dream, he was lying in bed when a figure appeared in his room. "I recall seeing an alien standing at the foot of my bed."

The figure was about five or six feet tall, gray skin, big eyes, and many of the characteristics of typical gray aliens, which Carson had seen in pop culture. Except there was one bizarre difference. "The only thing that was different is the one thing that I now find odd. It was wearing what appeared to be a three-piece suit."

Carson was baffled by the detail, having never heard of such a thing. "Anyway," says Carson, "this thing reached out to grab me from the foot of the bed, and it scared the living you-know-what out of me and woke me up yelling . . . My girlfriend woke up to my scream and calmed me down."

Carson was confused by the dream. He had never dreamed about aliens before. He's had scary dreams, but they'd never woken him up yelling.

Then again, why would an alien be wearing a black three piece-suit? This detail, says Carson, "put a big lump in my throat." It made no sense. Was this a dream or an actual encounter? Later, after doing some investigation into other people's encounters, Carson learned that others have also reported this detail. He used to think the experience was a dream, but after learning about this detail, he says, "It's making me wonder."[46]

Basalt Entities

As investigated by William Plunkett of the investigative group *UFOs Northwest*, on the evening of April 26, 2009, Charlie (age eighteen) had sneaked out of his parents' home in Basalt to visit a friend. Around 2:30 a.m., as he walked back home, he noticed a large light following him. Suddenly the light approached closer and shined a beam of light on him. He ran to his house, and the light followed. As he climbed through a window into his bedroom, the light shined in and he found himself temporarily unable to move. He could now see a large craft hovering outside. It was U-shaped with three lights on either end and a large section in the middle. Suddenly he saw small beings approach. They appeared to be about four feet tall and had "legs that were reversed."

At this point, around 2:30 a.m., Charlie's parents woke up to hear a tornado-like roar outside the house. Neither of them investigated; both returned to sleep.

Charlie told his friends, but didn't tell his parents. When one of the friends told Charlie's parents, they questioned their son and he revealed what happened. They checked for any evidence outside the house, but found none. Charlie, however, was clearly shaken. Says the mother, "My son always slept with his window unlocked, but now both of his windows are locked. I know this has scared him, and me too in so many ways."[47]

By Intelligent Design

Noah (pseudonym) is a C6 quadriplegic, bound to his wheelchair in his Colorado Springs home. On the evening of July 5, 2011, he woke to notice an odd "hieroglyphic-like" symbol on his right hip. Hot to the touch, it appeared almost branded into his skin. Over the next three weeks it scabbed over and began to heal.

It was a strange symbol, with one vertical line on the left side, three horizontal stacked lines in the center, three dots in a vertical line on the right, and stray markings below it. "At first my aide mentioned it," says Noah, "and I figured it was nothing until I saw it in a mirror. It was shockingly unnatural, and I felt a deep conviction it was made by intelligent design."

Noah wracked his brain. What could have caused this symbol on his hip to suddenly appear? There was nothing in his environment that could have caused it.

And yet there it was.

"All of a sudden in the shower it hit me," says Noah. "A 'dream' from the previous night. I remember being in a bright room or area, feeling very calm, and not scared. This was induced, and I was artificially numb to what I was encountering. An entity proceeded to ask me questions about my spinal cord injury . . . I was asked specifically about my hands, fingers, and arms. Why were they as such? What was done to try and fix me? Why was one side stronger? I answered without hesitation."

What happened next remains unexplained. "I was very psychologically level," says Noah. "Then I felt pain, looked at my right hand. All fingers were straight and spread. This isn't possible without lengthy splinting. Next my left hand and fingers did the same thing. This hurt, but it was good to see all the same. The entities seemed not to understand why I remained paralyzed, and I got the impression they were surprised/upset/confused as to what I can only guess they perceived to be primitive medical technology. This is all I remember from the dream . . . but had I not seen the mark on my skin I would never have recalled anything."[48]

A Black Silhouette

"Entities are causing me to pass out. I need help with this. This is not the first time I have had dealings with entities. I have had it with this problem and need help," writes an anonymous witness about encounters in her Colorado home (exact location not given.)

One of the scariest events occurred on July 20, 2012. The witness had just gone to bed when she had a strong feeling that somebody was in her room. Panic swept over her. She turned over to see if anything was there. "I look over," she says, "and I see a seven- or eight-foot-tall being. He/she is extremely dark, and I cannot see any detail but a black silhouette. It never moved or touched me, this time. It just stared at me. I have about a second of eye contact, and I unexpectedly—and like a rag doll—pass out and crumple in my bed."

She woke up the next morning to her dad shaking her until she finally woke. The witness has experienced three other similar events and is currently seeking help. As she says, "I'm tired of the stress."[49]

Alien Thief

Three days after the above encounter, at 3:30 a.m. on June 22, 2012, Natasha (pseudonym) of Thornton woke up to see an extremely slender figure almost seven feet tall standing in her room. It had a large head with an oversized forehead, and long arms that reached only a foot from the ground. Each of its fingers was a half-foot long and ended in a sharp claw.

"Fear took over my whole being," says Natasha. "We stared at each other for what seemed to be a couple of minutes." Natasha "jumped slightly," stared at it, and the entity went away. Had she scared it away? She looked at the clock and saw that only a few seconds had passed.

When Natasha woke up the next morning, she noticed something very strange: Her hair extensions were gone. She instantly remembered her encounter. She had the distinct impression that the alien wanted to abducted her to study her hair. "I feel like it wanted to abduct me," says Natasha, "but I woke up, and it didn't want to take me when I was awake. So they took my hair extensions instead. I would really like an explanation to why it was in my room and what it wanted with me."

Following the incident, Natasha began to suffer from "severe depression," and blocked out everything about the incident. Two years later she decided that she was ready to face everything, and she reported the incident to MUFON.[50]

Nightmare in Glenwood Springs

Lucy (pseudonym) of Glenwood Springs had rented a room in her home to a gentleman tenant. He had lived there for some time when strange events began to happen. On June 25, 2012, at around midnight, Lucy woke up to hear a thud coming from her renter's room. "I walked down the hallway toward his room," she says, "and called out his name. A bright yellow light was emitting from under his door."

She called his name again, but there was no response. She walked back to her door, looked again down the hallway, and saw that the bright light was now gone. Puzzled by what had occurred, she made a mental note to ask her renter about it in the morning.

Around 3:00 a.m., says Lucy, she woke up to see a dark black figure at her window. Her initial thought was: burglar. "Go away!" she screamed.

The figure changed shape into a large spider, which began to crawl along her window. "Get out of here!" she yelled.

The spider-thing swooped away. She looked out her window and saw that there were four odd figures outside, some short and stocky, others tall and thin. They stood just beyond her fence, and were silhouetted in an eerie blue light being cast down over her house and the neighbor's house.

"I then ran to the front of the house," says Lucy, "and saw two creatures crouching behind my neighbor's car, and two behind my renter's van in the driveway."

Following the event, she woke up her renter to tell him what had just happened. He explained that he had been abducted many times since he was a child, and proceeded to show her a mark on his body where he believed he had been implanted.

The next morning, he left to go camping, saying that he was going to "call upon good fairies and energy" to remove the darkness from Lucy's home.

The next night, on June 26, an apparition of a "skeleton" appeared outside her home. "I was looking out my window at night," says Lucy. "I saw it manifest itself and walk up to my bedroom window. It moved fluid-like and swung its arms like a man walking. I screamed for it to leave, and it just stood at the window."

"Be gone!" she shouted. "You are not invited and you have to leave."

When the figure continued to stand and stare at her, Lucy threw a pillow at the window. It promptly disappeared.

Lucy invited a friend over, and together they tried to clear her house with religious items, prayer, and burning sage. There were no strange events for days.

Then, on July 1, Lucy had another strange visitation. "I woke around 3:00 a.m.," she says, "and saw this Grey at my window. He had a bald head and the almond eyes . . . I told him to go away, he was not invited, and could not be there. I called on Warrior Angels to protect me and my home."

Lucy was shocked when her entire bedroom window began to glow with energy lines similar to a scrambled television signal. Outside, her backyard glowed with light. The being still remained. She screamed again for it to leave and threw a pillow. The being disappeared and the light winked out.

"I want help!" says Lucy. "I don't know what to do to get these beings to leave me alone. I am frightened to be alone at night. I am unable to sleep. How can I make these beings leave for good? . . . I am eager to be free of this nightmare."

Lucy had hoped her renter would be able to solve the problem, but as she says, "He is now missing. He left my home the morning of June 26, and has not been seen since. The search and rescue people here in Glenwood Springs did find his van at a local trailhead, but no one has found him yet."[51]

Pueblo Landing

In mid-December 2010, Oscar (pseudonym) was driving around 2:30 a.m. through the Pueblo area when he saw something very odd sitting in the middle of a field: a large diamond-shaped object. It appeared to be translucent, with an interior that was lighting up with chaotic, laser-like beams of green light. He watched it for about a minute when one of the strange beams came out of the object and hit the windshield of his car. "When that happened," says Oscar, "I made my turn and left the area as quickly as I thought was prudent." As he drove off, Oscar felt his adrenaline pumping through his body. He knew he had just seen "something abnormal in the extreme." Although he had a cellphone in his pocket, his fear of the object caused him to depart before he could take a picture.

When he returned to the field later, there was no evidence of the object. He drove by the field many times and never saw anything like it.[52]

Wildfire UFO

On June 9, 2012, a massive wildfire struck the High Park area outside of Fort Collins. On the second day of the fire, a nearby resident watching the progress of the flames saw what appeared to be a disk-shaped craft hovering over the southern end of the fire. It moved slowly around the area for about a minute, then disappeared. Shortly later, he saw another (or the same?) object on the southeast end of the fire.

He felt sure that he had seen something unusual. But the story wasn't over yet. Says the witness, "About four weeks later, something happened that confirmed to me what I saw. A voluntary firefighter showed me a photo of a burn area, just yards away from the forest burn area, that they could not explain. The photo showed a perfectly rounded burn area that no forest fire could have created, and he felt it was so strange that he took a picture of it."

He told the firefighter about the objects he had seen. The firefighter had no comment.[53]

Two Landed

On August 23, 2012, a young man was playing basketball near his home in Indian Hills. Around midnight, he decided to go home, and noticed five star-like objects zigzagging in the sky at very high altitude. He watched them dart at high speeds and at sharp angles. Sometimes they moved together, other times in different directions. Two of the objects darted across the horizon and disappeared. Another darted off and away.

The witness focused on the brightest one and watched as it darted to the east, stopped and hovered, and then emitted another object that dropped 50,000 feet straight down and appeared to land in the distance. Five seconds later, it released another object that flew down, landing an estimated twenty-five to fifty miles from the other.

The witness called his mother, who rushed to the scene. Together the two of them observed the three remaining objects as they darted around. They watched them for two-and-a-half hours before finally going to bed. The witness had the feeling that the objects were "trying to make themselves known on purpose."

Since that night, he has seen the objects on multiple occasions, often appearing to mimic the stars.[54]

Florence Donuts

On March 12, 2013, a sheep rancher in Florence retrieved his sheep and penned them up for the evening. The next morning, he let them back out into the fields. However, later when he went back to retrieve his sheep, he found inexplicable ring-shaped markings in the field, as if something had landed there. "There were about ten of the donut-shaped circles between nine and eleven feet in diameter. The outer circle, all vegetation, was gone for about eighteen inches. In the inside the vegetation is normal. I have lived here for nineteen years and never seen anything like this."[55]

Alien in Broad Daylight

"My background is retired military, and [I am] currently employed in the Department of Corrections in Florence," says a man who experienced a remarkable alien encounter while hiking along a mountain trail outside Canon City. It was the afternoon of May 23, 2013. He looked up. About one hundred yards ahead of him, a chevron-shaped craft hovered a mere five feet above the ground. The craft had an indentation around the perimeter.

Says the witness, "About fifteen feet from the craft were two aliens dressed in shiny silver uniforms. One had red boots, but the other two had boots the same color as the uniform. They were carrying what appeared to be an unresponsive third alien to the craft. They had dark gray skin, appeared to have trouble moving, and were somewhat uncoordinated. A beam of blue light was coming from the bottom of the craft. The aliens carried the apparently lifeless body of the third one into the beam; it appeared to take on a rippled appearance like water. Then the light went off and all the aliens were gone. Next the craft began to slowly rise until it was very high. Then it began to move quickly until I couldn't see it anymore."

The witness has no explanation for his experience and calls it "a mysterious, unique sighting of three aliens in broad daylight."[56]

A Flying Humanoid

On June 29, 2014, a woman was watching fireworks with her husband outside their home in Thornton. Suddenly, what they thought was a firework display confused them, as one of the lights suddenly froze in place. They were about to launch some more fireworks when they saw a black figure floating in the sky. "We saw what we believe [is] a flying humanoid," says the woman. "[It] was flying in a straight line, slowly, no motion, then started flying up and disappearing into the sky. It was about one hundred feet off the ground."[57]

Another Pterodactyl?

October 26, 2014, a boyfriend and girlfriend were taking an early evening walk through their hometown of Lakewood. Suddenly the boyfriend looked up and saw a triangle-shaped object flying at about 5,000 feet. "What the hell is that?" he shouted.

The girlfriend looked up just in time to see it move behind the tree-line. The boyfriend saw it clearly and says that it "looked like a giant prehistoric bird."

"We were both a little shaken by it," says the boyfriend. "Neither of us are really ones that believe in UFOs or anything like that. I, having military experience, believe it to be some sort of military secret, especially considering all the military bases of operation down south in Colorado. With that being said, I've never seen anything, experimental, stealth, or regular military aircraft that looked anything similar." He thought he may have seen very faint lights on the object, but isn't sure.[58]

Onboard UFO Experiences

Perhaps the closest of all encounters are cases in which people have been taken onboard. While onboard UFO experiences (often called UFO abductions) were once considered rare, today many researchers believe that such cases may number in the millions. While sightings and landings are reported in large numbers, abductions and onboard experiences are often so strange that witnesses are too frightened to report them to anybody, including within their own circle of family and friends.

And yet there are now thousands of such cases on record across the United States and the world. What follows are more than forty Colorado cases. Some involve only missing time with little recall of what happened. Others involve full-blown onboard experiences with near total recall. Some involve friendly contactee-type cases, while others involve more traumatic abductions.

The Case of Leo Sprinkle

In the fall of 1949, Ronald Leo Sprinkle and Joe Waggoner (both age nineteen) were students at the University of Colorado at Boulder. One day, says Sprinkle, "[we] watched a flying saucer, or daylight disc, moving over the campus . . . " Believing that "only kooks see UFOs," Sprinkle and Waggoner were confounded. They kept the sighting secret from everyone but each other. It impressed Sprinkle deeply. "It wasn't an airplane, and it wasn't a balloon," says Sprinkle.

He often thought about the sighting and its implications. However, it wasn't until seven years later on a summer evening in 1956, when he had another sighting, causing a radical change in his life.

Since the first sighting, he had graduated from college, completed four years in the Army, returned to Boulder to complete graduate school, and had married his wife, Marilyn Joan Nelson.

One summer evening in 1956, he and his wife were driving from Denver to Boulder when they saw a brilliant red light moving between them and the Flatirons in the Rockies. "We watched it for several minutes," says Sprinkle. "It would hover, then move, hover, then move. It had no sound, and no features that I could observe, but I knew something unusual was going on because I could hear the honking of the horns below us in Boulder."

The object moved off and disappeared. The Sprinkles were expecting a big news story the next day, but found nothing.

The sighting changed Sprinkle's life. He was convinced UFOs were real and felt that they deserved greater study. He decided to get a doctorate in Psychology. Before long, he became one of the first investigators to hypnotize abductees to help them recall their periods of amnesia. He was also one of the first academics to study the subject scientifically.

Sprinkle assumed that his own experiences with UFOs were limited to his own two sightings, and his interactions with UFO witnesses. However, strange vague memories of being onboard himself began to make him wonder. After going under hypnosis himself, he discovered that he was also apparently a contactee. Under hypnosis he recalled that as a child in Rocky Ford, he was taken onboard a spacecraft. He recalls looking out a porthole and seeing not only stars, but the image of the planet Saturn, life-like and close-up. A tall man stood beside him and told Sprinkle that he should learn to read and write well, and that as an adult, he would help other people to become aware of the purpose of their lives.

Sprinkle believes he was taken onboard a UFO and guided by friendly ETs. Since then, he has hypnotized hundreds of individuals and helped them recall their encounters. He was also the founder of the popular Rocky Mountain UFO Conferences. His pioneering efforts have made a long-lasting contribution to UFO research.[1]

The Elders

On a sunny day in 1952, eight-year-old Emily (pseudonym) went for a walk in the woods outside her home in Evergreen. Suddenly she was startled to see a circular shadow appear around her on the ground. Looking up she saw a large object. Suddenly, she found herself running back home, only now it was hours later. She had partial recall of going onboard and seeing strange beings. She told her parents, who replied, "Oh, you just have a big imagination."

Following the incident, Emily began to have dreams about it and remember much of what happened. As time passed, she was unable to get the incident out of her mind, and found herself in tears whenever she thought of it. In 1985, now forty-one years old, Emily decided to undergo regressive hypnosis. To her shock, the entire story emerged.

Emily remembered seeing the shadow, and looking up to find herself under the ship. Suddenly she was onboard the craft, laying on a table that moved along an oddly-shaped, brightly-lit corridor. Says Emily, "There was a small being walking beside me. He didn't scare me; actually I felt safe as long as he was there." Emily reports that the being had a very large head and large eyes.

As she went down the corridor, she saw what appeared to be a control room with a technological-looking panel board. She passed another room and saw taller figures who she calls the "Elders" as they radiated intelligence and awareness. In the room were several strange "floating spheres."

Emily didn't have a chance to examine further as she was taken to a different room where she saw another strange humanoid. She felt no fear. Instead her attention was drawn to a one-year-old baby sitting nearby on another table, undergoing some type of examination involving an instrument which descended from the ceiling of the craft.

The encounter continued. Emily found herself in another room in which she saw a young girl with a transparent helmet-like dome over her head.

Finally, she was taken to a darkened room with a group of other people. Strange lights illuminated the ceiling. Says Emily, "The whole ceiling and lights rotated and in the middle the lights were pulsing. After being in there, I couldn't remember much. It's as if they tried to erase my memory."

Following the incident, Emily had numerous sightings, both alone and with other witnesses, including her own family. Says Emily, "I'm not crazy. This has been happening to me all my life." She says that sometimes it feels as though she knows the aliens, as if she is a part of them and has been there before. At the same time, it scares her, especially as her young children have reported seeing an object much like the one she saw when she was their age.[2]

Was Grandpa an Alien?

"It doesn't matter whether you believe me or not," says Marty Minetto, then adds, "It did happen."

On April 9, 1955, Minetto (age five) was approached by his grandfather, Samuel, during bedtime. "Do you scare easily?" he asked.

"No," Minetto replied.

"Are you a strong young man and not afraid of new things if I am with you and take care of you?"

"Yes, Minetto said.

"I want you to go with me on a walk Saturday, and you will see great things. But you are to tell no one. You can never tell your mom or dad or brothers and sisters, because it could hurt grandpa and grandma, and they might have to move far away."

"I would never tell," Minetto told his grandfather.

His grandfather hugged him and asked, "Do you promise?"

"Yes," said Minetto.

Samuel often shared special stories with Minetto that were for him and nobody else. Many of the stories he didn't understand, other than they were about great wonders and people from far off places. And although he had many siblings, he shared a special bond with his grandfather and would never reveal his secrets.

Samuel called for Minetto's grandmother. He turned to her and told her, "I am going to show the boy tomorrow so he understands what I've been telling him. Tell his mom we will be okay, but we might be late getting home."

Minetto's grandmother began crying.

Minetto felt bad for her and asked, "What's wrong, grandma?"

"Nothing," she replied.

"Don't cry, Mama. It's okay."

She said, "I am crying because tomorrow you will know who you are. This is a good thing. Tomorrow is going to be a wonderful day for you. Stay close to Grandpa; listen to him and do just what he says. Do not be afraid of some things you might see. It's okay to always trust Grandpa."

She hugged Minetto and told him to go to bed. She warned Samuel that only Marty was to go and none of his other siblings could go or know anything about this. Samuel agreed.

Says Minetto, "That night was hard to sleep as what lay ahead for me the next day kept me awake most of the night."

The next morning after breakfast, Samuel approached his grandson. "Are you ready to go for that walk?" he asked.

Minetto was excited as he and his grandfather left the farmhouse, and walked down a dirt road. Eventually, they left the farmhouse behind them and were surrounded by fields. Suddenly Minetto was shocked to see a "very large, oval-shaped object" dropping down from the sky. It glowed orange, then turned bright white as it began to get low. A tripod landing gear descended and the object landed on the road in front of them. It was close enough that he could feel heat emanating from the craft.

As the craft settled on the road, the wind blew fiercely, kicking up a cloud of dust. Samuel picked up Minetto and said, "They're here, son. Please don't be afraid. They're my friends and yours. Trust Grandpa."

"I wasn't scared at all," says Minetto. "I don't know why, but I wasn't."

The craft hummed loudly. Samuel set Minetto down and said, "Be kind and respectful. Stand where you are and don't move until I tell you."

At this point, a door opened on the side of the object and two people walked out and moved toward them. Now, Minetto began to feel some fear. Samuel approached them and began to speak in a strange language unknown to Minetto. They touched hands and shoulders. After a few moments, the two men and his grandfather approached Minetto.

"What were you saying?" Minetto asked.

"It is the old talk," said Samuel, "from where Grandma and I came from." He pointed to one of the figures, a man with a blue shirt and white pants. "This person is a friend of Grandma's. I want you to touch his hand. Say 'hello' to Austino. Go with him and I'll meet you inside in a few minutes. You will be okay. No matter what, don't speak until they tell you to. Do you understand, Marty?"

"Yes," Minetto replied. Austino held out his hand, which Minetto took, and together they walked to the right side of the object where Minetto could see a large doorway.

Inside, Minetto was surprised to see that the object was huge, and filled with numerous people engaged in activity. Austino led him up a ramp into a room that reminded him of a doctor's office. There were tables and lights and metal walls. Another person picked Minetto up and put him on one of the tables. He then placed "this crown-looking thing with two bent prongs on the top" and put it on Minetto's head.

Minetto felt a brief flash of pain, then was surprised to hear the man speaking. "Do you understand what I am saying to you?"

"Yes," Minetto replied.

"Would you like to see a great wonder?" the man asked. "Your friends would like you to see your grandpa's home."

Minetto felt a soft movement and asked Austino if they were moving.

Austino replied that yes, they had been moving for some time, and would Marty like to take a look around the ship with him?

As they walked around, Minetto asked where his grandfather was. "He's with friends and will be with us soon."

A short time later, Samuel appeared. Samuel told Austino to go ahead and show Minetto the craft, but only the safe areas. Austino began to give Minetto a tour of the craft. Minetto was surprised by the sheer size of the craft, which he said appeared to be as big as a football field and was filled with human-looking people. It was, he estimated, forty feet high, 120 feet long, with two whitish-pink decks.

"Are you hungry or thirsty?" Austino asked.

"Could I have something to drink?"

Says Minetto, "He went over to this wall, put his hand on this thing, and water filled this container. I drank it, and let me tell you, it was great. I could not believe how good it tasted . . . He showed me if I pinched the glass in this spot, watch what would happen. I did, and the glass turned cold." Minetto says that the liquid appeared to be water, but tasted better.

"Can I keep it?" Minetto asked, holding the glass.

"No," Austino replied. "It has to stay here."

Next, Austino showed him the engine room, which made a low humming noise. He told Minetto that their engines ran on water with the aid of the Earth's magnetic field. He said that one day, people on Earth would learn how to use water and the magnetic field to power their vehicles. He explained that their own engines allowed them to go as fast or slow as they wanted, and that they could slip into and out of time at will.

Minetto was impressed and told Austino he wanted to become a pilot when he grew up. "Where do you come from?" Minetto asked.

"We come from between my time and yours . . . We come from a place here on Earth, but beneath your time, in a different phase. We are with you all the time. You will learn more as you get older. You are the first in a long time to come to know these things. We are a good people, and one day you will understand, but not now . . . Let's go to your grandfather."

They walked through the crowded hallways until they found Samuel, who scooped Minetto up into his arms. Samuel pulled the translator(?) helmet from his head and gave it to Austino.

There was a soft thump, and suddenly, Minetto found himself being carried outside by his grandfather.

The ship was still parked on the dirt road next to them.

Minetto tried to talk with his grandfather about the flying object and the strange men. The ship took off.

"Be quiet," said Samuel. "Say nothing, and one day I will talk about it. If you say anything now," he said, "The sheriff will take you away and you will not see your family again. I will go to jail, and your mom and dad, too. You can only talk to me about it. If you need to talk, you are to say, 'Papa, will you read me a book?"

It wasn't long before there was a second incident. Minetto recalls only being released from the craft and greeted by his grandfather. "The next thing I remember," says Minetto, "I was standing in the road with my cowboy boots in my hand."

"Do you know where you have been?" Samuel asked.

"I was right here," said Minetto. "And this plane landed."

"Well the whole town is looking for you," Samuel said, and told Minetto that it was now 1:30 in the morning.

They started to walk home when a car drove up, followed by several others.

Someone jumped out and ran to Samuel. "Are you Samuel Johnson?" they asked.

"Yes," he said, "I found him."

Soon cars and people were everywhere. Minetto kept his promise and told nobody where he and his grandfather had been.

Following the incidents, Minetto had several dreams about being inside. He asked his grandfather about the experiences, but his grandfather wouldn't answer, only to say: "Don't worry. You are going to see something so wonderful, it will change your life."

Further onboard encounters occurred as an adult, the details of which Minetto has not revealed other than to say, "What I've got to tell you would knock your socks off."

Years later, his grandfather spoke more with Minetto about the second childhood incident. "Just before my grandfather passed away, we talked about that night, and he said how he found me. He was walking to the shed and saw this very bright light on the road and went to see if one of the searchers had found me. He saw this thing lift into the air, and in the light on the road he saw me standing there with my cowboy boots in my hand."

"Why did you take your cowboy boots off?" he asked.

"They said I had to go, and that I didn't have time to put them on, as my feet needed to dry first."

Minetto still remembers watching the craft light up, change colors, and dart away in a flash. Since the initial incidents, Minetto has seen the same craft five times. "Not up close," he says, "but always from a distance."

Despite his grandfather's admonishment to remain silent, Minetto later shared his encounter with his family. The result was not good. They accused him of lying or being crazy. Fifty years later, Minetto reported his sighting to MUFON, writing, "Until now I have honored his wish, but I am getting older, and I felt I needed to tell someone. I have so much more to tell, but I just don't know if anyone would believe me. Before I pass away, I felt I should tell someone . . . thank you, at least, for reading this."[3]

Rangely Alien

In early May 1964, in the town of Rangely, Jill (pseudonym) woke in the middle of the night to find herself alone in the house. She was about five years old. She looked out the window and into the neighbor's kitchen and was shocked to see her neighbor sitting there. In front of the neighbor was "a being." Says Jill, "The being had something in his hand, and he jutted it toward my neighbor; my neighbor jerked, like being shocked. I gasped. The being immediately turned and looked at me."

Frightened, Jill tried to hide under her bed. A few moments later, she heard its footsteps. "The being was in the house," said Jill. "It came to the door and I believe stood in the door looking at me. I fainted."

This first encounter was soon followed by others. Her mother reported seeing a cigar-shaped craft. Later on a trip together, they both lost about two hours of time.

There were several other sightings. Jill also reports bizarre physical symptoms: "I had dental x-rays that showed a piece of metal in the front of my mouth below the teeth, in the gums. A few years later, another x-ray was taken that showed nothing."[4]

Livermore Abduction

On the afternoon of September 2, 1969, Shirley P. (a school teacher) and her dog, Spank, were taking a short walk on her farm in Livermore. Looking up, she was shocked to see a large dumbbell-shaped object hovering silently above her. It had a surface of polished chrome with no visible markings whatsoever.

The next thing Shirley realized, she was inside the object looking down on the roof of the farmhouse.

Much of her recall of what followed was obtained under hypnosis. After being taken onboard, she was met by an ET (not described) who asked if she wanted to see the ship.

Shirley agreed, but told the ET that she was worried about her dog, Spank.

"Don't worry," the ET said. "We'll take care of Spank. He'll be fine. He'll be right where you left him."

"Okay," said Shirley.

The ET took her to a large circular room. In the center was a large object that appeared to be molded seamlessly to the floor. It had a transparent gridded top. Several "people" were walking around it, doing things. As she watched, images or pictures rose from the bottom of the object.

Shirley was mystified by the device and had no idea what its function might be. She wanted to take a closer look, but the ET stopped her and said, "You don't need to look at that."[5]

The Precious Harvest

It was July 9, 1975, and sixteen-year-old Elaine (pseudonym), her mother, and siblings drove from their home to Denver to eat some pizza. Afterward they were returning when they saw a very bright light in a field off the road. They drove up to the light. Says Elaine, "We observed a very large cigar-shaped craft hovering over the ground. It appeared to be metallic and had two very bright lights on the front and back. My mother turned off the car and rolled down the windows, and it was silent except for a slight hum, which could have been the powerlines overhead."

Following the sighting, Elaine lost all memory of the event. When her mother and siblings talked about the sighting, Elaine assumed that she wasn't there. Her family disagreed, however, and reminded her that she was the one who saw it first and pointed it out to everyone else.

The answer to Elaine's amnesia may lie with a fictional story she wrote for English class four years later. "It is a story called 'The Precious Harvest,'" says Elaine, "and recounts the abduction of a young woman describing her examination and the explanation for the procedure done on her. She was told that our species had been planted on this planet long ago and that the aliens believed that in a short period of time we would destroy the planet and ourselves with it. They described themselves as the Guardians of Seed, responsible for making sure that our genetic material would be available to one day reseed another planet."

More strange events continued. Says Elaine, "My senior year of high school and first year of college, I received phone calls from a woman who consistently told me where I had been and what I was doing, making it clear I was being closely watched. The event was reported to the police and persisted for a year and a half. It got so bad I had to have a police escort to nighttime events on campus. Oddly the woman would often say when I asked why she was doing this: 'We love you and have always loved you.'"

Years later, the unexplained events occur regularly. Elaine reports haunted house-type activity, more UFO sightings, and says that she and her children "often wake with unexplained bruising and scratches."[6]

The Abduction of Tim Cullen

April 2, 1978, Tim Cullen (age twenty-seven) of Yuma, woke from a terrible dream. He dreamed he had been in a terrible car crash. Thankfully, it was just a dream.

Then, one week later, Cullen was driving when his car rolled five times. He broke his neck and suffered severe injuries. Seven weeks later, on May 30, 1978, his neck in a cast, Cullen was driving home from a doctor's appointment along Interstate 59 when he saw a strange dark shape fly below the high-tension wires and over the highway in front of his car. "It was about one hundred feet long, twenty feet wide, and ten feet high," said Cullen, "and looked like an inverted pie tin. It had lights—diffused lights, like they were shining through cellophane."

The object was utterly silent as it began to hover alongside the highway as if to land. Mesmerized by what he was seeing, Cullen stopped his car to observe.

At some point, he experienced a confusion about the time. The next thing he knew, the object was gone.

Two years later, he was driving through the same spot when he saw another UFO.

Years later, in 1994, he had a third encounter during which he saw blue and white lights hovering over the cemetery in Cope, forty miles to the south.

But it wasn't until 1998, that something happened that changed everything. Cullen was using a hammer when he smashed his thumb.

He went to the hospital for X-rays, and the doctors were puzzled to find a small metallic shard in his left wrist. The doctors asked Cullen about it, but he had no answers, other than that night he saw a UFO land next to him on the highway. He read about UFOs and was shocked to see how his story matched others. "I knew then what had happened," says Cullen. "I knew it was an alien implant from that first encounter in 1978. There was lost time that night. I have to assume I was abducted."

In February 2000, Cullen went to Los Angeles to meet with Dr. Roger Leir, DPM, specialist in alien implants. Cullen had his "implant" surgically removed, and learned that it was identical in appearance to several other implants found in the bodies of other abductees.

Convinced that he had been abducted, and armed with hard evidence to back up his story, Cullen went public. Cullen's story caused waves throughout his community, but to his surprise, most people accepted his account. Several spoke to him of their own encounters in the area. Cullen (a cement worker) is a religious man and was already well-respected by his neighbors and friends. "I'm not trying to cause trouble," he says. "I'm just telling the truth."

Cullen says that he has had several premonitions throughout his life and speculates that perhaps the ETs are interested in this ability and that's why he was targeted.[7]

"You Have the Key"

In November 1978, Lois was driving with her friend, Gina, from Denver to Phoenix when they saw a hitchhiker by the side of the road. Although Lois never picks up hitchhikers, she felt herself compelled to stop.

The hitchhiker was dressed in jeans and a plaid shirt. He had long blond hair, brilliant blue eyes, and a very warm smile.

"I'm so glad you've come," he told Lois in a lyrical voice, as they pulled over. "We've been waiting for you." Both ladies were unaccountably entranced by the stranger.

Lois isn't sure what happened next. At some point, the car seemed to float off the road and move toward a large craft in the sky. She was overcome with fear, but the blond stranger began to sooth her by speaking in loving tones.

Suddenly Lois found that she was now inside the craft. She was surrounded by short entities with large eyes and separated from Gina. "Their mouths were straight lines that I never saw open," says Gina, "but I seemed to hear voices, perhaps by telepathy."

Lois was undressed, given a gown to wear, and told to lie on a table for a physical examination. "I obeyed everything they said without question," Lois said, "It was as if I had been hypnotized or something. I just did whatever they told me."

The aliens examined her much as Earth doctors had done, taking samples of blood, hair, and skin. Says Lois, "I had a sense that a lot of the tests had to do with my fertility, or lack of it."

Meanwhile, the ETs seemed interested not only in Lois's physical condition, but in her belongings. "They still seemed to be examining my clothing, my purse, everything that I had with me. I had been really nervous when the hitchhiker brought us aboard the space vehicle, but he kept saying over and over that Gina and I had nothing to fear, that they would not hurt us."

After being examined, Lois was taken to another room with a soft couch and a large window that looked out to the night sky. Colors and lights swirled past the window and Lois had the impression that they had traveled to another world.

An elderly man with a beard and wearing a robe entered the room. He told Lois that they had taken her aboard the craft because she was one of them, and that in the fullness of time she would remember who they are.

They had examined her to confirm that she was well, the man told her.

"What do you care about me?" she asked.

"Because you have the key."

"I have a key? What key do I have?"

"You will remember when the time is right."

Lois has no memory of what happened next. The next thing she knew, she and Gina woke up in her car, which was now off of the highway on a lonely desert road. Both felt thirsty and hungry.

When they returned to civilization, they found that five days had passed and that their family and friends were frantic with worry.

Years later, Gina refuses to discuss the experience and feels that it was a spiritual encounter that shouldn't be analyzed. Lois, however, remains disturbed and curious about what happened during the five days of missing time.

Following the encounter, Lois suffered from a severe poltergeist infestation, with telephones ringing, lights going on and off, and more. Both she and her daughter began having strange dreams. The activity increased to the point that they were forced to move."[8]

The Little Brothers

Barbara Benara (pseudonym) was very sick. She had just been diagnosed with ovarian cancer and was preparing to be treated for the disease. Only one week after diagnosis, however, she had a visitation with strange beings she calls "the little brothers." All her life, Benara was visited by mysterious entities who only came at night. The visits started around age seven. She always knew when they came as she would have a bloody nose afterward. She was frightened by the visits, but was always reassured and comforted by one of the beings who told her not to be afraid.

While the visitations continued, they were always at night, and she had only vague memories. That all changed in 1978 after her cancer diagnosis. She felt restless that evening, and was having trouble sleeping. Suddenly she woke up to find herself lying on a soft table in a white circular room. She was paralyzed, but strangely calm.

"You need our help," a voice said.

"Can I see you?" she asked.

The beings moved around to the front of the table. "There were four of them," said Benara, "all identical. They were three to four feet tall, ivory white, and had large almond shaped eyes."

A fifth taller being appeared and stared into Benara's eyes, telling her not to be afraid. It was the same being from her childhood. Benara next found herself immersed in an L-shaped tank. A long arm-like device came out and inserted itself inside her. "It wasn't painful," said Benara, "but it didn't feel comfortable. I had to relax and trust the voice that kept telling me not to be afraid."

The next thing she knew, it was morning. She was exhausted. Four days later, she went to her doctor and asked for more tests. To the shock of both her and her doctor, she now appeared to be cancer free. "They cured me of cancer," says Benara.

It wasn't her last encounter. Five years later, on November 25, 1992, Benara (now age forty) felt suddenly compelled to drive seven miles away from her home. She was confused and couldn't understand what had taken over her. It was now 8:30 p.m., and she realized that she had left her children unattended. The next thing she knew, the inside of her truck was freezing cold, it was now 10:30 p.m., and she was suffering from a nosebleed. She knew instantly what had happened. "I don't remember anything during almost two hours in my truck," she says, "but I know it was the little brothers."[9]

Another Cancer Healing

Fifteen minutes before midnight on November 19, 1980, Michael, an art teacher, and his wife, Mary, were driving home from Denver to Longmont, when they heard a loud swishing sound. At that moment, a beam of bright, blue light locked onto their car. The car lights dimmed, the radio failed, and the car suddenly levitated into the sky.

The next thing they knew, they were back on the highway, only it was now five minutes before 1:00 a.m.; they had lost one hour and ten minutes of time.

When they got home, Michael, who had several large melanomas on his legs, found that they were greatly reduced in size and coloration. Mary (who was two months pregnant) found an inexplicable rectangular mark on her abdomen. A few months later, she contracted streptococcal pneumonia. The doctors were concerned about the health of her baby, who ended up being born two months early, but healthy and normal.

In an effort to discover what happened during the missing time episode, Michael elected to undergo regressive hypnosis, though his wife, due to her illness, postponed any sessions.

Under hypnosis, Michael recalled that after being struck by the blue beam of light, the car was drawn up into a domed craft. Once inside, he smelled an electrical odor. Meanwhile, a gray-skinned being with a bald head, narrow chin, and wearing a shiny, gold uniform appeared and led them both into a brightly lit area. The being separated Michael from his wife. Michael was undressed, laid out on a table, and physically examined by a "floating light."

Michael's memories were pulled from his mind, and the beings told him that there are multiple dimensions co-existing with our own. The beings, who communicated via telepathy, returned Michael and Mary to their car, placed the car back on the road, moving at fifty-five mph and returned them to full conscious awareness.

The investigation, which was being conducted by the J. Allen Hynek Center for UFO Studies (CUFOS), was halted when Michael began to experience psychological conflicts about the event.

The case was also investigated by Linda Moulton Howe and Richard Sigismond. The husband told them that he disliked the aliens who abducted them. The wife agreed and said that they had examined her body in a way that left her enraged. She felt as though she had been violated or raped.[10]

"I Was Abducted"

It has taken him years to piece together his memories and dreams, but Mel (pseudonym) is now certain that in August 1981, while at St. Malo summer camp near Estes Park, he was abducted by aliens. He was on a campout with the other kids at the camp. Each of them were in two-man tents. Mel was restless as he tried to fall asleep. Suddenly he noticed a "very bright light" outside the tent. Says Mel, "I tried with all my might to wake up my sleeping companion. His eyes sprang open, but they were motionless. I mean, they stared straight out, as in death. I then heard the zipper of my tent open. I had thought at first it was one of the campers with us, but 'it' waved at me and I felt motionless. I felt no fear."

Standing in front of him was a four-foot-tall figure with two large bug-like eyes, no apparent nose, a slit for a mouth and almond colored skin. "I heard something in my head," says Mel. "Not a voice, but more like an emotion. As if by autopilot, I was motioned outside the tent by hand. I was surrounded by white light. I felt a pinch on my arm."

At this point, Mel felt strange new emotions, as though he was somehow genetically unique and different from others, and that he needed to be specially watched. He experienced a period of missing time, and the next thing he realized, he was being carried back to his tent and set down where he had been sleeping hours earlier. It was now early morning. The next morning, he reported what he could remember to camp authorities and learned that he wasn't the only one who had complained about strange events.

Later Mel moved to Alaska where he had more experiences. He found a mark on his arm that "I cannot explain or remember otherwise."[11]

Time Travel

An unusual Boulder case comes from a letter written to Whitley Strieber by a Native American woman. Growing up in South Dakota, she began to experience unusual encounters with apparent ETs. When she moved to Boulder, the encounters continued, including an incident involving what appears to be time travel.

One day, Cora (pseudonym) woke up in her backyard to see a strange vehicle. She climbed into her assigned seat, and looking out the windows, the landscape blurred before her. Suddenly it was nighttime outside. The ship landed on a prairie next to a log house. Cora was surprised to see a husband, wife, and their two children, each of them dressed in old-fashioned clothes from American Pioneer times.

Cora was surprised to find herself participating in the abduction of the pioneer woman. One of the ETs (who had a hooded appearance) said that "she would have to leave with them if she was to live."

They pulled the woman into the vehicle, which took off up into the sky. Writes Cora, "Next thing I knew, I'm looking down on her house and watching her husband and children as they come home. I can tell he's calling for her. As I watch him head into the house, the children looked up and saw the vehicle we're all sitting in, but by that time the husband was in a panic because he couldn't find his wife. We watched as they looked all over the area around the house and into the forest a bit. But then we left."

Cora doesn't know what happened to the pioneer woman as she was dropped off back at her home in Boulder.

On another occasion, around 1982, Cora woke up to find that it was light outside. Thinking she must have overslept, she walked downstairs to find the back door unlocked and open. She closed and locked it only to find a little boy in her home. They played together for a short while, and afterward the boy left, promising Cora that they would meet again. Cora was surprised to find that morning had still not arrived and she went back to bed.

The unusual events continued. One evening Cora woke to hear the sound of somebody in their kitchen. Her parents weren't home and she was the oldest sibling, so it was her duty to investigate. She looked to the kitchen area. "All I saw," she said, "was a shadow that then took off into my brother's room." She ran after it into the room. The window was wide open. She looked out the window, but didn't see anyone. Her brother, however, reports seeing the same shadowy figure as it ran through his room and out the window.

Cora's encounters continue.[12]

Missing Time in Denver

On July 13, 1987, a man, his fiancée, and their two children were traveling to meet his wife's sister in Denver. It was a cloudy day, around noon, when the wife looked to her right and saw a reddish-orange globe that appeared to be pacing their car along the highway.

"It's following us," she told her soon-to-be husband.

"No, it's just the sun," he replied.

They continued driving until the sky began to clear of clouds. The sun, they now saw, was on the left side of their car.

"Look, there's the sun," she said.

"You're right," he said.

"So what is that?" she asked, pointing to the red globe of light which still seemed to be pacing them. Suddenly the object moved to the left side of the road and started to descend. They quickly approached the object, which they now saw was "as big as a stadium."

They both became very excited and anxious. The wife turned to wake up the kids. "As I turned," she said, "it seemed like slow motion. The kids were asleep. When I turned back, it was gone."

"What happened to it?" she asked.

"I don't know," he replied.

They looked all around them, but all signs of the UFO were gone. They pulled over at the first gas station and asked the attendant about the giant orange object down the road. Nobody at the gas station had seen it. It was then that they both noticed that their watches were one hour behind.

Baffled by the experience, they made a point to check out the area on their return trip to their home in Omaha, Nebraska. Unfortunately, there was no evidence that they could find of their encounter. Once at home, they decided to call Offutt Air Force Base to report their encounter to Project Blue Book. The officer at the base informed them that Project Blue Book had been shut down years ago, but that there was somebody else that she could talk to. She reported the encounter in detail.

Following this, the wife went to the hospital for a health issue. She was approached by a man claiming to be a doctor who wanted to hypnotize her. She refused and complained about him to the other doctors. None of them, however, knew who the mysterious doctor was.

"When I got home from the hospital," says the wife, "a woman called to make an appointment with this doctor. I said no. She was very insistent, so I hung the phone up. She called back saying I better come in. I unplugged the phone."

Strange events continued. The wife woke up one morning to see a black figure with a long head standing in the shadows of her hallway. She couldn't believe what she was seeing, and turned to wake up her husband. "My man was awake," says the wife, "and he was just staring at it. It ran down the stairs. You could hear the stairs creak."

"Did you see that?" she asked him.

"Yes," he replied.

They both described what they saw; their descriptions matched exactly.

"The kids!" she screamed. Her fiancé jumped up to check the kids, who were fine. They checked the whole house. All the doors were locked and the windows closed. "I have always wondered about this," she says, "and will never forget it. Someone please tell me something."[13]

A Totally Different Place

Late one evening in March 1989, twelve-year-old Melissa (pseudonym) had one of the strangest experiences of her life. She had fallen asleep on the couch of her home in Centennial. She woke up to find that the television had gone to static. She got up to turn it off when suddenly it switched back on by itself and continued to display static. Looking around, Melissa saw a "bright light" in the backyard.

At this point, she lost consciousness. Says Melissa, "I woke up sprawled out on the stairs between the main floor and the second floor with no idea how I got there." She has vague memories of talking and shouting before suddenly losing consciousness again.

"I woke up in my bed with no idea how I got there, and then lost consciousness."

When she woke up again, Melissa now found herself sitting on the toilet in the bathroom on the second floor. "I had no idea how I got there, and had total amnesia."

Interspersed with her memories from that night came other memories. "I had memories of coming from a totally different place, in a cavern, surrounded by strange beings, who told me that I had a different name than the one I was born with."

At some point, Melissa recalls being returned to her body, and sliding inside it. When she woke up, she had no memory of who or where she was, and it took a few moments for her to recall her identity and location.

There were other bizarre effects. Says Melissa, "I felt very ill, as if I had been placed in an oven and my insides cooked. My guts and intestines felt hot to me."

The next day she remained shaken, but was fine enough to attend school. She had no idea what happened and wondered if she had experienced some bizarre psychological event or weird dream. However, a few months later, it happened again, without amnesia. She recalled being taken from her body, back to the table in the cavern, where she was surrounded by "strange creatures" who examined her. The effects of the encounter were identical to the first time. "After I woke up," says Melissa, "I felt very ill again, as if my insides were heated up.[14]

Memory Loss in Colorado Springs

Serena (pseudonym) was nine years old when she had an incredible close-up encounter involving amnesia in Colorado Springs. It was the summer of 1989, and she was with her mother at the house of her mother's boyfriend. When the boyfriend and mother got into an argument, Serena and her mother decided to walk back to their home only a few blocks away. It was around 3:00 a.m., as the two walked hand-in-hand. They were approaching their trailer park when suddenly the landscape around them became lit up from above.

Says Serena, "We stopped and looked up, and directly above us was a large round craft."

She never saw it arrive. Suddenly it was just there, hovering about thirty feet overhead. It was utterly motionless and gray in color. It had three white lights in a triangle, with rows of orange and green lights around the perimeter. The bottom of the craft had tubing, grills, and other strange devices. Serena and her mother stood still and watched it.

At this point Serena felt "a familiar happiness." Suddenly her memory ends. "Next thing I knew," she says, "me and my mother were walking up the porch steps to our trailer."

Serena was baffled and confused. Her mother put the key in the door, looked down at Serena and asked, "Did we just see what I think we saw?"

"Yes," Serena nodded her head.

"We shouldn't tell anybody," her mother said. "Don't ever talk about it."

"The next day it ended up being all over the radio and television news that somewhere around 200 people had been calling in UFO sightings all throughout the night, many of whom lived in our general area of the city."[15]

I Was on a Craft

John Smith doesn't want his name to be used. He is a retired US Air Force crew chief who served at Altus Air Force Base in Oklahoma as chief on the KC-135 tanker. In 1991, he moved with his family to Colorado Springs to serve his military reserve requirements at Peterson Air Force Base. At 1:00 a.m. one evening in November 1991, he saw a large, silent triangular craft move at an altitude of 250 feet above his home, heading toward Fort Carson. Afraid to go outside, he watched the craft from the window of his home. It was completely silent, the size of a jumbo jet, and its bottom was crisscrossed with a series of intersecting I-beams creating a geometric diamond-like pattern. "It was just completely out of this world," he says.

Following the low fly-over by the UFO, the Smiths began to experience inexplicable electrical problems in their home. Lights started to go on and off by themselves. The microwave beeped for no apparent reason. Then one evening their Christmas lights began flashing on and off, and they weren't even plugged in.

The Smiths decided to go out shopping. On their way back, they saw what appeared to be the same craft again. At first it looked like a helicopter, but as they approached, they saw it was the triangular craft.

"At a stoplight I'm looking under the thing, and it's sitting right there about 200-250 feet above the ground, on an open lot right next to a Wendy's restaurant. My daughter saw it, I saw it, and my wife saw it. And it just sat there motionless. There was a blue light on one tip of the triangle, a red light in the middle, and white lights on each corner."

John turned to his eight-year-old daughter. "What does that look like to you?" he asked.

"Daddy, that looks like a big triangle."

"Yeah," said John. "You are absolutely right. That's exactly what it is."

All three of them were amazed. "My wife was dumbfounded," says John. "She couldn't believe it."

Then came the "dream." About a month or two later, John had what he first thought was a dream, but now believes may have been an encounter. "It was very vivid," he says, "like I was right there. And I was on a craft that looked like a circular room. The people in it were hybrid-looking. They looked human, but kind of alien and kind of not. I really can't describe it. Their heads were bigger, and the eyes farther apart. Other than that, they looked human—I remember one that had kind of orangish-blond hair. My biggest question was: What was your method of propulsion?"

As a crew chief, John was uniquely qualified to comprehend engine design. After asking the question, John was surprised by the response. "He showed me a light—a pure white light. And they said, 'This is our method of propulsion.'"[16]

Four Hours Gone

Missing time can come swiftly and without warning. On the evening of March 29, 1994, three brothers from Rifle drove to town to check on their dog who was at the local shelter. Says one of the brothers, "As we were going up the road behind our home, there was a red flash of light. Then the car slowly pulled into the driveway, and we had lost four hours. It felt like we were gone only twenty minutes."[17]

The Experiences of Connie Isele

Connie Isele moved to Divide in 1994. Formerly from Sacramento, California, Isele has had UFO experiences her entire life. They have plagued her family for generations. Her experiences continued in Colorado, where she continued to experience missing time, waking up with bruises and cuts, and more. Her daughter reports the same things. Most recently Isele had a period of missing time and woke up missing a patch of hair. Says Isele, "It's scary, but because of it I learned a lot about myself, and the world, and in that sense I wouldn't wish that it didn't happen. Before I'd find all these excuses, psychologically, for what's going on. Now I'm looking at it as reality."[18]

Red Feather Lakes Encounter

One evening in February 1995, Scott, a professional health worker, was driving home from his place of employment in Red Feather Lakes when he noticed his headlights weren't functioning. He felt strangely disoriented.

Suddenly he noticed a cupcake-shaped UFO hovering over the local schoolhouse. It was 500 feet in diameter and had a raised disk on the top. He thought to himself: "That looks like a UFO. What is that doing there?"

He had been on Hiawatha Road. The next thing he knew, he was on Red Feather Lakes Road and was thinking to himself that he was about to see a UFO up ahead.

At some point, he began to "receive" information about how the craft's engines worked. "The bottom of the UFO had opposing rows of magnets running simultaneously, one group going clockwise, and the next group running counterclockwise." He also received the impression that the top dome part of the object was "the observation area."

As he drove by the object, Scott's memory of the event became jumbled. At some point, he remembered looking up through his windshield to see the object hovering directly over his truck. He remembered seeing the UFO from an angle where there were no roads. According to his recollection, he never stopped driving.

"As I was driving to and away from the UFO, time seemed to stop. The UFO shot away at a sharply upward and oblique angle going in a southwest direction. In a blink, it was gone. I saw it shrink into a dot in less than a second and disappear. I don't remember any noises. My sense of time was all shot to hell during this whole experience. At times I seemed to be in fast-forward, and at other times, I was in very slow motion."

When Scott arrived home, it was close to midnight. He normally arrived home at 10:00 p.m., and this time was unable to account for two hours of time. He has no memory of any ET contact, and although he was frightened to see the UFO hover over his truck, he felt that the experience was "a good one."[19]

Mountain Man Encounter

As investigated by Christopher O'Brien, Larry Williams is a "mountain man" who lives in a small trailer at 9,000 feet of elevation in the Sangre de Cristos Mountains, in a remote area in the Rio Grande National Forest and Wilderness Area. Williams told O'Brien that throughout June and July 1995, he observed strange lights on "an almost nightly basis." He also noticed increased helicopter activity, and even more strange, the water level in a local stream rose and fell inexplicably. Strangest of all, in early August he found a large number of animal skeletons on his property including elk, deer, fox, raccoon, and cattle, a problem he had been dealing with for more than a year.

The strangeness continued. "I've been waking up at exactly 2:00 a.m., and seeing lights pretty near every night since June," said Williams. "We've found little, tiny four-toed tracks walking around the perimeter of my place."

August 15, 1995, he was returning home after visiting a town when he saw another strange light. Seeing the light approach, he grabbed his camera and began snapping photos. It was 8:45 p.m. when he took sixteen photos in a row as the object moved directly overhead. As he took the sixteenth picture, he could see that the light was actually a large boomerang-shaped craft, which now appeared to be hovering overhead.

Suddenly, Williams realized that the craft was gone. He looked at his watch and saw that more than a half-hour had elapsed. He was unable to account for about thirty-five minutes of time. Confused, he exited his truck and found that it was now sitting "six inches away from its tracks." It looked as though his truck had been lifted up and set a half-foot to the side. The tops of the trees nearby had been sheared off sixty feet high. Not only was his truck moved, but his bulldozer and trailer were moved the same distance.

Williams also discovered a strange mark on his body, a four-inch-wide wart, which had to be surgically removed.

On the same evening that Williams reported his missing-time encounter, a family near the area, heading east on Highway 160, saw an extremely bright ball of light surrounded by helicopters.

The day following Williams' encounter, a dozen helicopters flew at low level over his home, and then his trailer was broken into and ransacked. The intruder was apparently interested in his photographic equipment; his film and camera equipment had all been stolen. "I am positive they were looking for those pictures I took the night before," said Williams.

Over the next two weeks, Williams reported a weight loss of twenty pounds. He also noticed that his "pet black bear" was missing.

Williams called local authorities who conducted a brief investigation. Williams found further evidence of intruders in the form of boot-tracks, cigarette butts, and a mirror that had been moved from its mounting. O'Brien spoke with authorities who confirmed the robbery and also told him that they had received reports from other people of strange lights in the area. Williams said that his photos showed the light and the craft, and some of them showed a strange "post" and other images that he did not remember taking.

O'Brien was unable to investigate further as other researchers heard about the case and revealed Williams' true name and identity. Williams cut off all contact with investigators and refused to talk any further about his experiences.[20]

Alien Dreams

August 22, 1997, three witnesses observed two lights over the Rio Grande area, immediately north of New Mexico. The lights looked like "huge car headlights." They watched for about ten minutes, during which time they saw a third light, large and golden-colored to the south over the state border.

Christopher O'Brien spoke with the witnesses, one of who told him that on the evening of the sighting, he went to bed and "knew they were coming back" to get him. That night he had a lucid dream during which he remembered being "taken out through the window and aboard a small ship," where he saw "aliens," and then was taken "up to a larger ship." The dreams continued for three nights in a row, convincing the witness that he had been truly contacted.[21]

A Plain-Clothes Alien?

July 7, 1998, Tracy, her friend Carol (pseudonyms), and Carol's two children, decided to travel to the parks outside of north Denver to observe the buffalo herd kept there. They spent the day there and around sunset were picnicking outside when Tracy noticed somebody looking at the sky. "I looked west toward the setting sun," said Tracy, "and thought at first I was watching an airplane. But then I realized it was round, metallic, and very bright."

Tracy pointed the object out to her friend, Carol. At this point, the object began to skip across the sky, darting back and forth at high speeds. Frightened, several of the people around them began to pack up and leave. They joined the rush to escape and quickly left the area.

For some reason, instead of taking the interstate, they decided to take the slower scenic route back to Denver. "It was a weird decision," says Tracy, "because the freeway was right there."

As they drove down the road, a strange phenomenon occurred: Outlines of fluorescent, olive-green, geometric patterns appeared in front of the car, coming in waves. The children became frightened when the adults were unable to identify what was happening.

Suddenly they came upon a switchback to find a man standing there. "He was in plain clothes," said Tracy, "and he was just watching us. We drove by him. I couldn't get a good look at his eyes, but he was so very still."

Finally, they reached the end of the scenic route, only to find that it was now nighttime. In addition, the brakes had to be replaced, which made no sense as new brakes had been installed less than a week earlier.

Once at home, they were surprised to see several helicopters fly over the house. Following the incident, the children had a series of dreams about that night. Tracy and Carol, however, "just kind of laughed about it, but we don't know what really happened, or what we saw."[22]

Confused on Highway 106

As investigated by Christopher O'Brien, following a number of sightings in the area, on October 8, 1998, a female witness was driving east near Mount Blanca on Highway 160 in the San Luis Valley when she saw an amber-colored light in the shape of a half-circle hovering above the mountains. When the object jumped upwards, the witness pulled over to observe.

At this point, she became confused. She believes she had watched the object for several minutes, but became disoriented when she experienced a memory lapse. The next thing she knew, the craft was flying directly over her car. She could now see a "triangle-shaped array of white and amber lights" beneath the object, which quickly moved away.[23]

The Abductions of Tim

In 1998, Edward Burke, a field investigator and director for Colorado MUFON reported on the case of Tim, a lifelong abductee from Colorado Springs. While the details of his case were not revealed, Burke shared that Tim suffers from chronic fatigue, and wakes up with "ugly bruises" on his body. Tim told investigators that he has been repeatedly threatened by strange women, that he and two friends witnessed the recovery of a "meteorite," which caused burns on their hands and arms, and that he believes he has a tiny object, possibly an implant, in his cheek. Burke says that Tim's case is one of the most unusual he has ever researched.[24]

Missing Time in Bailey

One summer evening in 1999, Taylor and his friends were camping at Lost Park campground in Bailey. Around 1:00 a.m., they were all surprised to see a "bright reddish light" hovering almost at ground level about a half-mile away. They decided to leave the campfire and investigate. As they approached they saw that the object was actually above the trees. It cast down a "reddish-orange-purple" light, which varied in intensity. It was totally silent. They watched it for about ten minutes until it suddenly "shot into the sky at speeds I didn't think were possible."

"The next part is what really scares me even to this day," says Scott. "We went back to the campfire and started to talk about what we just saw . . . when I looked at my watch, it was 4:00 a.m. Somehow three hours had gone by without anyone noticing . . . what was literally a ten-minute experience was actually three hours in real time. I just can't explain it."

While Taylor and his friends had been drinking, he feels certain that this doesn't account for the missing time. "We all experienced the same thing," he says.[25]

Mummy Mountain Encounter

In June of 1999, two friends decided to go camping and climb to the peak of Mummy Mountain outside Estes. They were camping 500 feet from the summit when one of them woke to urinate. While outside the tent, he saw what appeared to be a person walking toward them with a flashlight from the summit. He woke up his friend and warned him that somebody was coming. They were nervous, as they had not gotten a permit to camp there.

The light approached to within a hundred feet at which point it "went straight up from the ground, vertically into the air, and we watched this thing fly out of sight. It was just a white circular orb . . . "

The two men became overcome with fear. They found themselves having a strange hazy feeling, as though they had been drugged. They had trouble speaking and crawled into their tent where they fell into a deep sleep.

The next morning, they were climbing down the mountain when four men wearing army camouflage uniforms and riding horses appeared behind them and followed them down the mountain, staying about 150 feet behind them. Finally, one of the army men approached the climbers and asked, "How are you guys doing? Are you guys okay?"

"Yes," they answered. The army men followed the climbers for the next six hours until they reached the base of the trail. They got in the car and found that the radio wouldn't turn off and was randomly changing stations.

When they got home, one of the climbers noticed a "very strange diamond-shape" mark on his shoulder. He said that he had a dream that aliens had taken a chunk out of his arm. Following the experience, whenever he walks under a streetlight, it flashes off.[26]

Healed by a UFO

On December 29, 1999, Natalie (pseudonym) was driving down 13th Street in Denver on her way home when she saw a strange-looking object hovering very low in the sky ahead of her. It was rock-still, with two blue lights on the outside, and a red light in the center. It couldn't be a plane, because the lights were too still. It must be a helicopter, she thought. Then she drove under it, and changed her mind.

"As I passed under the object, I saw a grayish-black boomerang-shaped object. My mouth hung open, and I said aloud to myself, 'What in the #@*!% is that?'"

She wanted to slam on the brakes and jump out of her car, but seeing other vehicles behind her, she turned off at the next street, pulled over, and got out. Only thirty seconds had passed, but the object was now gone. She pulled a U-turn and kept looking. She turned around a third time, but the object was nowhere to be found.

Convinced she saw a genuine UFO, she reported her sighting to NUFORC, and also reported it to a MUFON investigator. Not long after the sighting, Natalie began to exhibit a number of alarming medical symptoms. Says Natalie, "About two months after my encounter, all of the moles on my body began to fade, then completely disappear. To date, five moles have completely disappeared, and nine more are in different states of fading. About five months after the event occurred, all of the hair on my arms and legs began to change to light blonde."

Normally Natalie had brown hair. She thought perhaps she was turning prematurely gray, but she's only twenty-nine years old. The hair changed color from the root upwards, turning from brown, to reddish, to blond over a period of about five days. The hair also became much finer.

Natalie had suffered from spider veins in her legs for several years. "About two months ago," she says, "my spider veins in my legs began to fade. Now one that I have had for about five years is completely gone, and another is fading rapidly."

Then came the "dreams." Says Natalie, "Since this has occurred, I have had 'dreams' almost nightly of entities who talk to me and claim to be an intelligent species from somewhere else. They keep trying to give me strange information I don't understand. I have woken up a few times and caught myself uttering some language that I have never heard before. But I have ruled out speaking in tongues because this 'language' seems to have structure and form."

Natalie has also noticed other changes. "Throughout the day I have feelings of hot and cold in different parts of my body. I get pulsating feelings on the bottom of my feet and up my legs and down my arms and on the palms of my hands. Sometimes this pulsating becomes so intense, it is painful. I have also felt this heat/pulsating feeling right below my eyes, between my eyes, and in the front of my brain. I am very upset and confused as to what is going on with me."

Natalie is hoping to work with more investigators to deal with the effects of her encounter.[27]

Trucker Abducted

In March 2001, Judy Messoline, owner of the UFO Watchtower, was visited by a truck driver and his wife seeking help about a suspected UFO abduction. Writes Messoline, "He remembered traveling 285 toward Saguache when he saw a bright light in the sky. All of a sudden, the light was in front of his truck. He remembers slowing down and starting to pull over to avoid hitting whatever it was. The next thing he remembered was driving 285 past Saguache toward Monte Vista. When he got to Monte Vista's Truckstop he starting filling out his logbook . . . he was missing four hours. From that time on he was claustrophobic in his truck and was having violent nightmares."[28]

The Saga of Stan Romanek

On September 20, 2001, Stan Romanek was working as the assistant manager of a retail store in Denver. Shortly before closing time, several customers ran inside saying that a UFO was floating outside. Romanek ran outside and with several others observed a large glowing sphere about thirty feet across, hovering a few hundred feet over the building. Suddenly it shot straight up.

Romanek was shocked. It was the third sighting he had had in less than a year. Months earlier he and a group of other people sighted a metallic object at Red Rocks Park. He came upon several parked cars with people looking up at a shiny metal object with rotating spheres. He kept driving and was shocked when the object followed his van. Remembering he had a video camera with him, he pulled over and started to film it when the object suddenly darted away.

A few months later, Romanek was traveling across the US by car with two friends when they all saw "a classic disk," which made several appearances during the trip and appeared to be following them. During one appearance, they pulled over and observed the object with binoculars. The object followed them through two-and-a-half states, darting in and out of clouds and playing a cat-and-mouse game of peek-a-boo before disappearing for good. Or so Romanek thought. Now, as he exited his place of employment in Denver and saw the sphere hovering above the building, he began to wonder what was going on.

That evening he had his first abduction experience. Around 2:30 a.m., he woke up to hear knocking on the front door. He found his sister in a trance, standing at the front door, which was open. Three figures walked inside. They were skinny, short, with large almond-shaped eyes and massive heads with thin white hair. He thought at first they were wearing masks. When he realized they weren't, he became consumed by fear. They began to lead him through the house. He fought with them, and suddenly fell unconscious. His next memory was waking up the next morning.

He thought it all must have been a dream until he discovered strange marks on his body. He had scoop marks on his back, abrasions on his wrists and ankles. The wounds healed quickly but fluoresced under a blacklight for weeks.

In addition, Romanek's sister said she recalled having a dream where three strange men dressed in pinstripe suits had woken her up by knocking on the front door.

Two days after the visitation, on September 22, 2001, Romanek saw a glowing ball of light following his van. The object was also viewed from his friends who were sitting in the park waiting for Romanek to arrive.

One week later, on September 30, 2001, Romanek was driving home when he saw the UFO again. He pulled over and began filming. Soon a crowd of people gathered and all watched the object until it darted away.

Romanek released his footage to the media and soon started receiving phone threats. He decided to go under hypnosis to explore the visitation incident. Under hypnosis, he recalled being taken into a rounded room where he was held to the wall by copper-colored bands around his wrists and ankles. Blue-white light lit the room. In the center was a strangely-shaped doctor's table.

He was consumed with fear. One of the beings told him, "It's okay. You need to calm down."

The beings examined him. Romanek peppered them with questions, but the only answers he received were unintelligible images and symbols in his mind. One of the beings told him, "Something significant is about to happen," then filled his mind with images of natural disasters, "images of winds so strong, they scoured the roads and highways off the Earth, and tidal waves covering entire cities; there were fires everywhere—the whole planet seemed to be in convulsions as disaster after disaster overtook it."

It was following this regression, that Romanek began writing strange alien symbols and long complex mathematical equations. It was strange, as he had never been a great student, and the equations looked extremely advanced.

From this point, Romanek's case started to increase in complexity. His wife, Lisa, started receiving letters from a secret informant who claimed to have information about Romanek's case. Romanek examined his past and remembered at least three separate incidents in which he was visited by a very strange woman with huge, blue, almond-shaped eyes.

In their home they started to hear strange sounds and see little balls of light darting around. Romanek began to wake up to discover he had been writing equations in his sleep. The equations, he later learned, were accurate representations of chemical elements and astrophysics.

More abductions began to occur. On November 17, 2002, Romanek woke up to find himself sleeping in his backyard. All the doors were locked. There was no way he could've gotten out by himself and locked the doors. He had a bloody nose and new scoop marks on his back. At the side of the house, they found large circular impressions on the grass. He had intense pain in his chest.

They went to the doctor who told him that it appeared his rib had been cut and re-set. It was baffling, as there was no sign of incision where it looked like he had had surgery. They took samples of the soil where the grass had been swirled. The scientist studying the sample said that the soil appeared to be exposed to a microwave-like energy.

In the months that followed, they saw more UFOs outside their home. In April 2003, Romanek saw somebody peeking inside his window. After it happened several times, and he was unable to catch the peeping Tom, he set up a surveillance system.

Romanek was able to catch videotape of the visitor who turned out to be a gray-type alien. Romanek's videotape was one of the few instances in which an ET has been caught on videotape, and it caused a sensation in the UFO community. But as the visitations continued, Romanek was able to capture further footage. Soon it became clear that the ETs were allowing him to photograph them. On one occasion, their camera went missing. When they found it, they were shocked to see two images of an alien who had apparently taken a selfie!

The visitations continued. One time he was returned to his bedroom wearing a woman's nightie. His wife, Lisa, confirmed that it was not hers.

Romanek had an implant removed from his body, which was studied by scientists. They were shocked to find that the implant produced a solution that appeared to be a type of amino acid used to coat artificial joints and pacemakers so that the body wouldn't reject them. The implant appeared to have an internal structure that was only discernable by electron microscope.

As time went on, Romanek gathered more evidence, including photographs of ETs lurking outside his house and more complex equations. On May 4, 2006, he fell from a ladder and badly injured his leg. A short time later, he was abducted and healed of his injury. Again, the ETs left visible landing marks in the backyard.

By now, Romanek's case was garnering considerable attention within the UFO field and also by apparent government agents. While he was receiving offers to speak about his encounters, he was also being continually harassed and threatened.

He received more channeled messages warning of future disasters, messages warning of a profound shift in human consciousness.

Romanek wrote three books about his experiences. His wife also wrote a book. The case has become one of the best documented within the UFO literature, containing multiple eyewitness testimonies, medical evidence, landing trace evidence, implant evidence, photographic evidence, and more.

In 2014, Romanek was accused by the Department of Homeland Security of trafficking in child pornography. Romanek and his family vehemently deny the charges. They claim that he is innocent and is being framed by the secret government who is upset about the fact that he continues to display his physical evidence of his UFO encounters. The outcome of the trial is still pending.[29]

The Missing Wife

Around 10:00 p.m. on the evening of June 5 2002, Judy (pseudonym) of Federal Heights decided to take a nighttime walk around the small lake in Bell Roth Park near her home. Judy was on the east side of the lake when she saw three orange lights performing aerial maneuvers. They appeared to be heading toward her. Soon they were over her head and getting closer. Says Judy, "I was terrified and I began looking for a place to hide. I ran toward the children's playground at the base of the berm. One of the objects emitted a white beam of light. The beam switched off and the lights were gone."

Judy returned back home to find her husband frantic. "Where have you been?" he asked, and told her that he had just walked around the lake three times looking for her. Says Judy, "I was confused and felt like I'd been drugged."[30]

Hunter Abducted

In the middle of July 2002, Messoline received a brief but remarkable report of a possible UFO abduction. Says Messoline: "I had a young man walk into the shop; he was hanging his head and very quietly said, 'I think I was abducted.' He proceeded to tell me that he had been hunting last fall over by Gunnison. He had laid down to rest on a rock with his rifle across his chest. He remembers looking down at the trees around him. He felt like he had a bit of amnesia. When he came out of it, he was missing three hours. The gun that was laying across his chest was found about twenty feet away."[31]

Two Nederland Abductions

Located high in the Rockies at 8,200 feet of elevation is the small town of Nederland, population 1,500. On August 18, 2003, Dennis X was camping with his friend, Jason, and both their families on Caribou Mountain just north of Nederland. They had set up camp high on the slope of the mountain, just below the snowcap near the summit. After dinner, they were sitting around the campfire drinking hot chocolate and making s'mores for the children.

Suddenly Jason cried out, "What the hell is that?"

Dennis turned and looked. "I observed a glowing object rising out of the mountains, going straight up. I instantly tried to determine what this object was, but when it stopped above the mountaintops and started pulsing different colors (red, blue, green, orange, yellow), I didn't know what I was seeing. Everybody was mesmerized and all camping activities stopped as we watched the object meander its way higher and higher in the sky until it was over our heads almost straight above us at an unknown altitude. Then it stopped, started hovering, and the colored pulsing became faster and brighter."

At this point, things went from strange to bizarre. The object emitted about ten red lights, which lined up in a row to the left. Says Dennis, "As the main object remained stationary and continued to pulse the rainbow colors, the red objects began to dart about the sky in ways I've never seen any aircraft move. Some seemed to be chasing each other; some seemed to go off by themselves flying erratically . . . it seemed as if they were playing like children in the playground, running around their mother."

Anyone who had a cellphone or camera pulled it out and tried to take pictures. But as it was nighttime and the objects were darting about, they were unable to get any photos.

They did have a pair of binoculars that they passed around to observe the objects. For the next few hours, the objects remained overhead. Finally, the red objects lined up to the left of the main object and returned back inside it in the same manner they had exited.

The main object slowed down its pulsing and slowly descended just behind the peak of Caribou Mountain, not far from their campsite. Holding the binoculars, Dennis began to walk up and around the mountain.

"What are you doing?" somebody shouted. "Don't go over there!" said somebody else. By this point, the kids were frightened and hiding in their tents. Says Dennis, "I admit I was scared to death too, but the curiosity I felt was overwhelming. I had to see what this thing was. As I rounded the mountain, the object was still there hovering. I stopped and tried to get a look through the binoculars . . . I could see the hull of the craft through the glow. There were no lights that I could see; it was as if the hull itself was glowing. It was silent, no sound at all. I was now within fifty feet of this thing.

"As I inched closer and closer," says Dennis, "every hair on my body began to stand on end. Then the object moved further around the mountain just out of view, and my hair laid back down. I walked a little farther, bringing the object back in view; my hair stood back up, and then suddenly the craft came directly toward me and flew right over my head within twenty feet or so. That scared the crap out of me, and I screamed out loud as the object passed over me without a sound.

"Oddly, the next thing I remember is standing next to the campfire, everyone sleeping in their tents, and the sun coming up. I climbed into my tent and went to sleep."

Dennis isn't sure what happened, if he was abducted or not. There were eight people there that night, but they spoke about it only a few times among themselves. When they shared it with others, they were "scoffed at and laughed at like we were all crazy."

Dennis eventually reported his case to MUFON, writing, "One thing is for sure, what we saw that night changed my life forever, and I'm sure the same goes for everyone that was there. Although I don't have any evidence of our encounter, I think about it every single day . . . I do have nightmares about things that are hard to admit, but it's just something I've learned to live with."

Two years later, another UFO abduction occurred in the same area. It was July 15, 2005, and twenty-year-old Jay (pseudonym) decided to go camping with two friends in Nederland. They found an attractive spot about three miles out of town, and then set up a tent and started a fire. They talked long into the night about various subjects. Suddenly one of them shouted, "Holy sh-t! Look! Look at that!" He pointed to a bright glowing sphere.

Jay looked up and saw a bright white light tinged with red and purple. They were amazed but became very confused about what happened next. Says Jay, "The next thing I knew, we were all sitting around the campfire as before. I felt very tired all of a sudden. I looked at my watch and it was 6:00 a.m. I felt dumbfounded. It seemed like I just checked my watch and it was 2:50 a.m. I went to bed. The next morning, we discussed it [and] no one could explain the missing three-something hours. We all knew we had witnessed something."

Jay found himself deeply affected by the encounter. "In the weeks after the event," he says, "I must have gone over it in my mind a million times. I couldn't find any answers, and I put it out of my mind. It's only recently that I've been researching what happened that night . . . I believe my companions and I were abducted by aliens."

Jay is interested in undergoing hypnotic regression in the hopes of finding out what happened, but at the same time, he feels some trepidation. He tried to contact his friends to see what they recall, but he had lost touch with them and was unable to find them.[32]

"Where Is She?"

One evening in March 2006, Clay (pseudonym) was with his sister and her boyfriend at the Sunnyvale condominium complex in Longmont. Around 11:00 p.m., he went on the balcony to smoke a cigarette when he saw what he first thought was a plane. But as he looked at it closer, it started to look strange. He began to wonder if he was seeing a UFO.

He rushed inside and called his sister, accidentally waking up her boyfriend who became angry. Together Clay and his sister went outside to observe the object. It now appeared much larger than a plane, it was moving too slowly and was way too low in the sky. It looked weirdly flat and had blue and orange lights. When it moved directly over their condo, they ran from the balcony, through the house, and out the front door. Again they woke up her boyfriend, who again became angry.

They watched it from the front door and noticed that it was so large it blocked out the stars from the sky. They watched it move slowly for about fifteen minutes when a green light came on, all the other lights went out, and the object moved out of sight.

After the object went away, Clay and his sister returned inside. She went to bed, and Clay retired to his bedroom.

About ten minutes later, Clay heard the boyfriend running through the house. Finally, he stormed angrily into Clay's bedroom. "Where is she?" he demanded.

"My sister?" Clay asked, confused.

"Duh? Where did she go?"

"She went to bed ten minutes ago."

Now the boyfriend was confused. He returned to her bedroom and found Clay's sister. Says Clay, "She was on the floor next to the bed in a disoriented state."

"Where were you?" the boyfriend asked.

"Here in bed," she said, not realizing that she was actually lying on the floor.

Clay is not certain, but he wonders if his sister was abducted by the UFO that had just passed over their home.[33]

Marked by Aliens

Around 2:00 a.m. on October 16, 2008, Anna (pseudonym) had left her place of employment and was driving to her home in Fort Collins. As she arrived, she was surprised to see a giant orange orb hovering between the tops of two trees. She stopped her car and observed. "It seemed to hover for such a long time," she says, "then it moved up and away across the street." The object continued moving off to the east and out of view.

Anna went inside and found her twenty-five-year-old son sleeping on the couch in front of the television. He woke up and together they watched television until about 4:30 a.m., then they both went to bed.

In the morning, Anna was woken up by her son. "My arm is burning," he told her, and asked her to look at it. Says Anna, "He had three marks on it like pods that were raised in the shape of a triangle."

The mark was no surprise to Anna. She revealed to her son that she also experienced the same mark, and had a long history of UFO encounters. In the early 1990s, while living in the Fort Morgan area, she saw a triangular craft, had a visitation with two beings in her home, and experienced a "missing fetus."

In 2005, Anna's daughter became pregnant. During the pregnancy, Anna was shocked to see the same mark on her daughter's body. Her daughter had a healthy baby boy. When Anna's grandson was three years old, Anna saw that he also had the same triangular mark.

Many times, said Anna, UFOs have followed her car from a distance.

After her son's mark appeared in October 2008, he complained that it ached and itched. Says Anna, "It was hard to prevent him from scratching it until it bled. I kept telling him to leave it alone until it finally disappeared. I had to calm him down . . ."

Anna speculates that the marks may indicate the presence of an implant. Anna told her case to MUFON, writing, "Thanks for letting me report this. I am truthful with this report."[34]

Encounter in Greeley

As reported to the MUFON Case Management System (CMS), December 16, 2011, a man was getting ready for bed in his Greeley home when he saw what he thought might be an unusually bright star or planet. He was going to take a picture with his phone when it disappeared and reappeared much closer and lower in the sky. As it descended into the woods behind his house, he grabbed a knife, put on a jacket, and went outside to approach the object. The way it descended, he knew it couldn't be a plane. And when he saw it, "it wasn't a helicopter."

The witness hid in the bushes and watched the object for about five minutes when it suddenly landed. "People came out in these uniforms," he says. "They had big round eyes; one had almond-shaped goggles on. I hid there for about twenty more minutes before they took an animal or something into the plane. I felt like the one with the goggles was looking at me; he like smiled . . . I was scared, but when he looked at me I felt comforted."

The next thing the witness knew, he blacked out and woke up in his yard. He saw a quiet helicopter going by, and thought perhaps that was what he had seen. At this point, he forgot much of the incident. But a few days later, he remembered that it wasn't a helicopter, and that it had landed. He hasn't recalled everything, but he remembered some of it. Says the witness: "I remembered it. I had to take the day off work because I was too shaky to write."[35]

Lakewood Encounter

When Laura (pseudonym) first met her husband, Nick, he warned her that he had had unusual experiences. He didn't want to talk about it, but he cautioned her that sometimes his ears bled, and he also had a sensitive mark on his back. It wasn't until September 2012, that she finally understood. They were with their two dogs in the basement of their home in Lakewood when they heard something outside. Nick went outside with the two dogs to investigate.

Says Laura, "The dogs came running back downstairs, which isn't like them to run from something. And Nick locked up the house and came down dumbfounded. I could see it in his eyes; he was terrified. He refused to tell me what was wrong."

They sat down to watch TV when Laura's parents phoned and asked if Nick could help them, as they were stranded with their truck and trailer about fifteen minutes away.

Nick then explained to Laura what was wrong. He told her that years ago in Arvada he had seen "a strange raccoon" creature. He told her that it was back, and that it was here for him. He said he would go help her parents, and the creature would follow him and leave her and the kids alone. Laura wasn't sure what he was talking about, but it clearly wasn't a raccoon.

He told her to stay away from the doors and windows and keep all the lights off. Then he left.

A short time later, he called his mother and told her that something was following him.

Laura called up Nick, and he said that the street lights were turning off when he drove under them. He then told her that his car was malfunctioning, and he wasn't going to make it to her parents.

"What's happening?" she asked him.

"This is so weird," he said. "I don't know what is happening, but the jeep is breaking down."

She said she was going to get the kids and go find him. He told her to stay, that his Jeep just died, and he would call her back.

Next, Nick's mother texted him and he texted back that his jeep had broken down and that something was happening.

She texted him back and asked about the jeep, but he didn't understand. Says Laura, "He didn't know what she was talking about. He didn't remember the jeep breaking down. He said he didn't know why, but he was standing on the side of the road in the ditch, and the Jeep was across the road. When he walked up to it, it started on its own."

When Nick came home, he refused to talk and went straight to the shower. Says Laura, "When done, he still wouldn't answer my questions and went to bed shivering uncontrollably. I wrapped him in blankets, and wrapped around him trying to get him to warm up and calm down. It took about ten, maybe fifteen minutes before his shivering stopped and his breathing went to normal, and he finally fell asleep."

The next morning, Nick still had no memory of the Jeep breaking down. He only remembered finding himself standing by the side of the road with no explanation.

Several months later, on March 17, 2013, Nick and Laura were playing cards when the Jeep car alarm went off. Nick came back inside and said there was something outside, but refused to elaborate. He said his ears were ringing loudly, and would probably be bleeding the next day.

They heard their children crying, and Nick became frantic, and said that they needed to get to them because "they don't take long. It doesn't take long."

"Who are they?" Laura asked. "What doesn't take long?"

Nick told her to check on their daughter tomorrow, and that it was important she didn't forget. He insisted on locking everyone up in their bedroom, and warned Laura to keep the lights off and stay away from the doors and windows. Says Laura, "Before we fell asleep, he told me not to talk to him about it tomorrow, and made me promise."

"As of this morning," says Laura, "he doesn't remember anything. He didn't know why he woke up to both dogs and children in our bed, and why everything was closed and locked up. He doesn't even remember the Jeep car alarm going off."

When Laura checked her daughter, she found unexplained scratches on her back. Thankfully, they healed quickly.

"Something has been doing things with my husband," says Laura. "And he is fully aware of it while it's happening, and after. The next day, he doesn't remember anything. I need to talk about this, as I can't talk with my husband since he can't remember anything."[36]

Encounter in Grover

"It's hard for me to talk about this. I'm an oilfield worker, and also a truck driver. I haul crude oil for a living. My job takes me to remote places out in the middle of nowhere."

Around sunset on June 25, 2013, the witness was working in the Pawnee Grasslands outside of Grover. He was loading up his truck with crude oil from the Critter Creek oil well. Shortly after he hooked up the tanks, he noticed a round object floating toward him from the western horizon. His first thought was that it was a plane, until he saw its shape. Then he thought it was a balloon, but quickly discarded the theory as it was moving at a low altitude on a steady course straight toward him, despite the fact that there was a powerful crosswind blowing.

"I'm a grown man," said the oilfield worker, "but I began to get a little nervous and even a little freaked out by this thing; at the same time, I was excited as well. I started saying out loud to myself, 'What the heck is that?'"

He could now see that the object was actually a blue-gray perfectly round sphere. As it passed overhead, the hydraulic lines pumping oil from the well to his truck mysteriously shut off. The oilfield worker grabbed his phone and climbed to the top of his truck to get a better view and maybe take a picture.

The object was smooth, featureless, and utterly silent. He was about to take a picture with his phone when suddenly he thought, "No, don't worry about it."

He watched it pass overhead, move steadily off into the distance, and disappear over the horizon.

"I was on the top of the tanks watching this thing when it passed over me and disappeared over the horizon. The next thing I remember after it moved out of sight is standing next to my truck with the pump running. I looked at my gauge on my tanker and I was almost fully loaded up. I think maybe I was in shock or something, and don't remember walking down the ladder from the top of the tanks to my truck. Even stranger, when I finished loading, putting everything away, and was getting ready to leave, I climbed in my truck and found my phone sitting on the driver's seat. I'm sure I had it in my pocket."

The witness is confused about the incident. He doesn't understand why he didn't take a photograph, how he got from the top of his truck to the ground, how his phone got onto the driver's seat, and why he doesn't remember filling up the tanks. He wonders if the shock of the incident did something to his memory. He speculates that the object might be advanced military technology. Either that, or it was a UFO.[37]

Trucker Encounter

July 21, 2013, a long-haul trucker was passing through a remote area on Highway 285 near Saguache when he pulled off the highway to take a nap. Shortly after he lay down he heard a strange pulsating sound. He looked outside, but seeing nothing lay back down. Without warning, he began to hear the pulsating sound in his head. He fell asleep and began dreaming that he was in "a very large white empty room," like a warehouse. He was standing next to his truck. Suddenly he felt himself being levitated. His truck disappeared. Then the room became filled with colored lights, and his truck reappeared. He woke up a short time later. Says his wife, "He stated that the impression he had afterwards, was that he was just another trucker passing through as thousands of other truckers do in this area, and that he was not a person of interest to whatever it was that was occurring."

The trucker has no interest in UFOs or the supernatural and took the experience in stride. His wife, however, has had a lifelong fear of and obsession with UFOs and aliens. She saw a UFO at a very young age and ran inside terrified that they were coming to get her. Around that time, she began having dreams of being examined, and seeing the Earth from above. The sightings and dreams continued throughout her life, and she believes she is probably an abductee. She has had numerous gynecological problems resulting in total hysterectomy. "I truly wish to understand what all this means and conquer the fear I have," she says. "This is what I work on now, to combat fear."[38]

Low Level Sighting

July 10, 2014, a nineteen-year-old young man was on the back deck of his mother's home in Colorado Springs when he felt an odd feeling and looked up. Six feet above his head was a twenty-five-foot saucer with glowing white panels and bright golden-orange lights. The teenager had been dealing with abductions and entities for two years and instantly recognized the object. He screamed for his mother to come outside. "The object seemed to notice that," he said, "and silently flew toward Pike's Peak."

His mother came outside, angry that he had been shouting. He told her to look at the object, but she was unable to see it before it moved out of view. "It was not long after this that my hair started to recede," said the witness. "I felt surprised, aggressive, and a little disappointed and angry that my mother did not see it, nor did she really care. I've been dealing with UFOs and entities since I was seventeen. There are many other events like this I can report."[39]

A Strange Effect

October 4, 2014, a man was visiting his friend in Colorado Springs. When he smelled the odor of ozone, he became puzzled as the weather was clear. He went outside around sunset, and after looking around for a while, was surprised to see a bright star-like light darting around in the sky at about 50,000 feet altitude. At one point it flashed bright, disappeared, and reappeared in a different location. It repeatedly began to flash, disappear, and reappear. The man called for his friends to come outside, but was able to persuade only one of them who came outside, looked at the object, and said, "I don't know what it is."

The object stopped blinking, hovered, and began to zigzag. The friend became frightened and ran back inside and refused to talk about it. The main witness stayed outside and watched as the object darted a few minutes longer, then began to move away. It was quickly intersected by a second object, both of which moved off into the distance. "The whole event seemed to take only about seven or eight minutes," says the friend, "but when they were gone, I went in and discovered nearly an hour had passed." He later found out that other people in Colorado Springs had also reported UFOs on the same night.

Stranger events were to follow. "For several weeks, a strange effect on my eyesight was very noticeable. Occasionally I could see for miles with almost binocular-like vision."[40]

Missing Time in Denver

Around 7:00 p.m. on September 10, 2015, two brothers were walking to a Safeway store in Denver. Afterward they picked up snacks at the local dollar store and started walking home. They saw a black helicopter. They turned around and saw a bright white light, followed by a blue glow. When they got home, they discovered that two hours had passed. During that time, their mother had gone to the store and back looking for them.

The older brother reports having other similar incidents. Once he woke up in the middle of the night and remembered seeing strange lights outside the bathroom window. The next thing he knew, he was waking up in the morning super-tired.

Following the missing time incident at the Safeway, he began having dreams of a human-looking female with green eyes and long silver hair who warned him about the world's problems and told him that he had been chosen to be a "peacekeeper." The brother does not feel as though it was a bad experience, but as he says, "I don't know if it's real or not."[41]

As can be seen, there have been many cases of direct contact with extraterrestrials. There is little doubt that this is a physical phenomenon. We have examined cases involving landing traces, body markings, injuries, healings, implants, video-tape, and more. And yet, it's also apparent that little attention is being paid to these accounts. To complicate the situation, many of the witnesses remain fearful of talking about their accounts because of how people might react.

Thankfully, many people have come forward and revealed their cases in detail. And given the fact that most people don't report their encounters (especially if it involves an extreme encounter), it's safe to say that there are many other cases out there.

Onboard experiences give us a glimpse into who the aliens are, why they are here, and what their agenda is. Onboard experiences are perhaps the closest of all types of encounters, except, perhaps, UFO crashes.

CHAPTER 9

UFO Crash Retrievals

Once thought to be extremely rare, some researchers have reversed their opinions and now believe that UFO crashes happen fairly regularly. Colorado has at least a half-dozen possible cases, at least one of which has gained considerable notoriety. Colorado also holds the distinction of being one of the first places involving a remarkable incident of government disclosure regarding UFO crashes. The incident involves a group of science students and a few teachers who had the fortune to hear a lecture from a scientist allegedly involved in the Aztec, New Mexico, UFO crash.

As we have seen, UFOs are flying through our skies. They are landing on the ground. They are taking people onboard. And in some cases, they are crashing.

A Most Unusual Lecture

Among the first ordinary citizens to receive knowledge about UFO crashes in the United States was a group of 350 college students at the University of Colorado of Denver. Originally, the lecture was to be given to a group of ninety science students on the condition that there would be no publicity. But when the subject of the lecture leaked out, the number of attendees tripled and included several professors.

On March 8, 1950, Silas Newton (who claimed to be a Texas Oil millionaire) revealed that the US military was in possession of an actual flying saucer that had crashed in the New Mexican desert near Aztec. Newton explained that his friend, "Dr. Gee," was one of the scientists brought in to study the craft and the occupants. Originally, Dr. Gee was supposed to speak but got cold feet. Newton agreed to speak in his place. Both the scientist and Newton believed that the US government was on the verge of going public with the information, a fact which apparently played a role in their decision to reveal what they knew.

Columnist Frank Scully wrote about the incident in his book, *Behind the Flying Saucers*, part of which was devoted to the Aztec UFO crash. According to Scully, Dr. Gee didn't actually exist and was a combination of several scientists who studied the craft, which had been found only two years earlier.

Writes Scully of Silas Newton: "He delivered what was probably the most sensational lecture about this earth or any other planet since Galileo said, 'It moves!' He gave the whole inside story of a flying saucer, which he said had landed within 500 miles of where he was now talking, and he described the shape of the ship and its personnel in such detail that the undergraduates and faculty members left the lecture room with their heads spinning."

Newton had been brought in by George T. Koehler of KMYR Rocky Mountain Radio. His name was not revealed to the students. And when Newton began his lecture, he explained that there was much he couldn't talk about as the scientists involved were under security oaths. He started by telling the listeners that flying saucers are real and that the military had three of them in their custody. Together the three saucers had held thirty-four humanoids, each about three feet tall with fair complexions. They were all bald except for some who had a fine "peach fuzz" on their heads. They each had perfect teeth, and each wore identical uniforms and caps with no insignia or markings. A thread from one of the uniforms was tested, and according to Newton, it took 450 pounds of weight to break the thread.

One of the craft (now known to be the Aztec craft) held sixteen burned bodies. The second craft also held sixteen bodies, while the small craft held only two. The scientists involved believed that the object and the humanoids inside them were extraterrestrial, but they were not sure of their actual origins. He said that at least two unknown metals were currently being studied; one of the metals was very light and withstood 10,000 degrees and was impenetrable even with diamond drills. Onboard one of the saucers were instruments that seemed to measure lines of magnetic force. They believed the craft somehow used magnetics to power their craft. Only one of the craft showed slight damage, a small hole in a porthole, which apparently caused decompression. The scientists believed the three craft had come in for a guided landing and did not actually crash.

He said that the first craft was 99.9 feet in diameter, the second was seventy-two feet, and the third was thirty-six feet. Each disk had revolving rings of metal with a central stabilized cabin. The smallest one had a tripod landing gear built into it.

There were no weapons found onboard, though they did find sleeping quarters, as well as stored food and water. The food appeared to be in concentrated pill form. The water was discovered to be "heavy water." They found other devices which they were unable to identify. Doorways and storage spaces in the saucers were not visible until opened with a button. The largest ship appeared to contain a bathroom. The smallest craft had only two bucket seats and a panel with buttons, apparently to operate the ship.

Newton spoke about the recent death of Thomas Mantell, who been killed two years earlier while chasing a flying saucer over Godman Air Force Base in Fort Knox, Kentucky. He said that it would have been a simple matter for the ETs to use their knowledge of magnetics to disable Mantell's plane.

Newton wrote notes, diagrams, and pictures on a chalkboard, detailing what he was saying. The chalkboard and notes were preserved and a copy has been published in the book *The Aztec Incident* by Scott and Suzanne Ramsey.

Newton spoke for fifty minutes and spent fifteen minutes answering various questions. He then fled the area to catch his plane. Following the lecture, the audience's reaction was divided. Half of those who heard the lecture remained skeptical, while the other half were convinced Newton was telling the truth.

Despite the promise of no publicity, news of the lecture spread across campus like wildfire. According to Scully, within two hours of the lecture, military officials showed up to question the teachers and students in an attempt to determine the identity of the lecturer.

Nobody, it turned out, knew who the man was. It seemed that only Koehler knew his identity, and Koehler wasn't talking. Scully writes that the military spared no expense to identify Newton, going so far as to examine all the passenger lists of every commercial plane leaving Denver on that day.

Soon there was backlash at the faculty of the University of Denver. The Chancellor issued a directive saying that all future speakers would now be carefully screened.

Meanwhile, the story spread to newspapers, including a series of articles in the *Denver Post* and other newspapers, causing further headaches for intelligence officers. At the same time, a recorded tape of the lecture was making its rounds.

Frank Scully not only heard the tape, but knew the principals involved, interviewed them in depth, and devoted a portion of his book to the subject.

From this point, events become controversial. Scully's book was viciously attacked. Silas Newton and the mysterious Dr. Gee (later identified as Dr. Leo GeBauer) were accused of defrauding investors by claiming that they had an instrument based on alien technology that would/could detect oil underground. The men were convicted, and were jailed and fined. The Aztec case fell into disrepute for years. Later, researcher William Steinman revived the case and raised a convincing case that the whole affair was an attempt to discredit Scully and the entire Aztec UFO crash by providing disinformation and attacking the main witnesses.

Newton knew that he was disgorging military secrets and that he would likely pay dearly for it. Writes Newton: "As to my talk, it wasn't long before the finger of persecution began pointing my way, and they've scorched my hide already. But I haven't recanted."

Today many researchers believe the case to be genuine, while others still feel it was a hoax. In either case, the students who heard the lecture were amazed by revelation, and the lecture remains one of the first "security leaks" about UFO crashes. Today, UFO crash retrievals have become the cutting edge of UFO research.[1]

The Great Sand Dunes UFO Crash

As we have seen, the Great Sand Dunes in the San Luis Valley has been the location of many dramatic encounters. With so many encounters in one place, it's not too surprising that one of the UFOs might malfunction, or perhaps be shot down by the military.

According to researcher David B. Clemens (a MUFON state section director) in 1969, a family of four was conducting archaeological site surveys near the Great Sand Dunes for a major university when they saw a cylindrical object that appeared to be disabled. The object came swooping into the area, apparently trying to escape a military jet fighter that was chasing it. It flew overhead at an altitude of 500 feet and then crashed, only to be immediately recovered by the US military.

The mother of the family contacted various agencies "complaining vigorously" and was reportedly visited by a series of US Navy officers. Writes Clemens, "This story was independently verified by Monument employees."[2]

What Crashed in Eagle?

Gerald Best (a building inspector) and his wife, Vera, live on Spring Creek, just south of the Eagle County Airport. Just after midnight on July 24, 1988, Best and his wife observed what they thought was a low-flying aircraft with landing lights or strobe lights. They watched as the unidentified aircraft moved over a hill southeast of the airport. Moments later, they observed a large reddish-orange glow as though the aircraft had crashed and exploded.

They promptly called the sheriff's office, who contacted the Colorado National Guard at Eagle.

There were no reports of any missing planes. However, at daybreak, a plane was sent out from Eagle County Airport to investigate. They immediately said they saw a "white V-shaped" object on the north slope of Hardscrabble Mountain. This was looked into and was reportedly not anomalous, or part of any aircraft.

Colorado Civil Air Patrol planes also joined the search, as did two ground vehicles from the Vail Mountain Rescue Group. The search was concentrated between Blowout and Hardscrabble Mountains, and was later expanded toward the Seven Hermits.

After searching all day, however, nothing was found. At 5:00 p.m., the search was officially halted. No explanation of what crashed was found.[3]

NORAD UFO

One of Colorado's best possible UFO crash cases occurred over Greenie Mountain in Rio Grande County. In late December 1993, and early January 1994, there had been a wave of fireball sightings, orb sightings, and mysterious sonic booms in the area. Then, on January 12, 1994, a NORAD official called the Rio Grande County Sheriff's Office to report an explosion and heat source they had detected by satellite on the north face of Greenie Mountain. They told undersheriff Brian Norton that the satellite wouldn't have registered for anything less than a three-acre fire, and asked him to investigate. "A guy from NORAD told us to expend all efforts to find out what it was," Norton later told reporters.

Meanwhile, two hours later, Lt. Colonel Jim Lloyd (a retired fighter pilot) was driving on State Highway 67, forty miles east of the San Luis Valley, when he saw a group of six or seven unidentified objects race overhead, heading in the direction of Greenie Mountain.

Undersheriff Norton began his investigation by confirming that no planes were reported missing in the area. Next he drove there himself and searched the area for hours, but found no evidence of any fire.

When he phoned NORAD to tell them, he was routed to a supervisor from FEMA who told him to forget about the incident. When Norton asked for more information, the officer became belligerent.

The next day, two separate witnesses independently reported seeing a "soft green light" falling out of the sky toward Greenie Mountain. One of the witnesses said the green ball of light appeared to strike the mountain.

Three days later, the same gentleman reported seeing three B-52 bombers fly low over the site and then move away.

On January 17, the sheriff's office received three calls from people who saw a "blue flare" in the same area.

The following night, Deputy Mike James was patrolling the area when he saw three helicopters flying only 300 feet apart.

Events continued to progress. January 19, another man called to say he heard two loud explosions. Two days later, on January 21, another resident reported his sighting of an unmarked black helicopter searching the area. Norton sent out a deputy, but the helicopter left before he arrived.

Norton called NORAD and asked: "What's all these helicopters we're seeing up here?"

NORAD responded: "That's confidential information."

Norton was puzzled by all the activity. "It's strange," he told reporters. "I really can't make head or tails of it." He suspects that something crashed on the mountain, perhaps a cruise missile. But according to White Sands spokesman Jim Eckles, they have not lost any cruise missiles. "We know nothing about the source of this phenomenon up in Colorado," he said.

"Something was there," insists Norton. "This valley is not known for choppers. We don't have any in the valley, and I'd like to know where these are coming from and what they're doing here."

What crashed? Nobody seemed to know, and if they did, they weren't talking. "At first we were just thinking it was a downed plane or something," said Norton. "Then the longer it went, the story kept changing. We tried to come up with our own conclusions in this matter. But we didn't have any. We just kind of stood around, scratched our heads, and looked at the sky."

While most of the activity stopped by January 21, the mystery remained unsolved. Norton called NORAD and other military facilities throughout Colorado and even New Mexico. Nobody had any answers. "Somebody knows what happened," says Norton. "I think they located it, and now it's over with."

But the drama wasn't quite finished yet. Over the next year, several reports of unexplained lights came in to the sheriff's office at irregular intervals. Just over a year later, in March 1995, the Rio Grande County sheriff's office received reports of lights at Rock Creek on Greenie Mountain. Undersheriff Brian Norton, two Monte Vista police officers, a sheriff's deputy, a detention officer, a search/rescue member, and a volunteer fireman from Del Norte all observed the lights, which glowed red, blue, and white in random sequence. The lights hovered silently and unmoving at treetop level. "We were using field glasses," said Norton, "and we couldn't identify what they were."

In his research of the event, Christopher O'Brien learned from "a source close to the NORAD event" that two weeks following the original incident a newly promoted captain at the base (who was pregnant in her third trimester) was found in her garage dead of carbon monoxide poisoning. Allegedly, she had committed suicide.

O'Brien was able to confirm the event when he later talked to another NORAD employee who told him that the captain's death was, in fact, related to the NORAD event, and that two other people involved in the case also died under similar suspicious circumstances. O'Brien asks, "What could be so secretive as to warrant death?"

What indeed?[4]

Penrose UFO Crash

According to an anonymous report posted on NUFORC, one evening in August 1996, fourteen witnesses in two independent locations observed a UFO being shot down by the military in the Penrose area. The object was shaped like a building, hovered at 2,000 feet and was about the size of a football stadium. A single orange light rotated around the circumference of the craft. According to the report, "The craft was approached by two military helicopters, which came within very close proximity to it. The helicopters closed on it briefly, then backed off to a distance of about 200 yards and maintained their positions. Three separate missiles, apparently ground-fired from the Fort Carson military installation were seen to impact the object, causing it to fall to the ground. The line of sight prevented anyone witnessing the actual impact of the craft. The helicopters then left the area, following the route they had come from."

According to the report, ten people observed this event just north of their location, while four others saw it from about twenty miles to the north.[5]

Golden UFO Crash

It was just before midnight on June 10, 1997, when Jennifer (pseudonym) and her boyfriend were driving along Interstate 70 east toward Denver. They were approaching the exit to Golden when Jennifer saw a "large bright, white object" hurtling through the sky. It was too fast for a plane, but too slow to be a meteorite. Perfectly round, it descended at a forty-five-degree angle over the interstate and crashed to the ground behind the city of Golden. "About one minute later," says Jennifer, "I saw a flash of light coming from the same town. The flash was so bright that the mountain behind the town lit up."

Jennifer wanted to stop and look for it, but they were already in a hurry to get to Denver. The next few days, she searched the newspapers for reports about the incident but found nothing. Inquiries with several people also produced no results. Two years later, Jennifer reported the incident to NUFORC.[6]

Carbondale Crash Landing

Around 9:00 p.m., March 14, 2008, Rex (pseudonym) was driving home on Highway 82 heading to his home in Glenwood. Looking up, he saw something falling from the sky. "It looked like a giant drill," says Rex. "And it had bright green lights on it, so bright that it lit the night sky green. It looked like it either crashed or landed; it was hard to tell."

The object came down northeast of the highway in the mountains. "Later on that night," says Rex, "a lot of military jets and helicopters went in the same direction the ship crashed, or landed."[7]

Loveland UFO Crash

It was 9:30 p.m., June 19, 2016, when a Loveland resident went outside to check on his sprinklers. Instead he saw a bright orb-like object with bright, colored lights. Says the witness, "My first thought was it appeared to be in distress. The orb was ejecting lightning-like lights from the bottom of the orb, and it appeared to be slowing."

The object was silent. The lights flashed in a quickening pulsating pattern, then began to flicker, and suddenly went dark. There was a full moon that night, and the witness could now see the shape of the craft, which appeared rounded and about 250 feet across. He and two others watched as it descended, hovered, and changed directions. It came closer and lower. They watched it move at low altitude over the house across the street and over the tops of the trees. Seconds later, they saw an "impact flash." They immediately went looking for the craft. The witness was familiar with the area as he had hunted there before. "However," he says, "We were unable to locate any evidence of landing or possible crash due to night, and vast rural areas adjacent to foothills."[8]

As can be seen, Colorado has had more than a few mysterious UFO crash events. The NORAD event is by far the best-verified. Likely there are other cases that have not been well-publicized. While proof of UFO crashes remains elusive, the fact that there are multiple accounts lends credence to the possibility that UFOs crash more often than most people think.

The Mutilations

One of the strangest aspects of the UFO phenomenon has come to be known as "cattle mutilations" or "unusual animal deaths" (UADs). While many cases involve cattle, the reports involve a wide variety of animals. Before 1967, reports of animal mutilations were virtually non-existent. Around that time, a rash of mutilations occurred in southern Colorado, which began to cause buzz among the locals. As Peter Davenport of NUFORC says, "Reports of other mutilations south of Florence, Colorado, were circulating as early as June 1967, a fact that I know from personal experience there."

Colorado contains vast areas of ranching country, particularly with cattle. The state was about to find itself the focus of a disturbing mystery that would soon spread to New Mexico, other surrounding states, and eventually the world. Colorado and New Mexico, however, seem to be the primary target area.

The first case of an animal mutilation to receive any widespread attention occurred September 9, 1967, at a remote ranch outside Alamosa, in the vast San Luis Valley. It came to be known as the mutilation of "Snippy." In fact, Snippy was the victim's mother, and the actual horse's name was Lady.

The Mutilation of Lady

Ranch-owner Harry King had been having problems with strange activity over his ranch for a long time. Located at the foot of Mount Blanca outside Alamosa, throughout the mid-1960s, he saw numerous strange lights, vehicles, and flying saucers moving over his ranch and the surrounding area. Among these were low-flying, unmarked helicopters and even B-52 bombers that would make mock runs over the Great Sand Dunes where King was employed. He complained to the Air Force about it, apparently to no effect, as the activity continued.

One evening in May 1967, King was driving on the ranch when a UFO emerged from behind some rocks and began to follow him, staying 150 feet above him and 150 yards away from his car. King stopped his car, and the object stopped. He began moving, and so did the UFO. It followed him for about a mile before suddenly leaving. He later discovered that two other witnesses saw what was apparently the same object on the same night.

Then on the morning of September 8, 1967, a horse on his ranch, Lady, was missing. The horse was owned by his friends, Mr. and Mrs. Burl Lewis, but Lady spent most of her time with two other horses on the King Ranch. When she didn't show up at the watering hole, King knew something was wrong.

Searching the ranch the next morning, he found her carcass about a quarter-mile from the ranch. He was baffled by what he saw. Lady's head was stripped of flesh and the brain was missing. Also missing were her spine and internal organs. There was no evidence of any blood. Nor could he find any tracks around the animal.

About forty feet away, there was a smashed bush. Surrounding the bush, he found eight strange, circular depressions in the ground.

In another direction, a bush 150 feet away from the body also looked like it had been squashed flat. Surrounding it was a twenty-foot area that appeared to have been swept clean.

Puzzled by the lack of tracks around the animal, he circled the area looking for any evidence of Lady's most recent tracks. He found them easily. The tracks of all three horses on the ranch showed them grouped tightly together, running at full speed toward the ranch house. Suddenly Lady's tracks veered from the other two and simply ended. The tracks of the other two horses continued to the ranch house where they were found. Lady, it appeared had been lifted into the sky. Her body was dropped several hundred yards beyond where her tracks ended.

King reported the incident to the Lewises, the owners of Lady. The Lewises arrived and were also shocked. Mrs. Lewis reported a strange sweet odor. Investigating the area, she was able to locate a tuft of Lady's mane in a bush 150 feet away from the body, where she also found a small chunk of flesh.

They called in the police to investigate, but the police were skeptical and reluctant to get involved. They contacted Duane Martin of the forestry service who was able to bring a civil defense Geiger counter. After testing the area and surrounding test areas, Martin found that the area where Lady was mutilated contained radiation well beyond normal.

Soon the press caught wind of the story, and they came to investigate. Newspaper articles were written, some of which went national. Most of the articles, as mentioned before, called the horse "Snippy," who was actually Lady's mother. Regardless of the horse's name, the story garnered considerable attention.

Ten days later, Dr. John Altshuler, then a professor of medicine and pathology at the University of Colorado Health Sciences, went to investigate the carcass.

He was shocked by the surgical neatness of Lady's wounds. Examining the edges, he concluded that the cuts had been done using some type of surgical cauterizing-blade. Years later, when lasers became available for surgery, he was struck by the similarity of the tissues. "Most amazing was the lack of blood," wrote Altshuler. "I have done hundreds of autopsies. You can't cut into a body without getting some blood. But there was no blood on the skin or on the ground. No blood anywhere. That impressed me most . . . How do you get the heart out without blood?"

Hearing about the UFO sightings in the area, Altshuler decided to investigate. He went to the Great Sand Dunes where there had been recent activity. "About 2:00 to 3:00 a.m.," he said, "I saw three very bright, white lights moving together slowly below the Sangre De Cristo mountaintops . . . At one point, I thought they were coming toward me because [they] got bigger. Then suddenly, they shot upward and disappeared . . . "

Dr. Altshuler was in a state of near panic. When he concluded the investigation, he was thoroughly shaken. "I was unbelievably frightened. I couldn't eat. I couldn't sleep. I was so afraid I would be discovered, discredited, fired, no longer would have credibility in the medical community. My experience in 1967 was so overwhelming to me, I denied the experience to everyone, even to myself."

Altshuler didn't realize it at the time, but he had actually been visited by aliens. He later underwent regressive hypnosis and recalled having a face-to-face encounter with the beings from the craft. "They were not the typical kind of gray creatures," he said. "They were different. I don't know if that's simply a figment of my imagination or not. I don't know. They have huge heads—huge, with a very small body. The head had four definite wrinkles on the forehead. The eyes were wide open, literally."

Altshuler's life would never be the same, and he would be thrust into the forefront of cattle mutilation research.

Meanwhile, APRO investigator Don Richmond was on the scene four weeks after the incident and made a careful recording of the landing traces. He also found several strange burned areas, each only a few inches in diameter, leading in straight lines from the body.

Around this time, two students from the University of Colorado in Boulder and another friend heard about local sightings in the San Luis Valley and decided to travel there. One of the friends, Raymond Ingraham, was a photography buff. The other, Mike Kellenbarger, was a member of APRO and a UFO buff.

They were able to meet Harry King and visit his ranch. Raymond Ingraham, writes, "He took us to the spot where Lady was found, and even then, so many months after the event, one could plainly see the outline of the horse, as nothing would grow there."

Even more startling was what happened next. Ingraham noticed a gray station wagon parked down the road that appeared to be watching them. He raised his camera to take a picture, and the car suddenly screeched away at high speed. King told Ingraham that such things had occurred for a long time, but had increased since he reported the mutilation of his horse. King made it clear that he was sorry he had ever reported the mutilation in the first place.

Ingraham and his friends left. They saw no UFOs during the trip and eventually lost contact with each other. Three years later, in January of 1970, Ingraham was drafted into the US Army. Still an avid photographer, he was accepted in the Army Intelligence section with a specialty in photo reconnaissance.

It was then that his innocent foray to Harry King's ranch came back to haunt him. "I proceeded to Fort Leonard Wood, Missouri, for basic training," says Ingraham. "In my initial screening/clearing interview, I was asked point-blank why I had gone to Alamosa in 1967, and what was I doing there? Needless to say, I was flabbergasted (a) that they knew I was there and (b) why on earth it concerned them. When the discussion of APRO ensued, they asked me if I had joined, to which I honestly replied, 'No.' This apparently satisfied them."

Ingraham was eventually denied entrance due to an ulcer and was discharged two months later.

The mutilation of Lady was the seminal case that foretold decades of similar incidents throughout Colorado, New Mexico, and the world.[1]

The Wave Begins

Throughout the late 1960s, Deputy Sheriff Gene Gray of Saguache County quietly investigated more than a dozen mutilations in the area. "There would be absolutely no evidence of foul play whatsoever," said Gray. "I even looked for disturbed grass and burn spots from a ship."

Gray had been on duty for twenty-two years when the mutilation phenomenon first struck. He had never seen a UFO. Once the mutilations began, however, he had his first sighting. One evening, during the rash of mutilations, he saw a huge red glow "like a saucer or something. I watched it take off like a scalded cat across the valley disappear off to the west."

One of the cases occurred on the ranch of Duane Flickinger of Norwood. The rancher found two cows missing their lips, tongues, and anuses. They appeared to have been cut with a razor. The cows were found a fourth-mile from their original location, and appeared to have been picked up and dropped.

In the early 1970s, Costilla County Sheriff Ernest Sandoval received several reports of mutilations in the area. In some of these cases, ranchers reported sightings of helicopters at the time and place of the mutilations. In one particular incident, Chama residents were chased by helicopters away from Sanchez Reservoir all the way to Chama, a distance of seven miles. Several mutilations occurred in the area on that evening.

By the mid-1970s, the number of mutilations increased dramatically. The wave was now in full swing. While the culprit remained a mystery, the incidents were becoming more brazen. On July 6, 1975, a cow that was due to calve in two months was discovered at the NORAD entrance gate. Sergeant Robert Stone of the local sheriff's office reported that the mutilation could not have been done by predators such as coyotes.

On September 13, 1975, as reported by Officer Hart of Garfield County, a Hereford cow from Mesa County was discovered dead, mutilated, and missing its sex organs, rectum, and one ear. In another nearby case, a mutilated steer was found missing its ribs and heart.

Mutilation researcher Frederick W. Smith conducted a study of mutilations in Colorado, which, along with New Mexico, was harder hit by the phenomenon than anywhere else in the United States. In 1975, a number of the cases took place near Colorado military bases, such as Ent Air Force Base, Fort Carson, Peterson Airfield, Lowry Air Force Bombing Range, the US Air Force Academy, the Buckley Air National Guard and Naval Air Station, the Rocky Mountain Arsenal, and more.

One such case occurred on October 21, 1975, at Cheyenne Mountain Zoo, immediately north of the Cheyenne Mountain Complex, whose duty is to track all objects entering US Airspace. A female buffalo was discovered mutilated, missing its sex organs, one ear, and four square-feet of hide. Zoo director Dan Davis said, "There is no doubt the animal was mutilated with some sort of sharp instrument handled by man."

The question is, why are these mutilations taking place so close to military bases, particularly Cheyenne Mountain?

Writes Smith, "Someone thought this would be a neat place to have a cattle mutilation . . . someone has been delivering a message to the American people, to the government, the intelligence community."

In October 1975, rancher Emilio Lobato Jr. of Costilla County suffered one of the worst recorded losses. During a two-week period, he lost forty-seven head of cattle. Seventeen of them were found mutilated, and the rest were either shot or stolen. A carload of witnesses observed a helicopter landed on the ground next to a cow lying on its side. They saw a man leaning over the cow holding metal tubes which protruded from the animal. The incident occurred on Lobato's ranch.

By the end of 1975, the *Denver Post* reported that statewide, ranchers had reported in excess of 200 mutilations of cattle and horses. This figure was confirmed by the Colorado Bureau of Investigations. Their investigation ultimately concluded that the mutilations were caused by predators, lightning, toxic plants, and disease—something which is strongly disputed by virtually all ranchers and mutilation investigators.

Elbert County undersheriff George Yarnell had provided the CBI with several samples of tissue from mutilated cows. The response was always the same: predators. Frustrated, he sent some tissue that he sliced himself with a knife. The conclusion came back: predators. He now knew that the CBI was either incompetent or flat-out lying.

Pete Espinoza served for eight years as a Costilla County sheriff and deputy. He says: "Every ranch in Costilla County had at least one mutilation case."

The year of 1975 was perhaps the worst on record, even to the present day. Writes researcher Linda Moulton Howe, "Sheriffs in Logan and Elbert Counties in Colorado were investigating as many as three mutilations a day that summer. Some of these mutilations appeared to have strange UFO-type landing marks next to them." Sheriff Tex Graves came upon such a site involving three mysterious holes in the ground. Says Graves, "We found one set that had gone in the ground roughly eight inches. It would take a good post-hole digger or a shovel to dig in like this. It indicated something very heavy had set down in this area, and yet there were no tracks leading from it nor to it."[2]

Rocky Mountain Ranch

Some of the answers to what's going on in Colorado may be provided by Jim, a former US Air Force Security Officer. His friend, John, was a manager at a large corporation and married to Barbara. In the mid-1970s, the three of them pooled their finances and purchased a large ranch in the Rocky Mountains of Colorado. The three of them, and John and Barbara's two teenage sons moved and settled in. Almost immediately strange events began to occur.

One evening in 1975, their coon-hound began barking, and the cattle began braying. Going outside to investigate, Jim saw a large glowing object hovering above a nearby dam. "It was orange and trapezoidal-shaped. I was going to see what it was, and I got about halfway there when I realized that whatever it was, I didn't want to know."

During this time, cattle mutilations were being reported in large numbers. Following this incident, Jim learned that a reward had been offered for the arrest of whoever was responsible for the cattle mutilations. One evening, he decided he would go out with his shotgun and search the area. Jim suddenly found himself paralyzed. He sat on the couch, unable to move, feeling as though he had been drugged.

Suddenly he heard his wife screaming. This broke Jim's paralysis. He ran to his wife who was unable to speak and stuttering in fear. When she regained her composure, she reported that she had experienced a uniquely strange episode. Without warning, her heart had begun to race and her mind began to scroll through a flood of memories, almost as though someone else was controlling her thinking patterns. This occurred exactly when Jim felt his paralysis. It took them both several minutes to fully recover.

Some days later, the teenage sons were outside when they discovered the mutilated body of one of their cows only 600 feet from the house. Feeling like something was following them, they rushed home. The next morning, they examined the body. "The udders were removed surgically," says Jim. "One eye was missing. One ear was missing. And that was it. There was no blood—all the blood had been removed . . . the rectum was also removed."

There were no tracks next to the animal. However, they did find something strange: large Bigfoot-like prints about eighteen inches long led from near the body of the cow to the horse barn, following the route the teenage sons had taken when they first discovered the cow.

Jim reported the incident to the local police, who declined to investigate. Two weeks later, a neighbor's bull was mutilated and killed, with its organs apparently surgically removed.

This time, Jim drove into town and met the police directly, and asked them why they weren't investigating. The officer told him that they knew who was doing the mutilations and had known for some time. He told Jim that there had been 400 reports in this county alone, and that they had consulted with the FBI about the problem. "It's being done by extraterrestrials," he said.

Jim was skeptical. Meanwhile, the strange events continued. One evening, two friends and a neighbor were visiting the ranch when they heard strange noises at the cistern southeast of the house. They looked towards the source of the noise and saw a large creature running down the hill toward them. They retreated into the house. Later, they went outside and found footprints. Jim took photos and collected hair samples that he found. He sent them to a bio-geneticist in Denver who was unable to match it to any known species. Says Jim, "By then, I was getting more and more upset about the activities. One law officer was encouraging me to keep my mouth shut about it because he didn't want a full-scale panic in the county. I told him I wasn't interested in panics—I was interested in finding out who was mutilating my cattle."

Jim and the entire family were being affected. Jim slept near the front door with a gun ready. One evening around 2:00 a.m., he heard a strange humming noise and saw a disk-shaped object fly by the house. Several other occasions, he saw what appeared to be a Bigfoot-like creature run by. Usually he took no action, though once he jumped out and shot it at close range. Sure that he hit the creature, he chased it to the neighbor's property while it made an odd whining-beeping noise.

Other strange events occurred, including fly-overs by Air National Guard interceptors who were apparently searching for UFOs. One night, nine disks landed on the property, and were observed by Jim, Barbara, and another friend. Jim walked outside to take a closer look, while Barbara watched from the window. Another witness, upstairs, heard the people in the house talking about the disks, but found himself paralyzed. As Jim approached the disks, Barbara was struck by an unseen force and knocked to the ground. Jim retreated inside.

One time, the lights in the house went out, and a voice came over their stereo saying, in part: "Attention. We have allowed you to remain. We have interfered with your lives very little. Do not cause us to take action which you will regret . . . "

Finally, the day came when Jim had face-to-face contact with the apparent ETs who had, it seemed, taken up residence on their ranch. He noticed a light in the trees outside the house. Going up to investigate, he saw two male figures, each about five-and-a-half feet tall, wearing tight-fitting jumpsuits that flashed brown and silver. They were fair, blond-haired, with large eyes, fine features, and an almost effeminate appearance.

They acted with complete confidence. They thanked Jim for coming and apologized for the inconveniences they had caused. Jim wanted to ask questions, but instead told them that they should stop mutilating cattle as they were drawing attention to themselves. He saw the Bigfoot creature that he had seen before, and was surprised to see the ETs order it around. Jim spent about five minutes with them, at which point they said that a "more equitable arrangement" would be worked out, and that they would "come back and talk again."

At first, Jim assumed he was dealing with government people. Their ranch was next to a military base. However, noting the strange appearance of the men, and the fact that a UFO was landed right next to them, he later concluded that they were aliens, and that they had some kind of permanent installation on his ranch.

"I'm reasonably sure that they play rough. It's not big brothers from space who are interested in us as spiritual beings or whatever. I'm absolutely convinced that they couldn't care less if we live or die . . . I have no doubts they are mutilating the cattle— none at all. The cattle are being lifted into the air, they are being drained of blood, they are being mutilated, and they are being lowered. If they wanted to do just biological research on cattle, they could have disposed of the remains without them being found. It is obviously some intent to instill fear and it has been quite successful."

Jim later discussed the mutilation problem with an officer at the Air Force base near his ranch. The officer told him that the base had experienced a number of troublesome UFO incidents, and that they had directives on how to deal with them. When Jim mentioned the Bigfoot encounter, the officer admitted that they had similar directives for it as well.

Dr. Leo Sprinkle and the other investigators came away from their investigation feeling that the witnesses were sincere. "They truly were puzzled by the events," he said, "as were we."[3]

Not From This Planet

The mutilations continued. In May 1978, Saguache County Deputy Lynn Bogle examined a mutilation on a ranch in Center. A three-year-old cow was missing its eyes, rectum, and heart. There was no evidence of blood. At the time, Bogle speculated that the US military was responsible.

By the close of the 1970s, Colorado was suffering badly from the animal mutilations. However, beyond the local area, almost nobody was talking about it. That was all about to change. In the late 1970s, mainstream journalist Linda Moulton Howe heard about the cases and began her own investigation. She interviewed ranchers and visited animal mutilation events immediately after they occurred.

In 1981, Howe released her ground-breaking film *A Strange Harvest*, which was the first documentary to examine the mystery. The film earned her an Emmy Award and began to bring public awareness to the plight of the Colorado and New Mexico ranchers. During her investigations, Howe discovered that UFO sightings were sometimes reported in association with mutilation events. However, she also discovered that many people were also reporting strange, unmarked black helicopters. Was this the government monitoring the situation? Were they responsible for the mutilations?

Says Howe: "I talked to Lou Girardo, who was the chief investigator on mutilations in the DA's office in Trinidad, Colorado, throughout the 1970s. One night in his office, in October of 1979, with my film camera running, I asked him about the helicopters, and this was his answer. He said they had so many reports of completely silent helicopters that he had come to the conclusion that they were dealing with something not from this planet. These were his words: 'creatures not from this planet.' One of the possibilities for these silent, strange helicopters was that this life-form had some kind of technology to camouflage themselves however they wanted to, and in some cases chose to look like a helicopter that didn't make any noise. Now, that was a law enforcement officer's perspective after several years of investigating mutilations."

June 5, 1980, the Sutherland family were having dinner when they saw an old-fashioned whirlybird helicopter land on their property, then take off, flying directly over their home. The next morning, they found a 1,700-pound bull dead. Its eyes were missing, a one-inch plug was missing from its brisket, and its rectum was cored out. The Sutherlands researched the helicopter and found that they were no longer in official use. The bull was untouched by predators, including flies, and took years to fully decompose.

September 16, 1982, Bill and Linda Dzuris (who own a ranch thirty miles east of Colorado Springs) found a dead and mutilated cow on their property. They had seen the cow alive and healthy that morning. About five hours later, they found the body. Half of the udder was cut out, the rectum had been partially removed, and the eyes were bulging out strangely.

April 13, 1984, rancher Kenneth Knight of Morgan County reported the mutilation of one of his cattle. According to the *Denver Post*, there had been no reported mutilations in Morgan County for four years.

One evening in fall 1985, rancher Myron Scott (age twenty-three) was feeding hay to his livestock when he saw strange lights hovering over a field about two miles away. He went to investigate the area the next day and discovered that one of his 600-pound steers had been bizarrely mutilated. The animal's horns and spine were broken, as if it had been dropped from the air. Its tongue was missing. Most strange, the animal's hide had been pulled up over its body "like you'd roll a cigarette paper," explained Scott.

August 24, 1986, the dead and mutilated body of a yearling bull was found by its owner on his ranch in Trinidad. The nose and lips were removed in a 360-degree cut. The tongue had been completely severed and removed. One eye was missing. There was one cut from one side of the rib-cage to the other, and two strange cuts leading to the rectum, removing a large triangle of hide and flesh, as well as the rectum and sex organs.

Sheriff Lou Girardo of Las Animas investigated the incident. He learned that three nights before the mutilation occurred, neighbors observed strange red lights in the sky about two miles from where the body of the bull was found. Three weeks later, on September 18, 1986, two teenagers in the area saw a circular light hovering over their home.

May 20, 1987, rancher Bob Walker found a two-year-old steer dead and mutilated on his ranch in Pueblo. The left ear was removed, as were the sex organs.

In August 1987, in Denver, a security guard protected the grounds of a large corporation when he was startled to see a large circle of lights hovering in place over a farm pasture a few hundred feet away. Fearing that he would lose his job if he reported a UFO, he decided to keep quiet. He came to regret this decision when he discovered that in the morning following the sighting, a farmer found two of his cows mutilated and killed in the pasture. The case was investigated by Linda Moulton Howe who spoke with the guard. "What kind of technology are we talking about?" asked the guard. "I never took my eyes off those lights. There was no beam, no sound—nothing. How did they do it?"[4]

If Cows Could Talk

While the mutilation phenomenon began in the 1960s, thirty years later, new cases continued to surface. Still investigators were no closer to solving the mystery. The 1990s proved to be particularly active, producing many bizarre cases across southern Colorado.

November 27, 1992, rancher Manuel Sanchez of Chama told local authorities and reporters that he found one of his pregnant cows dead and missing its eyes, bag, and rear-end. There were no tracks around the cow, not even from the cow itself. Says Sanchez, "Someone should be trying to find out what's going on. Small ranch operations like mine can't afford to lose a pregnant cow like this . . . my insurance won't cover it."

Also in November 1992, Las Animas County Sheriff Lou Gerardo investigated two "classic mutilations" about thirty-five miles west of Trinidad. The cows' eyes, bag, sex organs, lips, and tongue were all surgically removed, with no trace of spilled blood. One of the cows was owned by John Torres. When asked who he thought was responsible, Torres replied, "Well, as far as I'm concerned, it was aliens. Seriously, I really do think it was something from out of this world, to do something like that without leaving any evidence whatsoever."

During Thanksgiving week, around the time of the mutilation, numerous witnesses observed unexplained lights over the Great Sand Dunes. Says Luna Bontempi: "They bounced around unlike any type of plane or helicopters, at very fast speeds. You could see them in groups of three or four, like the points of a triangle."

More than ten other residents living in the area also observed unexplained lights around the same time.

David B. Clemens (New Mexico MUFON State Section Director) writes, "During late 1992, cattle mutilations and UFO sightings returned with a vengeance. In the year ending December 1992, over forty suspected mutilations occurred in the Sangre de Cristo Range."

Clemens investigated a case that happened on April 29, 1993, only hours after it had occurred. The cow was found within 200 yards of a ranch house in Chama. Its rectum had been cored out and its udders had been taken. Dr. Altshuler examined tissue from the carcass and found evidence that high heat had been used to make the incisions.

In May 1993, a fisherman discovered the dead and mutilated body of a 200-pound heifer. The cow's rectum and vagina were cored out, and the left eye had been removed. He reported it to Park County undersheriff Kevin Anderson, who began an investigation. Anderson located the rancher who owned the cow. The rancher told him that the heifer had actually died ten days earlier of pneumonia. Anderson suspects that cultists might be responsible.

In the summer of 1993, Garfield Torres found a mutilated cow on his ranch. Its ears, eyeballs, tongue, and uterus had been surgically removed. It was found in soft soil with no trace of footprints around it.

Also in the summer of 1993, a rancher in Mead found a dead cow. The cow had been pregnant. When the rancher found the cow, the fetus had been removed and stolen.

Around the same time, rancher Delbert Castor of Weld County found one of his cow's mutilated. Tissue samples were sent back to Colorado State University for analysis. The result came back that the tissue had been cut by sharp instruments.

In mid-June 1993, rancher Doris Williams of Weld County called the local sheriff to report the mutilation of her favorite horse, which she found mutilated and dead in a field about a half-mile from her home. One eye had been removed. There were slice-marks around the ear and jaw where a section of hide had been removed. The horse's tongue was also cut out.

The horse was sent to laboratories at the Colorado State University Veterinary Teaching Hospital for analysis. The result came back shortly later. The horse had died of a twisted bowel. The strange mutilations were caused by predators.

Williams disagrees. "I expected this kind of an answer. I guess the predators are carrying scalpels now. I'm getting madder by the minute as I think about their report, and I'd really like to see that report . . . My horse was eating well and in good health . . . Why was his tongue cut out? What happened to the pieces of hide that were taken? Just too many questions."

June 1993, a four-year-old Hereford cow was found mutilated on the Pinon Ranch owned by Alex McCulloch of Pueblo County. The cow appeared to have been shot above the right eye. The milk-sack, uterus, and tongue had been surgically removed. A small spot of blood was found fifteen feet from the body, though there was none where the body lay. The cow's newborn calf was found in good health, standing next to the body of its mother. Although officials suspected cultists, there were no accessible roads within two miles of the incident.

On December 14, 1993, Dale and Clarence Vigil lost a 1,700-pound bull missing its sex organs, rectum, and entire rear end. Broken branches with tufts of hair in the trees above the bull showed that the animal had been dropped from above. Dr. Altshuler investigated the body and found evidence of high heat where the cow had been mutilated.

About 150 miles north, in Eagle, Colorado, Bill Bradford found a cow on his ranch missing "an eight-inch plug out of its brisket." It was also missing a ten-inch equilateral triangle from the hide on its side. Bradford had lost a cow only a few months earlier on Thanksgiving. The hide on the left side of its face had been removed. On the same day, his neighbor, Lloyd Girard, found one of his cows inside a potato storage barn. It was missing its tongue, windpipe, and all the tissue from the left side of its face and neck.

May 9, 1994, several residents in Monte Vista saw a brilliant strobing white light moving at tree-top level. Undersheriff Brian Norton observed the lights himself and said they moved at a few hundred miles per hour. Cars were lining up along Highway 285 to watch it. Undersheriff Norton tried to chase the object, but it began to play cat-and-mouse games with him, mirroring his actions. When he moved north, it moved south. When he moved north, it would dart to the south. On that night, a farmer in the area had two of his cows mutilated. Next to the cow was a twelve-foot-wide burn mark.

Coincidentally, the group CSETI headed by Steven Greer, was in the area holding a workshop to try and make contact with UFOs.

In late October 1994, rancher Ermenio Andreatta lost three cows within a three-mile radius on his ranch near Middle Creek Road. Each cow was missing its anus, uterus, and left nipple. There was no evidence of blood, no evidence of any struggle, and no tracks around the body. Each cow exhibited a strange bruised mark on its chest.

In 1994, rancher Ted Hasenbalg of Simla found one of his bulls mutilated and killed. Twice before he had lost bulls to the mutilation phenomenon. "I've got to think it's UFOs," says Hasenbalg. "That's the only thing that's logical."

March 4, 1995, rancher Robert Kernan found one of his cows dead on his ranch in Del Norte. It had been mutilated in a very unusual manner; its spinal cord, brain, heart, lungs, and ribs were all missing. Normally, mutilated cows are missing ears, eyes, tongue, reproductive organs, and anus. In this case, those body parts were left untouched. Christopher O'Brien investigated the case and calls it one of the weirdest and most bizarre mutilations he has ever seen. "I find it inconceivable that the ribs and brain were removed in that fashion," he explained. He learned that the police had received a call from a neighboring ranch around the time the mutilation occurred about unexplained blue lights in the area.

When Kernan came upon the calf, he saw fifty of his cows standing around looking at it. "Boy, if those cows could talk," he said. Although he had been a cattle rancher his entire life, this was the first time he experienced a mutilation. "This always happens to the other guy," he says, "but this time it happened to me."

He is certain the cuts were not caused by predators. Not only were they too neat, no predators would even go near the carcass. "The dogs were afraid of it," he says.

On July 26, 1995, Allan and Vicki Dietel found three dead animals on their Douglas County ranch. Two steer and one deer were all found in a fenced-off, seventy-five-acre pasture. One steer was missing its genitals and its right front leg. The second steer was missing its nose and right front leg. Nearby, a body of a deer was found shot and dead, but otherwise, unmutilated.

Authorities suspected satanic cult activity, though no evidence of any trespassers was found.

September 22, 1995, UPS driver David Jaramillo was with his family in Antonito when they found a mutilated cow near their cabin. It was missing its udder, rectum, and tongue. Also a circular portion around its ear was missing, and the tip of the cow's tail was skinned. About one hundred feet away from the carcass they found three circles of crushed grass. Each circle was four feet across, and twelve feet apart in a triangular pattern. Around each of the circles were three four-inch-deep holes, also in a triangular-formation. In the center of the three large circles, Jaramillo found some tail hairs from the mutilated cow. Jaramillo took footage of the animal and the landing traces. His footage later appeared in a segment on the television program *Strange Universe*.

That same week, a rancher in Rio Grande County contacted undersheriff Brian Norton to report a mutilated cow on his property. He was exploring his ranch on his horse when he came upon the carcass of the cow, which lay dead in the center of a thirty-foot-diameter circle of swirled grass. His horse refused to enter the circle. The rancher noticed a fine white substance "like baby powder" on the animal's body and within the circle of crushed grass.

September 26, 1995, Huerfano rancher Larry Chacon found his old horse, Whiskey, had become victim to the mutilation phenomenon. Whiskey was missing his rectum, one eye, and half his tongue. Also his hair and hide was "blackened and stiff."

The case was investigated by researcher David Perkins. Christopher O'Brien spoke with Perkins and writes, "As per usual, no tracks, footprints, or signs of predator or struggle were noted. Only four days earlier, a dramatic sighting had occurred in the area involving a large triangle, which was part of a greater wave of sightings that began with the now-famous Salida sightings as filmed by Tim Edwards.

November 6, 1995, rancher Susan Nottingham found an 800-pound bull dead and mutilated on her ranch near Burns. The bull was lying on its side and was missing its genitalia, the left side of its mouth and lips, and one ear. The sheriff from Eagle County investigated and said that there were no signs of any struggle, and that vultures and prey animals had avoided the carcass. He found coyote tracks circling the body, but none came any closer than twenty-five feet.

Also in 1995, cattle rancher Clyde Chess found one of the heifers on his ranch, located in eastern El Paso County. Whoever killed his cow removed its lips, tongue, ears, heart, and sex organs. Chess theorizes that it's the US government, as they would be the only entity with access to the kind of technology used.

The mid-1990s continued strong. In January 1996, rancher James Richard White of Truckton found one of his cows dead, with no sign of any struggle and no tracks around the body. The only apparent injury to the cow was a missing eye socket.

Also in 1996, a New Mexico cattle inspector was examining a mutilated cow in Taos when he was overcome by strange fumes emitted from the body and had to be hospitalized.

In late November 1997, Ted Ruggles, a rancher north of Center, reluctantly called the Saguache County Sheriff's Office. He had just checked his herd of weaner calves and found one of them dead. The calf was missing its sex organs, rectum, and the right side of its face. The freshly fallen snow around it revealed no tracks.

"I don't know how it died," said Ruggles, "but you could tell right away that it had been cut on, or mutilated, or whatever . . . It was totally bizarre to me. Once Bill told me there was a dead cow, it just didn't sound right because I had checked the day before and everything was all right. When I found it, I said, 'Wow!' You can tell it's been cut because you can see the knife cuts."

"We're doing a formal report on it," said undersheriff Mike Norris. "At this point, all we have is an unexplained cow's death that wasn't predator-caused."

Christopher O'Brien investigated and was able to obtain samples for analysis.

One week before Christmas, in 1997, an Alamosa rancher found one of his horses dead, mutilated, and lying in the bottom of a dry canal ditch. The night of the mutilation, unexplained lights were seen over the area, which had become fogged in. The police were notified and Christopher O'Brien was brought in to investigate.

The gelding was missing the inside of its hindquarters and its sex organs. It also had two abrasions on its side. Some chamisa bushes near the body were smashed down, and they found a "blood splash" sixty feet from the ditch, and a few other blood splashes. "It looked real suspicious," said O'Brien. "It looked like it thrashed around before it died . . . We couldn't find any tracks near it."

Tim Miller owns a ranch near the Pike Stockade in Monte Vista. He had a herd of sixteen horses, only one of which was white. Unfortunately, the white horse was targeted by the mysterious mutilators. In early March 1998, Miller found the gelding dead and mutilated.

Christopher O'Brien investigated and found a "softball-sized hole" in the horse's chest. Part of its lower jaw was shaved of hair and cut open. There were other cuts on the face, and the horse's sex organs had been removed. Foam around the horse's mouth seemed to indicate that it had been running strenuously when killed. "It looks to me like they spotlighted it," says O'Brien, "ran it down, darted it, and lifted it."

There were no tracks around the body, not even its own.[5]

Current Cases

In mid-October 2004, Jacque Osburn contacted the Moffat County Sheriff's Office to report the mutilation of two steers and one heifer on the ranch near Craig and Moffat. Osburn's herd had about 200 head, and she had never had any troubles before. Each of her animals had only their genitals removed; no other marks were found on their bodies. The financial loss of the incident, she estimates, is about $2,400 dollars. Insurance will cover the costs only if it's proved that the animals died of lightning, drowning, hit by a vehicle, shot, or other natural causes.

In May 2005, a man was driving near Jaroso when he saw an unexplained "orange light." He returned to the area two days later and found "a mutilated cow."

One month later, a rancher found a mutilated cow on his ranch south of Monte Vista.

October 11, 2005, six horses and a burrow were all found dead and mutilated in a field near Calhan. Veterinarian John Heikkila ruled out storms, diseases, toxicity, and lightning. The only mark on the animals was a quarter-inch puncture hole. No evidence of bullets was found. Heikkila speculated that they must have been poisoned, but their owner, Bonny Blasingame, disagrees. "I've talked to several of my friends who think that it's aliens," she says. Blasingame remains undecided. Two weeks after the incident, a teenager spotted a UFO in the area.

Toxicology reports came back and found no evidence of poison. A team of veterinarians from Colorado and the State Veterinarian's Office said that no official cause of death could be determined, but that the general consensus was that the animals were killed in "a flash blizzard." They had no explanation for the mysterious puncture holes in the animals' bodies.

One horse survived the incident, a six-month-old filly by the name of Santanna, whose mother was killed. Blasingame says that Santanna has been very skittish since the incident. "I'd give anything if she could talk," said Blasingame. "She'd have a story to tell."

Two weeks later, Calhan was hit by what might be one of the worst mutilation incidents ever. Rancher William DeWitt found that sixteen of his forty horses had been killed. When he arrived at the scene, he found the horses all lying dead on their sides, strewn in various locations throughout his pasture. "I've never seen anything like it," said DeWitt (age seventy-two.) "I was shocked."

There were no marks on the bodies and no sign of trauma. A veterinarian was called in and could only speculate that they must have been killed by lightning strike. There had been lightning reported around the time the horses must have died. "If it was lightning," says DeWitt, "it would be the largest strike I've ever seen." In both of these Calhan cases, there were no organs removed as occurs in typical mutilation cases.

After a team of veterinarians researched the incident as well as the prior incident involving five horses and a burro, they concluded that the second Calhan incident was also weather related and that it must have been lightning.

According to reporter Amy Brouillette, "The lightning theory has riled some area ranchers."

DeWitt disagrees with the conclusion. He has seen lightning deaths before and says that his horses were spread over too wide an area to all be killed by lightning strike. And there were other problems with the lightning theory. "You normally would find burn marks on the ground or the animal's hair singed," he said. "They are grasping at straws."

Chuck and Sheri Bowen own a 13,000-acre ranch near Eads and Lamar that has been in their family since the 1940s. Back in the late 1970s and early 1980s, Chuck Bowen's grandfather lost several cattle when the mutilation phenomenon first became prevalent. More than twenty-five years later, first in February 1996, and then in April, the Bowens found two of their Angus cows from their herd of ninety dead and mutilated. The only apparent damage to the animals was the skin from the same side of both cows' faces had been surgically removed. "The grass around their legs was still upright, still tall," said Chuck Bowen. "When an animal dies, it usually thrashes around and disturbs the ground. This was like the cows had been gently laid down in the grass, like they'd been lowered."

The injuries on each cow was identical. "The cut was a perfectly straight line," said Sheri Bowen. "You could tell it was done with a knife."

Not only were there no tracks, the Bowens reported that the coyotes that roam the ranch refused to scavenge on the bodies. The Bowens own a metal detector that they sometimes use on the ranch. Placing it over the cows, they were surprised when the meter went off, registering "aluminum foil."

"Aliens killing our cattle just doesn't make sense," says Chuck Bowen. "Both cows had the exact same patch of skin taken from the same side of their face. And to be honest, it's a little creepy."

The Bowens also admit to seeing UFOs on their property throughout the years, including a sighting over the area where they had lost the cow. "A number of years ago," says Chuck Bowen, "in the same area, we saw a light going across the sky at an enormous speed. It would zig and zag across the sky. It would go up and down." It eventually disappeared in a flash of light.

Ninety miles north of the Bowens, outside of Kirk, Larry Brachtenbach owns a 2,000-acre ranch. The ranch has been in his family for years. They were first hit by the mutilation phenomena in 1973 when they found a bull calf that had been "turned out." Throughout the years, they would be hit over and over.

One of the more memorable incidents occurred in 1990 when Brachtenbach lost a Simmental cow. An autopsy was performed by a veterinarian who was unable to identify the exact cause of death, but did say that the cow's heart had been perforated with a hundred tiny holes. Says Brachtenbach: "She was lying on her side and there was a six-inch piece of hide taken out, as if it was taken with a cookie cutter. We had seen her just the day before. On her side was white powder. Her eyes, tongue, and female organs were missing."

On a few occasions, they found cows with their hides removed, with square incisions around the udders, which were left intact. Brachtenbach wonders if the mutilators are intentionally leaving "a sign" of their presence.

Most recently, in June 2006, they found one of their cows dead and missing its tongue and sex organs. It was, said Brachtenbach, at least the seventeenth head of cattle they had lost to mutilations.

A few weeks later, they found another cow lying between two soapweeds. It was missing its tongue and reproductive tract. Brachtenbach and his son, Matt, immediately noticed a broad trail of crushed bushes leading from the body upslope about ten yards. Clearly, the body had been dragged for about thirty feet. Otherwise, there were no tracks. They did find a two-foot area near the body that had been mysteriously dug up. "Like someone took a soil sample," said Brachtenbach.

While there was no apparent UFO or black helicopter connection, Matt Brachtenbach says that, in 2006, he viewed unexplained lights while traveling to Stratton.

In mid-July 2006, another mutilation occurred. Rancher Manuel Sanchez reported the mutilation of his five-year-old 1,500-pound, Limousin cow, which had been seen alive and healthy only a few days earlier. The Costilla County Sheriff's Office agreed to conduct an investigation. The cow, who had still been nursing her calf, was missing its udder, tongue, and rectum. Sheriff Roger Benton says, "I'm not positive, but I feel confident—from looking at the photos—to say this was a mutilation. I hope it's not happening again, but it's very consistent with the other ones I've investigated."

This was the third time Sanchez had lost a cow due to the mutilation phenomenon. "It's hard to say who or what did this," says Sanchez. "I know nobody from here could do that kind of work . . . It could not have been an animal. The cuts were clean. There was no blood, and the cuts are pretty strange. I've been a hunter and rancher. We don't do those kinds of cuts. It's a big loss; the meat goes to waste."

In October 2007, Darius (pseudonym) and a contractor he had hired were installing wood floors in his home in Wellington. The two men stepped outside for a break. Looking up, they were surprised to see the large number of contrails crossing east to west across the sky. Wellington is a rural area, and he had never seen so many contrails before. As Darius and the contractor studied the sky, they suddenly noticed something else. Says Darius, "As we looked up directly overhead, we both saw a small hovering object, right above us perhaps by a few hundred feet or more, hanging motionless. It was easily seen, in broad daylight. It was device unknown to me."

Darius had served in the military and been a candidate for flight school. Although familiar with aircraft, he had never seen anything like it. The object was a "very subdued, dark-green grey," had a faceted-shape, like a lunar lander but without legs, and had two globe-like protrusions on the underside.

"What is that?" asked the carpenter.

"I really don't know," Darius answered.

The object made noise as it hovered motionless for a few moments about 1,000 feet high. Then the globes beneath the object began to glow, and it slowly accelerated upward toward the northeast and off into the distance. "It was definitely not a conventional air vehicle," says Darius.

Shortly later, something else strange occurred. "Within a few days," said Darius, "we found a dead antelope about fifty-sixty yards from the southeast corner of the house. Antelope are very common in large herds in this area. This, however, was odd as it appeared to be a fairly young, healthy animal and was not attacked by predators. It was lying on its side, quite dead, with a large round hole in its left hindquarter, bigger than any firearm other than a 40-mm grenade launcher could make. No scorching, no blood, and no exit wound, just this big perfectly round hole."

Unlike most mutilations, predators soon devoured the carcass. Still, Darius wonders. "We have no idea what killed this animal," he says. "We do not know if there is a connection between the two events, but it is curious how close together they occurred."

March 8, 2009, rancher Mike Duran found a dead cow on his ranch near the Purgatoire River, west of Weston. The cow's udders and reproductive organs appeared to have been surgically removed. It wasn't the first time this has happened. He lost a cow under similar circumstances back in 1995.

March 17, 2009, Tom Miller, who owns a ranch with eighty head of cattle outside of Trinidad, found one of his young calves dead and mutilated. Almost the entire body of the animal had been taken. The only thing left was its spinal column, head, legs, and hide. "It's the strangest thing I've ever seen," said Miller. "I cut the hide, and the legs just fell off. All the bones were broken. It was just strange. An animal just doesn't clear out a carcass like that in one night. It would take several days to do something like that."

Miller was mystified for another reason. Normally, it would be very difficult to approach a calf. "The cows are too protective," he says. "If you went for a calf, the cow would be on top of you."

Who does Miller think is responsible? "I really don't know what it is," he says. "I think maybe it was a UFO. According to the circumstances, that is what it seems like . . . There are just too many strange things here . . . I really hope somebody can figure out what is happening to these things. It's scary."

This isn't pure speculation. Chuck Zukowski, a UFO researcher from Colorado Springs says he received a report of a "dark triangular craft" flying northwest over Colorado Springs. Says Zukowski, "That means it was coming from the Walsenburg/Trinidad area."

Five months later, in late August 2009, Jim Garren found one of his cows mutilated on his ranch southeast of Walsenburg. "The only thing we could tell about her was that her udder had been surgically removed," said Garren. "There were no other injuries to that cow . . . We searched and searched, and we could not find blood on the ground or on the cow. I just can't understand how anyone could surgically remove a part from an animal and not spill some blood . . . I don't see how any human could have possibly done this without leaving footprints or some prints where the cow may have struggled. It looks like she just laid down and died."

The cow was pregnant and due to give birth around the time the mutilation occurred. The mutilated cow was no longer pregnant. Garren searched his property and found the newborn calf, healthy and whole. He estimated that it had been born about ten hours before the mutilation of its mother.

Manuel Sanchez had already lost several animals to the mutilation phenomenon. In November 2009, he lost four more. Four calves were found in his pasture, located just north of the New Mexico state line. The calves had their hides peeled back and their organs removed. One calf was missing a tongue. As usual, there were no signs of predators, no tracks, and no blood.

According to a security worker on a ranch near Walsenburg, in 2014, there were multiple cattle mutilations in Huerfano County. In September 2015, he was on the night shift when he saw a "red orb" hovering over the area where the cattle mutilations had occurred. The orb made tight circles in the sky and zigzagged, flashing white, and turning back to red. "It seems to respond to thoughts somehow," says the witness.

Not long after he saw the orb, the witness (who has served eight years in the army) saw two black hawk helicopters surveying the area. The next night, the orb was back again and performed similar maneuvers.[6]

As can be seen, the animal mutilation phenomenon continues. Nor have investigators come any closer to solving the mystery than they were more than fifty years earlier.

People continue to attribute the mutilations to one of four theories.

1.   One of the most popular theories is that predators are responsible. This theory is rejected by virtually all current mutilation investigators as it doesn't even come close to explaining the evidence, including the surgical nature of the cuts, the use of a high-heat source, the lack of tracks, the removal of specific organs, not to mention the fact that most predators refuse to eat from a mutilated carcass. Despite this, those skeptical of the phenomenon still bring up the possibility of predators.

2.   Another theory is that Satanic cultists are responsible, a theory that seems logical considering the macabre nature of the injuries, with missing organs and lack of blood. Again, however, it fails to account for the lack of evidence, including tracks of any kind, or how such a thing could be accomplished without being detected. Nor does it explain the high numbers of incidents spread out over a very wide area.

3.   By far the most popular theory is that extraterrestrials are responsible. This explanation is supported by the number of accounts involving UFO sightings and/or apparent humanoids. The theory also explains the surgical nature of the injuries and the fact that the perpetrators have never been caught. Some researchers believe that the ETs abduct the animals for genetic purposes or perhaps environmental monitoring.

4.   The fourth popular theory is that some faction of the US Government is responsible, which would help explain why a portion of the cases involve strange, unmarked black helicopters, and the government's refusal to take the reports seriously, but fails to account for the reports of UFOs.

Some ranchers have raised the possibility that the explanation might lie with cultist aliens or cultist government officials. Whatever the explanation for the mutilations, the only thing known for sure is that each year will bring new cases.

CHAPTER 11

Current Encounters

Ever since the Modern Age of UFOs began in 1947, activity has continued strongly. Seventy years later, the parade of cases shows no signs of stopping. The UFOs, it appears, are not going away anytime soon. What follows are some of the more current Colorado sightings.

"It Was Changing Shape"

January 16, 2010, a wife and husband walking through a park in Fort Collins saw some people looking up at the sky and pointing at a large, black, slow-moving triangle. It was at a low altitude and appeared to be changing shape, though the husband thought it might be an effect from the reflecting sunlight. Says the wife: "I called my father-in-law who has a telescope, and he reported back that it was indeed changing shape. His initial sighting was of a stealth-shape triangle, but moving backward! As he watched, it shifted into a rectangular box before floating into a cloud." The wife snapped a cellphone picture which clearly shows the black triangle.[1]

"I Was in Awe"

March 4, 2010, a pilot with thirty-six years of experience was relaxing in his hot tub in his Colorado home (exact location not given), when he saw five lights moving across the sky. He first noticed them just after they passed overhead. To his surprise, the lights changed formation, and he wondered if he was seeing a triangular-shaped object or five separate anomalous lights. He heard no sound and watched as the objects turned to the northwest. "I was in awe when I first saw this," said the pilot, "as I have almost always been able to identify objects in the sky both day and night . . . I was very intrigued to finally see something that I was unable to identify."

The pilot reported his sighting to MUFON in the hopes that there were other witnesses.[2]

A Mysterious Bang

It was December 3, 2010, and Jacob (pseudonym) was house-sitting for his parents in Morrison. He was alone in the house except for his Australian Shepherd. At around 11:30 p.m., while he was in the kitchen, he saw two flashes of blue light in the backyard. He didn't think much of it until he saw a third flash, and his dog reacted by perking her ears and growling. Two more flashes followed. Then suddenly there was a "loud bang" in the bedroom upstairs. It sounded as though somebody had dropped a heavy box. Assuming there was an intruder, he called 911, then retreated to his parents' bedroom where there was a gun. About a minute later, the police arrived. Carrying his dog, he crawled out the window to meet them.

For the next twenty minutes, three officers searched in and around the house, but found nothing unusual. Jacob was telling one of the officers about the strange flashes of light, when the other two officers overheard and began to ask a series of questions about what Jacob saw. Surprised at their interest, Jacob asked them about it. They told him that they had received numerous calls the past year from other residents in the area who had reported the same phenomenon.[3]

Followed

December 11, 2010, a couple driving from Blackhawk to their home in Two Rivers realized that they were being followed by an unidentified flying object. It was a drive they had done twice a week for four years, and nothing strange had ever occurred. On this occasion, however, something did. It began in the Golden area when the wife noticed a bright light hovering toward the southeast. As they travelled east, the light also moved east. They speculated that perhaps it was a patrol helicopter from Aurora, where it was now heading.

However, as they turned north onto Highway 85, they were amazed to see that the object also veered north. They assumed it was still a conventional vehicle and would be landing at Denver International. "Well it didn't," says the wife. "It continued to travel north with us."

They drove past Fort Lupton and still the object followed. As they drove through Platteville, the object moved closer. Soon they approached the backroads leading to Two Rivers and their home. Still it followed. When they were ten minutes away from home, the object moved ahead of them.

By now, both were convinced that something was following them, but what? The husband believed it was a military aircraft, but had no explanation for why the military would be following them. The wife, however, believed it might be a UFO. She told her husband that she had recently become interested in UFOs and aliens and had seen some strange lights earlier in Black Hawk. She told him she thought it might be trying to communicate with them.

The husband was "uncomfortable" with that idea and still believed that the government was messing with them. He flipped his finger at them.

The wife insisted that they were law-abiding citizens, and there was no reason for the government or the military to follow them.

When they arrived home, the object stopped and hovered at a low elevation east of their house. By this point, they were both tired. They watched it for a little while longer, then went to bed. When they woke up the next morning, the object was gone.[4]

Another Triangle

March 25, 2011, Nick Vandervegt saw strange lights in the sky while driving to his parents' home in Lafayette. He rushed inside, alerted his father, Leroy, and together the two of them watched the UFO pass overhead. It had three lights in the shape of a triangle. "I don't know what they are," said Leroy. "It wasn't a satellite, it wasn't an airplane, and it wasn't a helicopter." The object was silent and seemed to hover at times. It moved at a slow rate of speed toward the southeast. The lights changed position slightly but remained in a triangular-shape. Leroy was able to videotape the object, which he posted on YouTube.

The Vandervegts weren't the only witnesses. Greeley MUFON section director, Doug Wilson, received four reports of what appears to be the same object. "It's unusual for us to have a single event with multiple reports," he said. "It's not just somebody pulling our legs."

Military Sighting

On March 14, 2011, two military police from Fort Carson on duty at Iron Horse Park near Colorado Springs observed "an odd light" approaching from the Pikes Peak area. The light was white at first, but as it zoomed toward them it changed to orange and then red. After zooming to the southeast, the object stopped, made a ninety-degree turn and "climbed out of sight at an almost unbelievable speed." Although the sighting lasted only forty-five seconds, it was enough to prompt them to call the police dispatch center to inquire about any known aircraft in the area. When they learned that none of the ranges were active, they decided not to officially report the sighting to their superiors, as they were afraid that they would be removed from their MP duties.

Not a Joke

September 15, 2011, a man and his wife were in their yard in Pueblo around 9:00 p.m. watching the stars. They saw five bright lights hanging high in the sky, and joked with each other that it was "aliens." It was just a joke, but two hours later, they were startled to see "very bright lights" shining through the trees in front of their house. To the wife, it looked as though a plane was about to crash. "We ran out into the street in a panic," said the husband. "There was a huge silver craft that was covered in flashing lights." The object was disk-shaped, about the size of a city bus, and flashed "every color in the rainbow." It hovered at treetop level and was moving slowly toward the north. The couple was awestruck and watched as the object remained in their area for about twenty minutes. Suddenly it shined a white beam of light at them. "We were so frightened," said the husband, "that we ran in our house and hid for the rest of the night."

This turned out to be the first of a series of sightings, including some during which they followed UFOs or were followed by them. Says the husband. "We have observed these objects many times. They can be seen regularly in the skies over Pueblo. I strongly urge anyone who is interested in UFOs to watch the sky above Pueblo, Colorado. There are strange things going on there on a regular basis."

A Black Disk

November 15, 2011, a woman from Lakewood experienced a sighting which inspired her to call authorities. "I was looking out my window," she said, "and saw what looked like a black disc flying through dark clouds. It was very hard to see, for it was very flat looking. It was moving much quicker than an airplane. When I saw it pass in front of a white cloud, I gasped because it was much bigger than I had thought! It looked about as long as a good-sized parking lot! All I could see was the edge, so I couldn't tell if it was a disk or a cigar-shaped craft. It came from the north and disappeared into the clouds on the east side."

Orange Lights

About two weeks later, on November 28, 2011 (also in Lakewood), a man was driving home when he saw a triangular-shaped object with orange lights. Never having seen anything like it before, he immediately thought: UFO. He had just been filming the sunset, so he took out his camera and filmed the object. The lights faded in and out several times as the object moved to the sound. "I was not scared," said the witness, "but rather intrigued." He remains uncertain if it was a genuine UFO or a conventional aircraft.[5]

UFO Rapture

Some UFO sightings seem to blend with religious elements. August 12, 2012, a woman from Denver was outside her apartment watering the plants when she saw a bright glowing object, much brighter than the stars. Having read about UFO abductions, she became fearful. She mentally sent a question to the UFO. "I asked if it was sent from the Christ (Jesus), and if so, would it blink off and back on," says the witness. "The star dimmed down and lit back up again. I then asked (again inaudibly, telepathically) if it was here for the rapture? It dimmed down and lit up again twice."

The star then moved slowly straight upward. At the same time, a dimmer more distant object also began to rise and move toward the first object. Together the two objects moved upward out of sight. The witness was so impressed, she reported her story to MUFON, investigator Linda Moulton Howe, and the *Coast-to-Coast* radio program.[6]

Colorado Springs Disk

May 11, 2013, a man went outside his Colorado Springs home to let his dogs out. Looking up, he saw three bright explosions of light overhead. About five minutes later, "a black cloud or shadow low on the horizon" started to move toward him. It was hard to observe as it moved closer and closer. It approached on a direct course and soon was passing one hundred feet directly overhead. "My dogs started to bark like crazy," says the witness. "All I could see was a black, dark shadow. I did not hear any noise other than my dogs barking. When it got over my carport and my next-door neighbor's house, the street light directly in front of my house came on . . . I immediately saw a dull gray object . . . it had no fuselage or tail and was smooth. There were no lights on it at all."

The object moved off into the distance and disappeared from view. The witness ran inside, got his camera, and climbed onto the roof of his house. By then, the object was gone. "I could not sleep," says the witness. "I don't understand what I saw."[7]

A Fleet of Orbs

Around 6:30 p.m. on February 12, 2015, a wife and husband driving to the Miramont Health Club in Colorado Springs noticed five orange orbs flying in from the southwest. They pulled over and got out of the car to watch. Soon, the occupant of another car joined them to watch the orbs. Next, a group of people came out of a nearby restaurant and began to watch. Shortly later, another driver stopped, got out of his car, and began talking about the orbs. A woman walking down the sidewalk came running up to them, asking if they had seen the orbs.

Soon two more orbs appeared, gliding together. A few minutes later, another orb appeared. After that, the last orb showed up, leaving the crowd of people buzzing and talking about what they had seen. Says the wife, "We said we hoped they were UFOs, because whatever it was, it would be difficult to explain."[8]

A V-Shaped Craft

It was around 8:30 p.m., March 21, 2015, when a young father from Longmont had "this sudden urge" to take his two-year-old outside to look at the stars. They had walked a few moments when his son looked up at the sky and pointed. Says the father, "What I saw shocked me. It was barely visible. I could barely see it, but could notice a very, very large, wide V or chevron-shaped craft just hovering completely still. It was a very clear night, no moon, and the stars were clear. This thing blended in with the stars. I could see the stars through this craft, almost as if it were glass or transparent. I only could see seven orange-yellowish, circular lights under it as it flew over us."

The object began moving a few seconds after they saw it. It moved overhead and off into the distance, making no sound. The father estimates that the object was no higher than 500 feet. "I mean, it was right there close, gigantic, in our face. It was bigger than our entire apartment building."

The father became spooked. Not only had he felt a strong urge to go outside, he felt almost as if the object was stalking him. As he says, "I have had a few other UFO encounters in the past few years. This was the scariest one."

As they walked home, he noticed headlights in a place where public vehicles aren't allowed. Beyond that he saw two SUVs parked with their headlights on alongside the road. Following this, he saw a "green laser-like dot" ahead of him on the road. He now wonders if perhaps he was part of a secret military operation.[9]

Keenesburg UFOs

On the evening of May 27, 2015, a family was driving through Keenesburg, heading toward South Dakota, when they saw a craft fly about a hundred feet overhead. It was triangular with bright lights down the center and red and blue lights on the side. They saw other cars pulled over on the interstate to watch. Soon they saw more objects move overhead. For the next forty-five minutes, a group of the objects followed them until they pulled off the highway to get gas. One of the objects was still in view. It appeared to be about the size of two football fields. One of the family members took video of the object, which appeared to show a door opening and figures moving around inside. They were thinking about stopping to observe more closely, but the niece became frightened and begged them to keep driving. They drove on and reached their destination. They had seen a total of eight UFOs.[10]

Pulsating Lights

April 3, 2016, three friends and one of their sons went winter camping at Handcart Campground in Pike National Forest outside Grant. While the six-year-old son went to bed early, the adults stayed up around the campfire, drinking a few beers and talking. They stayed up until about 10:00 p.m., then retired to their tents.

One of the men, Alec, admitted to an uneasy feeling, but disregarded it and tried to fall asleep. About 11:30 p.m., he woke up to urinate. He pulled on his boots, and still feeling uneasy, grabbed his pistol. "Something did not feel right out there," he says. "Words cannot describe it, but I was not at ease."

He returned to his tent and tried to fall asleep. Unfortunately, the wind was too loud and kept him awake. Suddenly he began seeing bright flashes of light outside his tent. He called out to one of his companions who offered a muffled response.

"For the next ten minutes, I stared at the roof of the tent, watching, terrified. My heart was racing, and try as I did, I could not get it to slow down." He felt as if he had been running, or was wondering if he was having a heart attack.

He heard his friends rustling around and called out again, but received no response. The lights flashed for about fifteen minutes, often in time with the gusts of wind. He tried putting his ear plugs in to calm himself down, but his heart still pounded.

At one point, the lights moved slightly and flashed green. "It was absolutely terrifying," says Alec, "and I didn't know what to think."

He again called out to his companions, but received no response. The next thing he remembers, it was the following morning.

As they broke camp, Brendan said that he thought he was going to have a heart attack, and began to describe exactly what Alec had experienced. Unlike Alec, however, he remembered hearing strange mechanical beeps. Like Alec, he also fell asleep while the lights were still present. The third friend and his son didn't remember anything unusual, other than it was an uncomfortable night.

Normally after camping for the night, they would make breakfast. This time they headed straight out. "Thinking of the event still makes me shudder," says Alec. "I'm still processing it. It terrified me. And as a lover of camping and the outdoors, it pains me to say that I have no desire to go camping again anytime soon."[11]

Three Copper Spheres

The year of 2017 produced dozens of sightings of unexplained lights and solid craft. One interesting report comes from Loveland. On the afternoon of April 9, 2017, a father and his kids went outside to fly a kite. Says the father, "When I was looking up at the kite, I noticed three spheres. The spheres were next to the kite but seemed far in the sky. The spheres looked copper-like and had a shadow."

The sphere's first appeared in a triangular pattern. But as he watched, two of the spheres changed their position so that all three spheres were now in a perfect line. At this point, the objects disappeared.[12]

Take a Picture

Not surprisingly, many people have been able
to capture amazing photographs of UFOs.
What follows are some of the better
photographic cases.

(Photo Credits: MUFON CMS)

1929-SlideWard-Colorado (Pline)

In 1929, Edward Pline photographed this object as it hovered over a Saw Mill in Ward.

August 27, 1995, Tim Edwards of Salida
videotaped a UFO that hovered above his
home. This image is a still taken from his
videotape.

August 2, 2003, a witness at a bus stop in
Boulder snapped a photo of these objects,
which appeared suddenly, hovered briefly,
then darted quickly away.

April 12, 2006, a man saw this cluster of objects over Golden. They appeared too large to be birds or balloons, had a metallic reflective texture, and moved in a strange "liquid" motion. Suddenly the group of objects veered apart into two sections and came together to form a triangle. He watched them for about five minutes until they "jetted off very quickly" toward the northwest and were gone.

May 18, 2006, a truck driver in Virginia Dale was taking pictures while driving. He spotted what he first thought was a plane, then realized it was moving too quickly. When it disappeared and reappeared in a nearby location, he knew it was unusual and quickly snapped the photo.

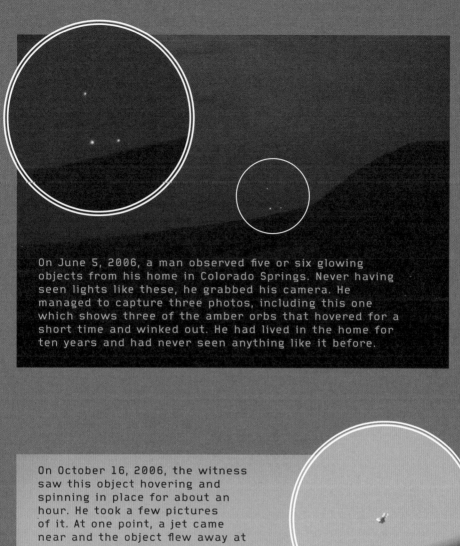

On June 5, 2006, a man observed five or six glowing objects from his home in Colorado Springs. Never having seen lights like these, he grabbed his camera. He managed to capture three photos, including this one which shows three of the amber orbs that hovered for a short time and winked out. He had lived in the home for ten years and had never seen anything like it before.

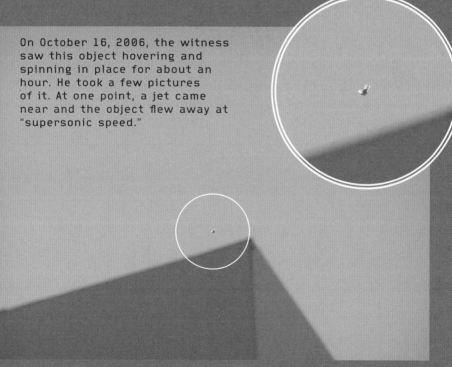

On October 16, 2006, the witness saw this object hovering and spinning in place for about an hour. He took a few pictures of it. At one point, a jet came near and the object flew away at "supersonic speed."

On the evening of June 6, 2006, ghost hunter, J. Muirhead joined a group of other ghost hunters in Ault Cemetery hoping to record paranormal activity. Instead they saw a small glowing saucer-shaped object moving around the top of a nearby tree. One of them quickly snapped the above photo. Afterward they saw other strange lights in the sky.

November 21, 2010, the photographer noticed a bright light over his neighborhood in Parker. When more objects showed up, he began to take pictures. The objects hovered briefly before leaving one by one in the same direction.

Around 6:00 p.m. June 2, 2012, a man and his son from Highland Ranch were standing out on their balcony when they saw three cylindrical-shaped objects in a triangular pattern moving slowly toward them. Suddenly the objects stopped and one of them extended a protrusion from its lower side. The father quickly snapped the photograph, at which point they "accelerated out of sight."

January 15, 2013, a woman was taking
pictures of a sunset in an unnamed location
in Colorado. Sometimes, it appears, the camera
is quicker than the eye. One of the photos
showed a bell-shaped object with a rim and a
tapered lower section. It was not visible when
she took the picture.

September 10, 2015.
The photographer was
taking a picture of
the sun setting over
Greeley and did not
see the strange object
until reviewing the
picture afterward.

Epilogue

As we have seen, Colorado's contributions to our understanding of the UFO phenomenon are undeniable. The mutilation of Lady the horse in Alamosa in 1967 brought the world's attention to the animal mutilation phenomenon. The August 1995, video footage by Tim Edwards of a UFO over Salida has been called some of the best footage ever taken. The Stan Romanek abduction case in Denver and the large amount of evidence it has produced continues to cause waves in the UFO community and beyond. The high levels of activity in the San Luis Valley have drawn researchers and UFO hunters from across the world and have even inspired the construction of Colorado's first official UFO watchtower. Finally, people are still talking about what crashed on Greenie Mountain back in 1994. While these cases had the fortune (good or bad) to become popular, most cases receive little or no publicity.

Colorado has a strong military presence with numerous military bases and the Cheyenne Mountain Complex which tracks all aerial traffic in the United States. And as we have seen, they are well aware of the high levels of UFO activity over Colorado. The many cases of UFOs over Colorado Springs makes it hard to believe otherwise, not to mention the reports coming from insiders.

What the future will bring isn't hard to guess. More people will come forward with photographs and videotapes. There will be more sightings and landings, more onboard experiences, and sooner or later, another UFO crash. Almost certainly there will be continuing waves of cattle and animal mutilations.

With trends escalating toward disclosure, the future might even bring about an admission of UFO reality from the government and even open official contact between humans and aliens.

Whatever happens, UFOs appear to be here to stay. Whether disclosure happens tomorrow or years from now, we will still have to learn to deal with these visitors who seem so different from us, and yet, in many ways, very much the same.

Endnotes

Epigraphs and Chapter 1: Early Encounters

1. Gavin Gibbons, *The Coming of the Space Ships* (New York: Citadel Press, 1958), 30.
2. Timothy Good, *Contact: Top Secret UFO Files Revealed* (New York: William Morrow and Company, 1993), 47.
3. Ibid., 46.
4. Arlene Shovald, "Edward's UFO Sighting Not Salida's First," *Mountain Mail*, (Sep 7, 1995), 2 (UFO Newsclipping Service [UFONS], Nov 1995, #316, 2).
5. MUFON CMS. Paris Flammonde, *UFO Exist!* (New York: Ballantine Books, 1976), 258; Bob Gribble, "Looking Back: May 1947," *MUFON UFO Journal #289*, (May 1992), 19; Jacques Vallee, *Anatomy of a Phenomenon: UFOs in Space* (New York: Ballantine Books, 1965), 55.
6. Dewayne B. Johnson and Kenn Thomas, *UFOs Over Los Angeles: The UFO Craze of the 50's* (Kempton, IL: Adventures Unlimited Press, 1998), 64. Frank Scully, *Behind the Flying Saucers* (New York: Henry Holt and Company, 1950), 227; Staff, "Oil Basin Folks Wonder, Did They See Flying Saucers?" *Rangely Driller*, (April 28, 1950).
7. Dewayne B. Johnson and Kenn Thomas, 202–203. Marc Davenport, *Visitors from Time: The Secret of UFOs* (Tuscaloosa, AL: Greenleaf Publications, 1992), 84; Flammonde, 308; Richard H. Hall, ed., *The UFO Evidence* (1997), 158; www.nicap.org/1952ad.htm.
8. NUFORC.
9. Ibid.
10. www.nicap.org/1955.htm; www.nicap.org/waves/1955fullrep.htm.
11. Bob Gribble, "Looking Back: May 1956," *MUFON UFO Journal #277*, May 1991, 16.
12. MUFON CMS.
13. Mark H. Hunter, "UFO Enthusiast Comes Home to First Site," *Valley Courier*. Alamosa, CO, Sep 10, 1994. (UFONs, Oct 1994, #303, p3).
14. MUFON CMS.
15. www.nicap.org/1958.htm; www.nicap.org/1957.htm; Milt Machlin, *The Total UFO Story* (New York: Dale Books, 1979), 99; MUFON CMS; Staff, "Weatherman Sees Flying Saucer," *Press*. Cleveland, OH, Jun 18, 1952.

Chapter 2: Sightings 1960-1969

1. Coral Lorenzen and Jim Lorenzen, *UFOs: The Whole Story*. (New York: New American Library, 1969), 224–225.
2. NUFORC.
3. Ibid.
4. Ibid.
5. Ibid.
6. www.nicap.org/1964.htm.
7. Coral Lorenzen, *Flying Saucers: The Startling Evidence of the Invasion from Outer Space* (New York: Signet Books, 1962), 238–239.
8. Brad Steiger, *Strangers from the Skies* (London: Tandem Books, 1966), 50–51.
9. Paris Flammonde, *UFO Exist!* (New York: Ballantine Books, 1976),16, 411; Raymond E. Fowler, *Casebook of a UFO Investigator* (Englewood Cliffs, NJ: Prentice-Hall, Inc, 1981), 54; Raymond E. Fowler, *UFOs Interplanetary Visitors* (New York: Bantam Books, 1979), 157–159.
10. Hans Holzer, *The UFOnauts: New Facts on Extraterrestrial Landings*. (Greenwich, CT: Fawcett Publications, 1976), 35; www.ufosnw.com/sighting_reports/older/coloradoufophoto/coloradoufophoto.htm.
11. Allen J. Hynek, *The UFO Experience: A UFO Experience* (New York: Ballantine Books, 1972), 22, 265.
12. Coral Lorenzen and Jim Lorenzen, *UFOs Over the Americas* (New York: Signet Books, 1968), 163.
13. NUFORC.
14. Major Donald E. Keyhoe, (USMC Ret.), *Aliens from Space: The Real Story of Unidentified Flying Objects* (New York: Signet Books, 1973), 214–215.
15. MUFON CMS.
16. NUFORC.
17. Ibid.
18. Lorenzen & Lorenzen, 1968, 162–166.
19. Ibid, 177.
20. NUFORC.
21. Ibid.
22. Ibid.
23. Ibid.
24. Ibid.

Chapter 3: Sightings 1970–1979

1. NUFORC.
2. Ibid.
3. Ibid.
4. Ibid.
5. Captain Kevin D. Randle, (USAF Ret.), *The UFO Casebook* (New York: Warner Books, 1989), 142–143.
6. NUFORC.
7. Ibid.
8. MUFON CMS.
9. NUFORC.
10. Ibid.
11. MUFON CMS.
12. NUFORC.
13. Ibid.
14. Ibid.
15. Ibid.
16. Ibid.
17. MUFON CMS.
18. NUFORC.
19. Bob Gribble, "Pilot Sightings and Radar Trackings," *MUFON UFO Journal #181*, (Mar 1983).

Chapter 4: Sightings 1980–1989

1. MUFON CMS.
2. NUFORC.
3. Bob Gribble, "Looking Back: 1981," *MUFON UFO Journal #276*, (Apr 1991).
4. NUFORC.
5. Ibid.
6. Ibid.
7. Ibid.
8. Ibid.
9. Kenneth Ring, Ph.D., *The Omega Project: Near-Death Experiences, UFO Encounters and Mind at Large* (New York: William Morrow and Company, 1992), 48.
10. Monty Gaddy, "Monty's Musings: Cattle Mutilation Phenomenon Remains a Mystery," *Ranchland News #304*, Simla, CO, Sep 15, 1994 (UFONS, Nov 1994).
11. NUFORC.
12. www.ufoevidence.org/sightings/report.asp?ID=8994.
13. MUFON CMS.

14. Ibid.
15. NUFORC.
16. MUFON CMS.
17. Christopher O'Brien, *The Mysterious Valley* (New York: St. Martin's Press 1996), 22–23.
18. NUFORC.

Chapter 5: Sightings 1990–1999

1. Tim Beckley, ed., "Asteroid Belt: Colorado's Mysterious Hum," *UFO Universe*, (Winter 1996).
2. Christopher O'Brien, *The Mysterious Valley*, 23–24.
3. NUFORC.
4. Christopher O'Brien, *The Mysterious Valley*, 24–25.
5. Ibid, 33–36.
6. Ibid, 27–28. David B. Clemens, "High Strangeness in a Colorado Valley," *MU-FON UFO Journal #313*, (May 1994); Christopher O'Brien, "Mutants and Mutilations," *Fate*. St. Paul, MN: Llewellyn, Sep 1995, 32–35.
7. Bill Briggs, "San Luis Valley Home to a Hotbed of Strange," *Post*. Denver, CO, March 15, 1994 (UFONs, May 1994, #298, 2); Christopher O'Brien, "Southern Colorado UFO and Mutilation Activity Update," *UFO Encounters* 1, no. 12.. Norcross, GA: Aztec Publishing, Volume 1, #12, 8–9.
8. Bill Briggs, "San Luis Valley Home to a Hotbed of Strange," *Post #298* . Denver, CO, March 15, 1994 (UFONs, May 1994, #298, 2).
9. Monty Gaddy, "Monty's Musings: Cattle Mutilation Phenomenon Remains a Mystery," *Ranchland News*, Simla, CO, Sep 15, 1994 (UFONS, Nov 1994, #304, 18).
10. NUFORC.
11. Kerth, Linda, "Strange Things in the Sky," *Rio Grande Sun*. Espanola, NM, Jul 4, 1996 (UFONs, Dec 1996, #329, 8–9).
12. Christopher O'Brien, *The Mysterious Valley*, 267–268.
13. NUFORC. D'Arcy Fallon, "UFO Sightings Transfix Residents." *Gazette Telegraph*, Colorado Springs, CO, Jan 7, 1996. (UFONs, Feb 1996, #319, 6); Major George A. Filer USAF, *Filer's Files: Worldwide Reports of UFO Sightings* (West Conshohocken, PA: Infinity Publishing.com, 2005), 126–127; Chris Hunt, "UFO Tape Analyzed," *Herald Democrat*, Leadville, CO, Sep 25, 1995 (UFONs, Nov 1995, #316, p11); MUFON CMS; Christopher O'Brien, "Sightings of Strange Objects Near Salida Continue," *Eagle*, Crestone, CO, Nov 1995 (UFONs, Jan 1996, #318, p1); Christopher O'Brien, *Enter the Valley*, (New York: St. Martin's Press, 1994), 55–84; Patrick O'Driscoll, "Salida's 'Close Encounter,' *Post*, Denver, CO,

Jul 7, 1996 (UFONs, Jul 1996, #324, p9); Arlene Shovald, "More UFOs Sighted over Salida," *Mountain Mail*. Salida, CO, Sep 26, 1995 (UFONs, Nov 1995, #316, p2); Arlene Shovald, "Salida Man Not Alone in Sighting UFO," *Mountain Mail*, CO, Sep 11, 1995 (UFONs, Nov 1995, #316, p2); Zack Van Eyck, "Colorado Man and His Films Bring UFO Meet Back to Earth," *Deseret News*. Salt Lake City, UT, Nov 30/Dec 1, 1995 (UFONs, Jan 1996, #318, 1); Murray Weis, "Edwards Gets More UFO Video from Salida," *Chronicle and Pilot*, Crested Butte, CO, Dec 15, 1995 (UFONs, Feb 1996, #319, 9); Thomas Wills, "Alien Lights and Black Helicopters," *Valley Chronicle*, Hotchkiss, CO, Dec 1995 (UFONs Jan 1996, #318, 6).

14. NUFORC.

15. Mark H. Hunter, "Center Man Shoots UFO Video," *Valley Courier*, Alamosa, CO, Feb 8, 1996 (UFONs, Mar 1996, #320, 3); Christopher O'Brien, "Unexplained Sightings Continue in Valley," *Eagle*, Crestone, CO, Apr 1996 (UFONs, May 1996, #322, p3).

16. Richard F. Haines, Ph.D., *CE-5: Close Encounters of the Fifth Kind* (Naperville, IL: Sourcebooks, Inc., 1999), 159–160.

17. NUFORC.

18. Tony Daranyi, "UFOs Sighted over Lone Cone," *Morning Sun*, Montrose, CO, Mar 11, 1997 (UFONs, May 1997, #334, 9).

19. Susan Baxter, "Suspected UFO Reported Over Snowshoe Mountain," *Valley Courier*, Alamosa, CO, March 28, 1996 (UFONs, Jun 1996, #323, p10); Erin Smith, "Bright Lights Cause Big Stir in Valley," *Chieftain*, CO, April 30, 1996 (UFONs, Jun 1996, #323, 10).

20. NUFORC.

21. MUFON CMS.

22. NUFORC.

23. Ibid.

24. Curt Sutherly, *UFO Mysteries: A Reporter Seeks the Truth* (St. Paul, MN: Llewellyn Publications, 2001), 203.

25. George Filer, "Filer's Files: Colorado," *MUFON UFO Journal #367*, Nov 1998, 13–14; George Filer, "Triangular UFO in Colorado," *MUFON UFO Journal*, Sep 1998, 21; NUFORC.

26. Sutherly, Curt. *UFO Mysteries: A Reporter Seeks the Truth*. St. Paul, MN: Llewellyn Publications, 2001. 203.

27. Filer, George. "Filer's Files: Colorado" *MUFON UFO Journal*, Nov 1998, #367, pp13-14; Filer, George. "Triangular UFO in Colorado" MUFON UFO Journal, Sep 1998, p21; NUFORC.

Chapter 6: Sightings 2000–2009

1. Bob Gribble, "Looking Back: Object Frightens Colorado Woman," *MUFON UFO Journal #385*, May 200018; Christopher O'Brien, "Stranger Than Fiction," *Eagle*: Crestone, CO, April 2000 (UFONs, Aug 2000, #373, 8) Deborah Frazier, "ET Watch," *Rocky Mountain News*: Denver, CO, July 23, 2000 (UFONs, Aug 2000, #373, 6–7); Erin Smith, "UFO Fans to Alight Near Hooper," *The Pueblo Chieftain*, Pueblo CO, Aug 3, 2003 (UFONs, Sep 2003, #410, 8.); www.ufowatchtower.com/.
2. NUFORC.
3. Randy Wyrick, "Close Encounters of the Eagle County Kind," *Daily*, Vail, CO, Jun 6, 2001 (UFONs, Jun 2001, #383, 4).
4. Ibid.
5. George Filer, "Filer's Files: Colorado Cigar-shaped UFO Reported," *MUFON UFO Journal*, April 2001, 11.
6. Randy Wyrick, "Close Encounters of the Eagle County Kind." *Daily*, Vail, CO, Jun 6, 2001 (UFONs, Jun 2001, #383, 4).
7. www.ufowatchtower.com/.
8. MUFON CMS.
9. George Filer, "Filer's Files: V-Shaped Object in Colorado," *MUFON UFO Journal #417*, Jan 2013, 15.
10. www.ufowatchtower.com/.
11. MUFON CMS.
12. Editor, "Durango Man Reports a UFO," *Post*, Denver, Colorado, Oct 28, 2003 (see UFONs, #2003, #412, 2); Patricia Miller, "Durangoan Reports He Saw UFO," *Herald*, Durango, CO, October 25, 2003 (See UFONs, Jan 2004, #414, 1).
13. MUFON CMS.
14. George Filer, "Filer's Files: Colorado 'Star' in Daytime Sky," *MUFON UFO Journal #436*.
15. George Filer, "Filer's Files: Huge Disc in Colorado," *MUFON UFO Journal #439*, Nov 2004, 18.
16. George Filer, "Large Object in Colorado," *MUFON UFO Journal #446*, June 2005, 12.
17. George Filer, "Colorado Pilot Describes UFO," *MUFON UFO Journal #465*, Jan 2007, 14.
18. George Filer, "Colorado Triangle Makes Passes," *MUFON UFO Journal #465*, Jan 2007, 14.
19. MUFON CMS.
20. George Filer, "Filer's Files: Colorado Dark Triangle," *MUFON UFO Journal #471*, July 2007, 20.
21. Ibid.

22. MUFON CMS.
23. Bill Jackson, "Strange Lights Reported in the Sky," *The Tribune*, *Greeley*, CO, May 1 2008 (See UFONs, May 2008, #466, 4).
24. MUFON; www.bing.com/videos/search?q=Denver+Airport+Conspiracy&&view=detail&mid=CF60A4CE14C1E1A48F4FCF60A4CE14C1E1A48F-4F&FORM=VRDGAR.
25. MUFON CMS.
26. George Filer, "Filer's Files: Trying to Create an Extraterrestrial Affairs Commission," *MUFON UFO Journal #483*, July 2008, 18; Extraterrestrial Affairs Comission. https://ballotpedia.org/Denver_Extraterrestrial_Affairs_Commission_Creation_Referendum_(2010).
27. Dan Cunningham, "UFO Reported in Colorado," *Bent County Democrat/Gate County News Service*, Fowler, CO, Jan 7, 2009 (UFONs, Jan 2009, #474, 7).
28. NUFORC.
29. Staff, "Broomfield UFO Sighting Lands on Web," *Broomfield Enterprise*, Broomfield, CO, Sep 2, 2009 (UFONs, Sep 2009, #482, 7).
30. Peter Jones, "Close Encounters of the Suburban Kind," *Centennial Citizens News*, Littleton, CO, Jan 21, 2010 (UFONs, Feb 2010, #487, 3).
31. Jones, Peter. "Close Encounters of the Suburban Kind." *Centennial Citizens News*. *Littleton*, CO, Jan 21, 2010. (UFONs, Feb 2010, #487, p3.)

Chapter 7: Landings and Humanoids

1. NUFORC.
2. MUFON CMS.
3. NUFORC.
4. MUFON CMS.
5. Christopher O'Brien, *The Mysterious Valley*, 49,
6. Gabriel Green, and Warren Smith, *Let's Face the Facts about Flying Saucers*. (New York: Popular Library, 1967), 8–10.
7. Green, 112–113.
8. Lorenzen & Lorenzen, 1968, 162-163.
9. Curt Sutherly, *UFO Mysteries: A Reporter Seeks the Truth*. (St. Paul, MN: Llewellyn Publications, 2001), 47, 55.
10. Jim and Coral Lorenzen, 1968, 177–178.
11. MUFON CMS.
12. Ibid.
13. Ibid.
14. Ibid.
15. Ibid.

16. Bob Gribble, "Looking Back," *MUFON UFO Journal #233*, Seguin, TX: Mutual UFO Network, Sept 1987, 19.
17. NUFORC.
18. NUFORC.
19. Curt Sutherly, 70.
20. Richard J. Boylan and Lee K. Boylan, *Close Extraterrestrial Encounters* (Tigard, OR: Newberg Press, 1994), 120–121.
21. Brad Steiger, *The UFO Abductors*, 139–143.
22. Christopher O'Brien, *Enter the Valley*, 208–209.
23. John Dicker, "The Aliens Among Us," *Independent #405*, Colorado Springs, CO, April 2003 (See UFONs, Jan 9, 200, 1–3)
24. Christopher O'Brien, *The Mysterious Valley*, 26–27.
25. Christopher O'Brien, "Sightings of Strange Objects Near Salida Continue," *Eagle,* Crestone, CO, Nov 1995 (UFONs, Jan 1996, #318, 1).
26. NUFORC.
27. Christopher O'Brien, *The Mysterious Valley*, 188–190.
28. NUFORC.
29. Christopher O'Brien, *The Mysterious Valley*, 250–251; Christopher O'Brien, *Enter the Valley*, 206.
30. MUFON CMS.
31. Christopher O'Brien, *The Mysterious Valley*, 254–255.
32. Christopher O'Brien, "Sightings of Strange Objects Near Salida Continue," *Eagle*, Crestone, CO, Nov 1995 (UFONs, Jan 1996, #318, 1).
33. NUFORC.
34. Mr. Morris, "More Sightings of Horsetooth Reservoir Creature," *Standard-Blade*, Brighton, CO, Apr 22, 1995 (UFONs, Jun 1995, #311, 18).
35. NUFORC.
36. MUFON CMS.
37. MUFON CMS.
38. George Filer, "Filer's Files: Colorado Sighting by Mackay," *MUFON UFO Journal #448*, (Aug 2005 16.
39. MUFON.
40. NUFORC.
41. UFO Casebook. www.ufocasebook.com/2011/marciaburke.html; Peter Jones, "Close Encounters of the Suburban Kind," *Centennial Citizens News*, Littleton, CO, Jan 21, 2010 (UFONs, Feb 2010, #487, 3).
42. MUFON CMS.
43. Ibid.
44. Ibid.
45. Ibid.

46. Ibid.
47. George Filer, "Filer's Files: Colorado Encounter with Light and Entities," *MU-FON UFO Journal #439*, May 2009, 17.
48. MUFON CMS.
49. Ibid.
50. Ibid.
51. Ibid.
52. Ibid.
53. Ibid.
54. Ibid.
55. Ibid.
56. NUFORC.
57. Ibid.
58. Ibid.

Chapter 8: Onboard UFO Experiences

1. Project 1947. http://project1947.com/shg/symposium/sprinkle.html; Ruth Montgomery, *Aliens Among Us* (New York: Fawcett Crest books, 1985), 30–31.
2. NUFORC.
3. UFO.net. https://ufo.net/2009/06/12/colorado-usa-1955/comment-page-1/; MUFON CMS; NUFORC.
4. NUFORC.
5. Haines, Ph.D., 401–404.
6. MUFON CMS.
7. Bill Briggs, "We're Not Alone: Tale of UFO Landing Not So Unusual in Yuma," *Post*, Denver, CO, March 12, 2000 (See UFONs, April 2000, #369, 3); Rich Tosche, "UFOs Make Yuma Man's Life a Pit Stop," *Post*, Denver CO, May 9, 2007 (UFONs, Jun 2007, #455, 5–6).
8. Brad Steiger, *The UFO Abductors* (New York: Berkley Books, 1988), 1–5.
9. Christopher O'Brien, *The Mysterious Valley*, 37–39.
10. Richard Hall, *Uninvited Guests: A Documented History of UFO Sightings, Alien Encounters and Coverups* (Santa Fe, NM: Aurora Press, 1988), 311–312.
11. NUFORC.
12. Whitley Strieber & Anne Strieber, eds., *The Communion Letters* (New York: HarperPrism, 1997), 158–165.
13. MUFON CMS.
14. Ibid.
15. Ibid.
16. Earth Files. www.earthfiles.com/news.php?ID=2426&category=Environment.

17. MUFON CMS.
18. John Dicker, "The Aliens Among Us," *Independent #405*, . Colorado Springs, CO, April 2003, (See UFONs, Jan 9, 200, 1–3).
19. MUFON CMS.
20. Christopher O'Brien, *Enter the Valley* (New York: St. Martins Press, 1999), 50–54, 317.
21. Ibid, 295.
22. NUFORC.
23. George Filer, "Filer's File: Colorado," *MUFON UFO Journal #368*, Dec 1998, 12.
24. George Filer, "Filer's Files: Colorado Abduction?" *MUFON UFO Journal*, November 2000, 9–10.
25. MUFON CMS.
26. Ibid.
27. NUFORC.
28. www.ufowatchtower.com.
29. Stan Romanek, *Messages: The World's Most Documented Extraterrestrial Contact Story* (Woodbury, MN: Llewellyn Publications, 2009).
30. MUFON CMS.
31. www.ufowatchtower.com.
32. MUFON CMS.
33. Ibid.
34. Ibid.
35. Ibid.
36. Ibid.
37. Ibid.
38. Ibid.
39. Ibid.
40. Ibid.
41. Ibid.

Chapter 9: UFO Crashes

1. Preston Dennett, *UFOs over New Mexico: A True History of Extraterrestrial Encounters in the Land of Enchantment* (Atglen, PA: Schiffer Publishing, 2011), 231–234; Scott and Suzanne Ramsey, *The Aztec Incident: Recovery at Hart Canyon* (Mooresville, NC: Aztec. 48 Productions. 2011), 103, 129; Frank Scully, *Behind the Flying Saucers* (New York: Henry Holt and Company, 1950), 1–30.
2. May Clemens, 13; David B. Clemens, "High Strangeness in a Colorado Valley," *MUFON UFO Journal #313*, May 1994, 13.

3. Staff, "Mysterious Glow Causes Search for Plane Crash," *Enterprise*. Eagle, CO, Jul 28, 1988 (UFONs, Nov 1988, #232, 12)
4. Bill Briggs, "San Luis Valley Home to a Hotbed of Strange," *Post*, Denver, CO, March 15, 1994 (UFONs, May 1994, #298, 2); Becky Dillon, "More Strange Lights Sighted at Rock Creek," *Prospector*, Del Norte, CO, Mar 29, 1995 (UFONs, May 1995, #310, 1); Dick Foster, "Fire on Radar Heats Up Mystery," *Rocky Mountain News*, Denver, CO, Jan 25, 1994 (UFONs, Feb 1994, #295, 10); Christopher O'Brien, "Mutants and Mutilations," *Fate*, St. Paul, MN: Llewellyn, Sep 1995, 32–33, 35; Christopher O'Brien, *The Mysterious Valley*, 226–232; Brad Smith, "Mystery 'Heat Source' Sparks Wonder," *Post,* Denver, CO, Jan 27, 1994 (UFONs, Feb 1994, #295, 10).
5. NUFORC.
6. Ibid.
7. Ibid.
8. MUFON CMS.

Chapter 10: The Mutilations

1. Good, 1993, 41–45; Lorenzen & Lorenzen, 1968, 148–158, 163; NUFORC; Christopher O'Brien, *The Mysterious Valley*, 65–86, 178; Week In Weird. http://weekinweird.com/2013/01/08/death-dunes-ufos-start-cattle-mutilation-san-luis-valley.
2. Monty Gaddy, "Monty's Musings: Cattle Mutilation Phenomenon Remains a Mystery," *Ranchland News*, (September 15, 1994). (UFONS, Nov 1994, #304, p18); Linda Moulton Howe, "UFO Mutilations, Crashed Saucers and Aliens in Government Captivity," *UFO Universe #1*, no. 1, (1988).; Christopher O'Brien, "Mutants and Mutilations," *Fate*, (September 1995); Christopher O'Brien, *Strange Harvest for the San Luis Valley: Cattle Mutilations Begin Again* Crestone, CO: Eagle, 1993) (UFONs, Mar 1993. #284, p20); Jacques Vallee, *Messengers of Deception: UFO Contacts and Cults* (New York: Bantam Books, 1979), 177, 189–190.
3. Good, 1993, 62–72.
4. Good, 1993, 58–59; Michael Lindemann, ed., *UFOs and the Alien Presence: Six Viewpoints* (Santa Barbara, CA: The 20/20 Group, 1991), 68; Linda Moulton Howe, "UFO Mutilations, Crashed Saucers and Aliens in Government Captivity," *UFO Universe*, New York: Condor Books, Vol 1, #1, 198818; Christopher O'Brien, *The Mysterious Valley*, 42–43, 48; Zack Van Eyck, "Horse's Death Brought Issue to Light," *New Mexican,* (September 18, 1994). (UFONs, Oct 1994, #303, pp18–19).
5. Tracie Cone, "Watch the Skies," *Mercury News*, San Jose, CA—Feb 2, 1997 (See also UFONS, March 1997, #332, p18); Angela Cortez, "Cattle, Deer Found Mu-

tilated," *Post*, Denver, CO, Jul 29, 1995 (UFONs, Sep 1995, #314, p19); Juan Espinosa, "Devil Worship? Mutilated Cow Found on Pueblo County Ranch," *Chieftain*. Pueblo, CO, June 25, 1993 (UFONs, Aug 1993, #289, p20); Dick Foster, "Officials Suspect Cultists in Latest Cow Mutilation," *Rocky Mountain News*. Denver, CO, May 28, 1993 (UFONs, Jun 1993, #287, p19); Mark H. Hunter, "Horse Mutilated near Pike Stockade," *Valley Courier*, Alamosa, CO, March 10, 1998 (See UFONs, April 1998, #345, p17); Mark H. Hunter, "Mutilated Horse Found Near Alamosa," *Valley Courier*. Colorado, Dec 30, 1997 (See UFONs, Feb 1998, #343, p20); Bill Jackson, "Mutilations Leave Many Questions," *Tribune*, Greeley, CO, Jun 27, 1993 (UFONs, Sep 1993, #290, p19); Becky Noland, "Apparent Calf Mutilation Has Officials Wondering, 'Who?' 'Why?'" *Post Dispatch*, Center CO, Dec 3, 1997 (See UFOs, Jan 1998, #342, p19); Christopher O'Brien, *Enter the Valley*, 130–132; Christopher O'Brien, *The Mysterious Valley*, 36, 39, 235–238; Christopher O'Brien, "Sightings of Strange Objects Near Salida Continue," *Eagle*, Crestone, CO, Nov 1995 (UFONs, Jan 1996, #318, p1); Christopher O'Brien, "Strange Harvest for the San Luis Valley: Cattle Mutilations Begin Again," *Eagle*, Crestone, CO, Feb 1993 (UFONs, Mar 1993. #284, p20); R. Scott Rappold, "Mysterious Animal Deaths, Mutilations Continue to Plague Colorado Ranches," *MUFON UFO Journal #454*, Feb 200619; Staff, "Andreatta Cattle Mutilated," *Signature*, La Veta, CO, Nov 3, 1994 (UFONs, Mar 1995, #308, p18); Zack Van Eyck, "Horse's Death Brought Issue to Light," *New Mexican*, Santa Fe, NM, Sept 18, 1994 (UFONs, Oct 1994, #303, pp18–19).

6. Associated Press. "Bizarre Calf Mutilations Found on Colorado Ranch," Nov 25, 2009 (UFONs, Jan 2010, #486, p20); Amy Brouillette, "Poison Ruled Out in 7 Animals' Deaths" *Post*, Denver, CO, Oct 26, 2005 (UFONS, Dec 2005, #437, p20); Amy Brouillette, "Town Baffled by Deaths of 22 Horses," *Post*, Denver CO, Oct 25, 2005 (UFONs, Nov 2005, #436, p20.); Dan Cunningham, "Cattle Deaths Mystify Colorado Ranchers," *AG Journal*, La Junta CO, Jul 7, 2006 (UFONs, Oct 2006, #447, p17); George Filer, "Colorado Mutilations Reported," *MUFON UFO Journal #446*, June 200515; Amy Hatten, "Sheriff Probes Mutilated Cattle," *Daily Press*, Craig CO, Oct 20, 2004 (UFONS, Dec 2004, #425, p18); Anthony A. Mestas, "Two More Cows Found Mutilated," *Pueblo Chieftain*, Pueblo, CO, Aug 29, 2009 (UFONs, Oct 2009, #483, pp19–20); MUFON CMS; Scott Rappold, "I've Got to Think It's UFOs," *Gazette*, Colorado Springs, Co, Jan 7, 2006 (UFONS, Feb 2006, #439, p3); Erin Smith, "Costilla County Officials Probe Cattle Mutilation," *Chieftain*, Pueblo CO, Jul 22, 2006 (UFONs, Sep 2006, #446, p18); Rick Tosches, "Theories on Recent Cattle Mutilations Sort of Alien," *Post*. Denver CO, May 24, 2006, (UFONs, Jun 2006, #443, p20.); www.chieftain.com/home/1470804-120/zukowski-carcass-miller-animal

Chapter 11: Current Encounters

1. George Filer, "Colorado Photo," *MUFON UFO Journal #502*, Feb 2010, 23.
2. Staff, "Colorado Pilot Unable to Identify Five Lights Passing Overhead," *National Examiner. Colorado*, Mar 6, 2010 (UFONS, Mar 2010, #488, 4).
3. MUFON CMS.
4. MUFON CMS.
5. George Filer, "Filer's Files: Colorado Disc," *MUFON UFO Journal #524*, Dec 2011, 14); George Filer, "Filer's Files: Colorado Triangle," *MUFON UFO Journal*, Jan 2012, 14); Sarah Kuta, "UFO Claims in Lafayette Baffle Some," *The Longmont Times-Call*, Longmont, CO, Mar 25, 2011 (UFONs, Mar 2011, #500, 1); MUFON CMS.
6. MUFON CMS.
7. Ibid.
8. Ibid.
9. Ibid.
10. Ibid.
11. Ibid.
12. Ibid.

Appendix

Colorado Unexplained
Blue Book Cases

Case 807	September 20, 1950	Kit Carson
Case 1405	July 9, 1952	Colorado Springs
Case 2013	August 29, 1952	Colorado Springs
Case 2138	September 29, 1952	Denver/Aurora
Case 3869	November 25, 1955	La Veta
Case 4841	July 27, 1957	Longmont
Case 5559	December 17, 1957	Fruita
Case 5852	June 14, 1958	Pueblo
Case 8973	July 27, 1964	Denver

Bibliography

Books

Boylan, Richard J., and Lee K. Boylan. *Close Extraterrestrial Encounters.* Tigard, OR: Newberg Press, 1994.

Davenport, Marc. *Visitors from Time: The Secret of UFOs.* Tuscaloosa, AL: Greenleaf Publications, 1992.

Filer, USAF, Major George A. *Filer's Files: Worldwide Reports of UFO Sightings.* West Conshohocken, PA: InfinityPublishing.com, October 2005.

Flammonde, Paris. *UFO Exist!* New York: Ballantine Books, 1976.

Fowler, Raymond E. *Casebook of a UFO Investigator.* Englewood Cliffs, NJ: Prentice-Hall, Inc., 1981.

—. *UFOs Interplanetary Visitors.* New York: Bantam Books, 1979.

Gibbons, Gavin. *The Coming of the Space Ships.* New York: Citadel Press. 1958.

Good, Timothy. *Contact: Top Secret UFO Files Revealed.* New York: William Morrow and Company. 1993.

Green, Gabriel, and Warren Smith. *Let's Face the Facts about Flying Saucers.* New York: Popular Library, 1967.

Haines, Ph.D., Richard F. *CE-5: Close Encounters of the Fifth Kind.* Naperville, IL: Sourcebooks, Inc., 1999.

Hall, Richard H., ed. *The UFO Evidence.* NICAP, 1997.

—. *Uninvited Guests: A Documented History of UFO Sightings, Alien Encounters and Coverups.* Santa Fe, NM: Aurora Press, 1988.

Holzer, Hans. *The UFOnauts: New Facts on Extraterrestrial Landings.* Greenwich, CT: Fawcett Publications, 1976.

Hynek, J. Allen. *The UFO Experience: A UFO Experience.* New York: Ballantine Books, 1972.

Johnson, Dewayne B., and Kenn Thomas. *UFOs over Los Angeles: The UFO Craze of the 50's.* Kempton, IL: Adventures Unlimited Press, 1998.

Keyhoe, Major Donald E. (USMC Ret.) *Aliens from Space: The Real Story of Unidentified Flying Objects.* New York: Signet Books, 1973.

Lindemann, Michael, ed. *UFOs and the Alien Presence: Six Viewpoints.* Santa Barbara, CA: The 20/20 Group, 1991.

Lorenzen, Coral. *Flying Saucers: The Startling Evidence of the Invasion from Outer Space.* New York: Signet Books, 1962, 1966.

Lorenzen, Coral, and Jim Lorenzen. *UFOs over the Americas.* New York: Signet Books, 1968.

—. *UFOs: The Whole Story.* New York: New American Library, 1969.

Machlin, Milt. *The Total UFO Story.* New York: Dale Books, 1979.

Montgomery, Ruth. *Aliens Among Us.* New York: Fawcett Crest Books, 1985.

O'Brien, Christopher. *Enter the Valley.* New York: St. Martin's Press, 1994.

—. *The Mysterious Valley.* New York: St. Martin's Press, 1996.

Ramsey, Scott, and Suzanne Ramsey. *The Aztec Incident: Recovery at Hart Canyon.* Mooresville, NC: Aztec.48 Productions, 2011.

Randle, Captain Kevin D. (USAF Ret.) *The UFO Casebook.* New York: Warner Books, 1989.

Ring, Ph.D., Kenneth. *The Omega Project: Near-Death Experiences, UFO Encounters and Mind at Large.* New York: William Morrow and Company, 1992.

Romanek, Stan. *Messages: The World's Most Documented Extraterrestrial Contact Story.* Woodbury, MN: Llewellyn Publications, 2009.

Scully, Frank. *Behind the Flying Saucers.* New York: Henry Holt and Company, 1950.

Steiger, Brad. *Strangers from the Skies.* London: Tandem Books, 1966.

—. *The UFO Abductors.* New York: Berkley Books, 1988.

Strieber, Whitley, and Anne Strieber, eds. *The Communion Letters.* New York: HarperPrism, 1997.

Sutherly, Curt. *UFO Mysteries: A Reporter Seeks the Truth.* St. Paul, MN: Llewellyn Publications, 2001.

Vallee, Jacques. *Anatomy of a Phenomenon: UFOs in Space.* New York: Ballantine Books. 1965.

—. *Messengers of Deception: UFO Contacts and Cults.* New York: Bantam Books, 1979.

Magazines/Newspapers/Journals

Baxter, Susan. "Suspected UFO Reported over Snowshoe Mountain." *Valley Courier.* Alamosa, CO: March 28, 1996.

Beckley, Tim, ed. "Asteroid Belt: Colorado's Mysterious Hum." *UFO Universe.* New York: GCR Publishing Group, Winter 1996.

Briggs, Bill "San Luis Valley Home to a Hotbed of Strange." *Post.* Denver, CO: March 15, 1994.

—. "We're Not Alone: Tale of UFO Landing Not So Unusual in Yuma." *Post.* Denver, CO: March 12, 2000.

Brouillette, Amy. "Poison Ruled Out in 7 Animals' Deaths." *Post.* Denver, CO: Oct 26, 2005.

—. "Town Baffled by Deaths of 22 Horses." *Post.* Denver, CO: Oct 25, 2005.

Clemens, David B. "High Strangeness in a Colorado Valley." *MUFON UFO Journal #313*, May 1994.

Cone, Tracie. "Watch the Skies." *Mercury News*. San Jose, CA: Feb 2, 1997.

Cortez, Angela. "Cattle, Deer Found Mutilated." *Post*. Denver, CO: Jul 29, 1995.

Cunningham, Dan. "Cattle Deaths Mystify Colorado Ranchers." *AG Journal*. La Junta, CO: Jul 7, 2006.

—. "UFO Reported in Colorado." *Bent County Democrat/Gate County News Service*. Fowler, CO: Jan 7, 2009.

Daranyi, Tony. "UFOs Sighted over Lone Cone." *Morning Sun*. Montrose, CO: Mar 11, 1997.

Dicker, John. "The Aliens Among Us." *Independent #405*, Colorado Springs, CO: April 2003.

Dillon, Becky. "More Strange Lights Sighted at Rock Creek." *Prospector*. Del Norte, CO: Mar 29, 1995.

Editor. "Durango Man Reports a UFO." *Post*. Denver, CO: Oct 28, 2003.

Espinosa, Juan. "Devil Worship? Mutilated Cow Found on Pueblo County Ranch." *Chieftain*. Pueblo, CO: June 25, 1993.

Fallon, D'Arcy. "UFO Sightings Transfix Residents." *Gazette Telegraph*. Colorado Springs, CO: Jan 7, 1996.

Filer, George. "Filer's Files: Colorado." *MUFON UFO Journal #367 & 368*, Nov 1998, Dec 1998.

—. "Filer's Files: Colorado Abduction?" *MUFON UFO Journal #291*, Nov 2000.

—. "Filer's Files: Colorado Dark Triangle." *MUFON UFO Journal #471*, Jul 2007.

—. "Filer's Files: Colorado Disc." *MUFON UFO Journal #524*. Dec 2011.

—. "Filer's Files: Colorado Encounter with Light and Entities." *MUFON UFO Journal #439*, May 2009.

—. "Filer's Files: Colorado Mutilations Reported." *MUFON UFO Journal #446*, Jun 2005.

—. "Filer's Files: Colorado Photo." *MUFON UFO Journal #502*, Feb 2010.

—. "Filer's Files: Colorado Pilot Describes UFO." *MUFON UFO Journal #465*, Jan 2007.

—. "Filer's Files: Colorado Sighting by Mackay." *MUFON UFO Journal #448*, Aug 2005.

—. "Filer's Files: Colorado 'Star' in Daytime Sky." *MUFON UFO Journal #436*, Sep 2004.

—. "Filer's Files: Colorado Triangle." *MUFON UFO Journal #525*, Jan 2012.

—. "Filer's Files: Colorado Triangle Makes Passes." *MUFON UFO Journal #465*, Jan 2007.

—. "Filer's Files: Huge Disc in Colorado." *MUFON UFO JOURNAL #439*, Nov 2004.

—. "Filer's Files: Large Object in Colorado." *MUFON UFO Journal #446*, Jun 2005.

—. "Filer's Files: Triangular UFO in Colorado." *MUFON UFO Journal #365,* Sep 1998.

—. "Filer's Files: Trying to Create an Extraterrestrial Affairs Commission." *MUFON UFO Journal #483,* Jul 2008.

—. "Filer's Files: V-Shaped Object in Colorado." *MUFON UFO Journal #417,* Jan 2013.

Foster, Dick. "Fire on Radar Heats Up Mystery." *Rocky Mountain News.* Denver, CO: Jan 25, 1994.

—. "Officials Suspect Cultists in Latest Cow Mutilation." *Rocky Mountain News.* Denver, CO: May 28, 1993.

Frazier, Deborah. "ET Watch." *Rocky Mountain News.* Denver, CO: July 23, 2000. (UFONs, Aug 2000, #373.)

Gaddy, Monty. "Monty's Musings: Cattle Mutilation Phenomenon Remains a Mystery." *Ranchland News.* Simla, CO: Sep 15, 1994.

Gribble, Bob. "Looking Back: 1981." *MUFON UFO Journal #276,* Apr 1991.

—. "Looking Back: May 1947." *MUFON UFO Journal #288,* May 1992.

—. "Looking Back: May 1956." *MUFON UFO Journal #276,* May 1991.

—. "Looking Back: Object Frightens Colorado Woman." *MUFON UFO Journal #385,* May 2000.

—. "Pilot Sightings and Radar Trackings." *MUFON UFO Journal #181,* Mar 1983.

Hatten, Amy. "Sheriff Probes Mutilated Cattle." *Daily Press.* Craig CO: Oct 20, 2004.

Howe, Linda Moulton. "UFO Mutilations, Crashed Saucers and Aliens in Government Captivity." *UFO Universe, Vol 1, #1.* New York: Condor Books.

Hunt, Chris. "UFO Tape Analyzed." *Herald Democrat.* Leadville, CO: Sep 25, 1995.

Hunter, Mark H. "Center Man Shoots UFO Video." *Valley Courier.* Alamosa, CO: Feb 8, 1996.

—. "Horse Mutilated near Pike Stockade." *Valley Courier.* Alamosa, CO: March 10, 1998.

—. "Mutilated Horse Found Near Alamosa." *Valley Courier.* Colorado: Dec 30, 1997.

—. "UFO Enthusiast Comes Home to First Site." *Valley Courier.* Alamosa, CO: Sep 10, 1994.

Jackson, Bill. "Mutilations Leave Many Questions." *Tribune.* Greeley, CO: Jun 27, 1993.

—. "Strange Lights Reported in the Sky." *The Tribune.* Greeley, CO: May 1, 2008.

Jones, Peter. "Close Encounters of the Suburban Kind." *Centennial Citizens News.* Littleton, CO: Jan 21, 2010.

Kerth, Linda. "Strange Things in the Sky." *Rio Grande Sun.* Espanola, NM: Jul 4, 1996.

Kuta, Sarah. "UFO Claims in Lafayette Baffle Some." *The Longmont Times-Call.* Longmont, CO: Mar 25, 2011.

Mestas, Anthony A. "Two More Cows Found Mutilated." *Pueblo Chieftain*. Pueblo, CO: Aug 29, 2009.

Morris. "More Sightings of Horsetooth Reservoir Creature." *Standard-Blade*. Brighton, CO: Apr 22, 1995.

Noland, Becky. "Apparent Calf Mutilation Has Officials Wondering, 'Who?' 'Why?'" *Post Dispatch*. Center, CO: Dec 3, 1997.

O'Brien, Christopher. "Mutants and Mutilations." *Fate*. St. Paul, MN: Llewellyn, Sep 1995.

—. "Sightings of Strange Objects Near Salida Continue." *Eagle*. Crestone, CO: Nov 1995.

—. "Southern Colorado UFO and Mutilation Activity Update." *UFO Encounters, Vol. 1, #12*. Norcross, GA: Aztec Publishing.

—. "Strange Harvest for the San Luis Valley: Cattle Mutilations Begin Again." *Eagle*. Crestone, CO: Feb 1993.

—. "Stranger Than Fiction." *Eagle*: Crestone, CO: April 2000.

—. "Unexplained Sightings Continue in Valley." *Eagle*. Crestone, CO: Apr 1996.

O'Driscoll, Patrick. "Salida's 'Close Encounter.'" *Post*. Denver, CO: Jul 7, 1996.

Rappold, R. Scott. "I've Got to Think It's UFOs." *Gazette*. Colorado Springs, CO: Jan 7, 2006.

—. "Mysterious Animal Deaths, Mutilations Continue to Plague Colorado Ranches." *MUFON UFO Journal #454*, Feb 2006.

Shovald, Arlene. "Edward's UFO Sighting Not Salida's First." *Mountain Mail*. Salida, CO: Sep 7, 1995.

—. "More UFOs Sighted over Salida." *Mountain Mail*. Salida, CO: Sep 26, 1995.

—. "Salida Man Not Alone in Sighting UFO." *Mountain Mail*. Salida, CO: Sep 11, 1995.

Smith, Brad. "Mystery 'Heat Source' Sparks Wonder." *Post*. Denver, CO: Jan 27, 1994.

Smith, Erin. "Bright Lights Cause Big Stir in Valley." *Pueblo Chieftain*. Pueblo, CO: April 30, 1996.

—. "Costilla County Officials Probe Cattle Mutilation." *Pueblo Chieftain*. Pueblo, CO: Jul 22, 2006.

—. "UFO Fans to Alight Near Hooper." *Pueblo Chieftain*, Pueblo, CO: Aug 3, 2003.

Staff. "Andreatta Cattle Mutilated." *Signature*. La Veta, CO: Nov 3, 1994.

Staff. "Broomfield UFO Sighting Lands on Web." *Broomfield Enterprise*. Broomfield, CO: Sep 2, 2009.

Staff. "Colorado Pilot Unable to Identify Five Lights Passing Overhead." *National Examiner*. Colorado: Mar 6, 2010.

Staff. "Mysterious Glow Causes Search for Plane Crash." *Enterprise*. Eagle, CO: Jul 28, 1988.

Staff. "Oil Basin Folks Wonder, Did They See Flying Saucers?" *Rangely Driller*. Rangely, CO: April 28, 1950.

Staff. "Weatherman Sees Flying Saucer." *Press*. Cleveland, OH: Jun 18, 1952.

Tosche, Rich. "Theories on Recent Cattle Mutilations Sort of Alien." *Post*. Denver, CO: May 24, 2006.

—. "UFOs Make Yuma Man's Life a Pit Stop." *Post*. Denver, CO: May 9, 2007.

Van Eyck, Zack. "Colorado Man and His Films Bring UFO Meet Back to Earth," *Deseret News*. Salt Lake City, UT: Nov 30/Dec 1, 1995.

—. "Horse's Death Brought Issue to Light." *New Mexican*. Santa Fe, NM: Sept 18, 1994.

Weis, Murray. "Edwards Gets More UFO Video from Salida." *Chronicle and Pilot*. Crested Butte, CO: Dec 15, 1995.

Wills, Thomas. "Alien Lights and Black Helicopters." *Valley Chronicle*. Hotchkiss, CO: Dec 1995.

Wyrick, Randy. "Close Encounters of the Eagle County Kind." *Daily*. Vail, CO: Jun 6, 2001.

Websites

www.mufon.com/
www.nicap.org/
www.nuforc.org/
http://prestondennett.weebly.com/

Index of Place Names